GW00728985

A WRITING LIFE

A WRITING LIFE

AUBREY MALONE

First published
Nov 2024

© Aubrey Malone

The author asserts his moral right to be identified as
the author of the work.

All rights reserved. No part of this
publication may be reproduced, stored in a
retrieval system or transmitted in any form or
by any means, electronic, mechanical,
photocopying, recording or otherwise, without
the prior permission of the publishers

ISBN 978-1-913144-62-3

Cover:

PENNILESS PRESS PUBLICATIONS
Website:www.pennilesspress.co.uk/books

Contents

Bookless   1
Trini-Dad   2
And So to School   24
Dear Dirty Dublin   35
Belfield   46
Getting Published   69
Floating   79
Twilight of the Gods   87
Teacher Man   96
Globetrotting   101
Partings   114
In Search of a Muse   127
Different Genres   135
The World of Books   154
The Life of Brian   165
Winding Down   171
Novel   176
Elvis   182
Thighland   189
Hemingway   199
Celebrities   205
Pub Culture   210
Wings of Poesy   217
Dumbing Down   225
Bukowski   234
Diversification   239
Sunset Boulevard   263
Piranha Fish   270
Resetting the Dial   276
Penniless Press   283
Brando   298
Burn Out   319
Time's Winged Chariot   333
Where To From Here?   351
Our Wonderful World   366

I like thin books because they balance tables, leather volumes because they can strop razors, and heavy books because they can be thrown at the cat.

Mark Twain

My earliest memory
is of being in a cot in the kitchen.
I remember having chilblains,
someone dropping marbles
on my feet.
Later on I'm under a table
with an embroidered tablecloth
where lots of people are sitting.
I'm crawling under their feet
as food is being served.
Then I'm being led up a hill to a building
with railings outside it.
A nun
whose face I can hardly see
behind a veil
brings me down a corridor,
her beads rattling as she walks.
Afterwards everything is hazy
There are people
coming into the house
at all hours
of the day and night.
My sisters are playing with dolls.

Bookless

"Books are a load of crap."

Philip Larkin's apothegm more or less summed up my attitude to them in childhood. I wasn't particularly sociable or sporty so one would have imagined I'd be a bookworm. Why wasn't I? I don't know. They just seemed irrelevant to my life.

I didn't have a torch that I kept under the bedclothes for dipping into *Gulliver's Travels*. I never read *Treasure Island* or *Black Beauty* or *Swiss Family Robinson* or *Huckleberry Finn* or any of the other books young people of my age talked about. I preferred comics. There had to be pictures beside the words to get me interested.

I remember a box of crayons I had as a child. They were chunky and all different colours. My first squiggles on a page were probably with them. I wasn't writing "To be or not to be" in those days, or "E=MC^2" I wasn't even writing "Lucy in the Sky with Diamonds." That was John Lennon's son Julian's comment to him one day when he saw him drawing a sketch and asked him what it was. It went on to become a hit song as you probably know.

I wasn't a Van Gogh as a child any more than I was a Shakespeare or an Einstein. Edna O'Brien said she wrote her first novel when she was eight. At eight I was still playing with my crayons.

Like many children I imagined other lives for myself – New York's Lower East Side with The Bowery Boys, some rain-soaked film noir world of swaying lampshades and sultry femmes fatales, or riding across the plains of Montana with Joel McCrea and Jeff Chandler. These worlds didn't come to me from books but rather films. That was where the magic was for me in those years – the cinema. It was where I wound down from school. Nobody could threaten me in those red velvet seats, not even yelping Indians or gruff police sergeants like Brian Donleavy. Such dangers were real but hidden behind a canvas screen. I had the best of both worlds.

Trini-Dad

My father radiated charisma, sucking the oxygen out of every room he entered. He wasn't large in stature but more than compensated for that by the richness of his personality. Nobody who met him ever forgot him.

He wasn't like other fathers I knew who acted like authority figures to their children. Instead he was fun with a capital F. When he recited poems he became the characters.

He had my mother on a pedestal, telling us he wouldn't give her toe for the world. His children were on pedestals too, all of us wrapped in cotton wool by him. He gave us all to believe we were God's gift to mankind. With his support we felt we could rule the world. "Win your spurs and wear them," he told us. He protected us from the cruel world outdoors in our edenic home of Norfolk. We looked up to him like an icon.

When he stood in a room he crowned it. Anytime he went up to the Convent of Mercy he charmed the nuns like some kind of visiting dignitary. They swarmed around him like bees around honey as he entertained him with his anecdotes.

He grew up in Ballina but spent most of his school years in Dublin. In the early 1920s he went to Trinity College to study law. It was unusual for a Catholic to be a student in this primarily Protestant university at that time. He had to get a dispensation to do his degree there.

He had his own room, Number 9. His mother sent him as much money as he needed, often without his father knowing. Imagine having a room in a prestigious college and enough money to indulge all your habits. "I loved sitting on the bars of the campus watching the pretty girls walking up and down Grafton Street," he confessed. It must have been like Ireland's version of the Jazz Age.

He graduated in his early thirties. By then he'd fallen in love with my mother, a beauty he said he chased all around Connacht before she said yes to his marriage proposal. It was time to leave Trinity. "The exams weren't getting any easier," he said, "and I wasn't getting any smarter."

Our young years form us. In some ways he never left Trinity

2

It was difficult for him to adjust to being a husband, a father, a breadwinner. I always thought he deserved more admiration for that. He burned the midnight oil in his first married home with my mother, Fuschia Cottage in Greystones. Afterwards he went back to Ballina to set up his legal practice. A plaque outside the door said, "Hugh Dillon-Malone, Commissioner for Oaths." As a young boy I imagined it had something to do with farming. I was thinking of oats.

Later on I thought he should have been a barrister. He shone in court, drawing on all his performing skills. They said he could have got Judas off with a warning.

He was an incorrigible exhibitionist, dressing in his Trinity gear right through his life. "Your father liked attention," a man said to me once.

It wasn't difficult to get it in a small town like Ballina. A "character" might not stand out in a city as he did there. Some people didn't like his flamboyant ways. They thought he was trying to lord it over them. It was only when you got to know him you realised it was all show. He wasn't really a snob. When you scratched him you found out he was a man of the people.

I was the youngest of his children, the runt of the litter. It made me a follower rather than a leader. I looked to him for guidance.

The youngest child of a family is often selfish - the "spoiled" one. We tend to forget what that term conjures up. I believe I stamped my foot to get what I wanted in youth.

I never liked my name. Aubrey sounded too formal. It might be okay for a writer but people aren't born writers. Parents pick names for their children without thinking of the consequences. Imagine if I was Bob Geldof's child and was called Fifi Trixibelle. Okay, so she was an "actual" girl.

I once googled "Aubrey Malone" and found there were dozens of them around the world, as there are of every name. I even found a character called Aubrey Malone in a book once, a book called *RB: The Game* written by someone called C.C. Colee in 2003. The character was female. That was the problem.

3

4

Hugh Leonard once said, "Evelyn Waugh never got over the fact of being christened with a girl's name. If a man called Evelyn is reading this, he'll probably hit me with his hockey stick." I know how Waugh felt.

Leonard had his own troubles with his name as he was illegitimate at a time when people didn't talk about such things. His actual name was Jack Keyes. Hugh Leonard was a pen name that he took from a character he created in one of his plays. I didn't have a pen name but rather a life one. In later years I asked people to call me Peter, which made them think Aubrey Malone was a pen name. In other words I did things the other way round to Leonard, who never liked being called Hugh. Only strangers addressed him like that. He was Jack to his inner circle.

I always felt children should have a right to change their names if they saw fit. It never entered my mind when I was growing up. In later years I discovered it was easier to change your surname than your christian one. That seems to be putting the cart before the horse. It's our christian name that's most often used.

In Muredach's, the college I attended, I was often addressed as "Malone." This was at a time when I was registered as Dillon-Malone. It may have been a way of trying to pull me down in case I had any notions about myself being "the solicitor's son." I never had. It actually made me more comfortable being called "Malone" than "Aubrey," or "Malone" than "Dillon-Malone" which I always found to be something of a jawbreaker.

I had four brothers. Keith, Clive, Hugo and Basil, and four sisters, June, Ruth, Audrey and Jacinta. My grandfather, PJ Malone, married three times, outliving his first two wives. The third one, Mary Dillon, wanted to be distinguished from his other two families so insisted the Dillon be kept as a form of reference. Thus Dillon-Malone became the moniker of the third family, the one my father came from.

He gave most of us English-sounding names. ("Norfolk" was even English). Keith came from the "K" of G.K. Chesterton, one of my father's favourite authors: Clive was from Clive of India. June was so-called because she was born on the last day of May: "The last of May saw the first of June."

Ruth was the character from the Bible who was "sick for home

5

amid the alien corn" an expression that proved prophetic after she emigrated from Ireland. Hugo may have been a derivation of my father's name, Hugh, or from Victor Hugo. I don't know where Basil came from.

My childhood was like everyone else's. I climbed trees, stole apples and played football wherever I could find a ball – or a pitch. Books were for school. I needed to burn off all the energy Murdeach's suppressed. Most of all I played snooker in a rundown hall called The Hibs.

Many of the people in The Hibs were from the Tech. I'd have preferred to go there than to Muredach's. Tech people could "do" things. In our own family, only Clive and Basil seemed to have that gift. Clive made us a table tennis table once. I also remember Basil working with wood. I don't know where they got these interests from. Certainly not my father. I couldn't imagine him having a piece of wood in his hand anymore than I could imagine him dressing in a jumper or a pair of jeans.

The Trinity gear, or "rig-out" as he called it, consisted of pinstriped suit, grey waistcoat, white silk scarf, and, when the occasion called for it, a tall hat, like in the photo opposite. He carried an umbrella even on the sunniest of days.

Most people in Ballina knew him to see even if they weren't acquainted with him personally. One day a friend of his from Trinity who dressed equally extravagantly said to him, "Let's go down the street, Hugh, and give the people a thrill." I think his name was Mido Cooligan. He wanted to be, as he put it, "Lord Knockemstiff."

His demonstrativeness wasn't to everyone's taste. The poorer people in the town could have been forgiven for seeing him as a show-off. I never thought of him that way. Like many performers he was a shy man at base.

One year there was a satire of him published in the *Western People*, our local paper, written by someone who called themselves Sean Bocht. Entitled "The Brolly Brigade," it referenced the "umbrella in summer" theme. None of us knew how much it affected him. He didn't talk about it but I think it devastated him.

Norfolk

My parents and Clive at his ordination

His sensitivity was often concealed under that larger-than-life personality.

He worked in an office in Bridge Street near the river Moy. It burned down in the 1960s, causing him to move back to Norfolk. The benefit for us was that we got to see more of him.

The dining room was converted into an office. He put his files on a mahogany table. After the work day was finished we put the files on shelves and played table tennis on it. After our games were finished we put them back again.

We had a girl called Tina who lived with us. She helped my mother with the cooking and other jobs around the house. I became close to her. Sometimes we went to "the pictures" together.

She brought me out on the back of her bicycle when she was shopping. When I started to read books it changed our relationship. I went into a different groove. One day I said to her, "Where are you going to park the bike when I go to university?" It became a family joke. Already I was being primed for that kind of life.

I don't remember my mother ever reading a book except prayer books. Women weren't encouraged to read as much as men when I was growing up. My aunt Nellie liked whodunits, or "whodidits" as she called them. People in Ballina didn't read highbrow literature, or at least the people I knew.

All four of my brothers became writers like I did. None of my sisters followed us into "the black trade." Maybe it was conditioning. Neither did I know any girls in Ballina who went to university apart from Mary Bourke. She was the daughter of our GP, the man who delivered me onto the planet. They were posh. Mary went to a finishing school in France. She would eventually become Ireland's president.

We weren't that well off, just comfortable. People might have thought we were rich because of our double-barrel name and our big house. That wasn't the case. It was tough on my father feeding so many mouths in a town that had more solicitors per capita than any other one in the province.

MATURE STUDENT
&
other poems
AUBREY MALONE

Belfast
Lapwing

All of boys in the family went to university but none of the girls. Ireland in the fifties was a terrible time for women. The thinking of the time was that they'd get jobs whereas boys would enjoy the fruits of those fancier things called careers.

Men got to travel the world whereas a woman's place was "in the home." At a certain point, probably in their mid-twenties, they'd marry. The alternative was to be left "on the shelf" – a horrible term. "Spinster" wasn't much better. ("Bachelor" sounded so much more exotic). If they were lucky they'd have the proverbial 2.2. children like all the other girls in the town. Not everyone could be a Mary Bourke - or Mary Robinson as she became after she got married.

Not everyone could be a Mary Robinson. Her success in society fortified her contrast to the fate generally advocated for less lucky women: Get a trade. Do a shorthand typing course maybe until Mr Right came riding along and scooped them off to his castle in suburbia. They'd give up their typing job and learn to cook Irish stew until he came home from his "career." And they'd all live happily ever after. He'd read "good" literature in the evenings while they busied themselves with potboilers or beach novels or airport ones, the recommended diet of the female sex.

My father was an avid reader. There were always books around the house. He read a few at a time. It was a habit I picked up from him in later years. I'll always remember his paperbacks by people like Chesterton and Hilaire Belloc.

The titles still stand out for me from the little cabinet where he kept them: *The Man Who Watched the Trains Go By. When the Kissing Had to Stop.* Maybe I liked the titles more than the books. He even had a copy of *Lady Chatterley's Lover*, probably the only one in the town. It was circulated among various personages. All of them got their time with Clifford and his grand dame.

My father didn't want any of us to become solicitors when we grew up. He saw too much of its bad side.

Like most solicitors in small towns, his cases were hardly dramatic. It was a simpler time than now. A person might not have had a light on their bicycle, or be caught cycling on the footpath instead of the road. He defended people for begging outside the bishop's palace. That was as serious as things got. No matter what he was presented with, he gave it everything. The courtroom was his theatre just like Norfolk was when he was doing his recitations.

Tina asked him if she could go to court to watch him in action once. She was impressed at the professional way he dealt with a witness. At one point he had to get stern with him. He was so gentle by nature, she was shocked by this. He said he had to do it as the prosecution was telling lies in the case. He always reminded me of Charles Laughton from the film *Witness for the Prosecution* when he put in his monocle.

At other times he showed his charm. I remember him telling me once that he addressed a guard as "sergeant." When the guard said, "I'm only a guard," he said, "A slight anticipation on my part." I'm sure it was this charm that secured the love of my mother when he was courting her.

He said he chased her all around Connacht to get her to say yes to his proposal of marriage. She had a quiet dignity that was the perfect contrast to his flamboyance.

He was always reading. A night owl, he scrutinised newspapers into the small hours. He was sad about the way the world was going, a world where people could "lie, cheat and steal" to get what they wanted. He was forever tearing articles out of newspapers to show us.

He wrote letters to the *Irish Times* about his frustration that the grand universe that existed in his father's time was now no more. It was being taken over by thugs and "teddy bears." We used to laugh when he said that. He meant "teddyboys." Pop music he saw as little more than noise. He preferred the Latin Mass to the modern one. It had more dignity for him. He talked about nuns "jumping the wildcat" up and down church aisles and priests playing guitars on altars. He hated the "kindness to the cat" theology, preferring the strictness of the church he grew up with.

There were also lots of books of quotations in the house. He loved quotations. The more colourful ones were recited to us. He'd draw himself up to his full height, put his monocle in and say something like "A little nonsense now and then/Is treasured by the best of men." Or, "There are none so blind as those who will not see." Or, "A man convinced against his will/Is of the same opinion still." Or "Memory is the only friend that grief can call its own."

My father (centre) in Runyonesque mode

He often quoted lines from Oscar Wilde or George Bernard Shaw. I remember his favourite one: "He hadn't an enemy in the world but none of his friends liked him." I can't remember whether it was Wilde or Shaw who said that. Let's say Shaw. (Here's another quote: "In times of doubt, ascribe all quotations to George Bernard Shaw.")

We loved comics before we got into books. My father bought these for us on the way home from his office when we were sick.

I read the ones everyone in the town read, *The Beano* and *The Dandy* and later *Tiger* and *Victor*. June and Ruth swore by *School Friend* and *Girls Crystal*.

If comics were more important to us than books in those years, so was music. We listened to the Top Twenty on Radio Luxemburg on a massive radio we had in the front room. The lights on it shone out like the Starship Enterprise. Some of the songs were instrumental. I particularly remember "Apache" by the Shadows. I wrote a poem about such nights:

> *We didn't need voices in those days.*
> *We didn't need words.*
> *We had Floyd Cramer*
> *playing 'Last Date.'*
> *We had Acker Bilk*
> *playing 'Stranger on the Shore.'*
> *We sat on the carpet*
> *in the front room*
> *with the curtains drawn,*
> *twirling the knob*
> *towards Radio Luxemburg*
> *as the rain lashed down outside*
> *like counterpoint.*
> *There were dozens of stations*
> *but that was the one we wanted.*
> *On the way to it*
> *we heard lots of voices*
> *some of them speaking English badly*
> *as the needle*
> *crept towards Number 208.*

It was our drug.
We didn't want
those Sunday nights to end.
We invited musicians
from England and America
into our room
to entertain us,
to be our friends.
The music pulsed through our veins
transporting us
from a world
where people told us
to build a future
based on other things,
things we jettisoned
as we turned the volume up
high
and the songs vibrated
through the floorboards.

My mother played the piano whenever she was stressed. It unwound her. Her favourite song was "Jerusalem." In later years she enjoyed pop songs. I remember her nodding her head at Bobby Darin's "Things" and saying, "I like that." My father had no time for modern music. Like many people of his generation he thought of it as little but noise. A "real" song was something like, "I dreamt that I dwelt in Marble Hall/with vassals and serfs at my side." In lines like that he championed his liking for the aristocratic life.

Keith and Clive left home in 1955. I was only two. Clive became a Jesuit and subsequently a university lecturer in Zambia. His visits home were few. Keith worked in Dublin and came home for holidays. I remember him for his love of Al Jolson's music. He mimicked his voice and acted out "Mammy" on one knee.

I remember Ruth playing Gene Pitney's "Looking Through the Eyes of Love," one of the most powerful songs of the time. June sang, "Fish gotta swim, birds gotta fly, I gotta love that man till I die, can't help lovin' that man of mine."

Hugo liked many singers, chiefly Frank Sinatra. I remember him going down to Byron's record shop one day and buying Tommy Sands' "That Old Oaken Bucket." Basil was a great fan of Cliff Richard, especially a neglected song of his called "A Voice in the Wilderness." It could have been the B-side of "Livin' Doll," his big hit. I went for anything by Elvis.

Singers were like our extended family. It was even better if they had only one name, like Fabian or Dion or Little Richard. Even if they had two, we often didn't bother saying the surname. Elvis was always just Elvis, not Elvis Presley. Cliff Richard was always just Cliff.

I wrote a poem comparing the time to the blandness of the present:

Elvis wore blue suede shoes.
Alma Cogan had a dreamboat.
Connie Francis saw lipstick on a collar.
Nina Simone's baby cared for her.
It was the fifties. We had singers then.
Tony Bennett with his blue velvet
Peggy Lee with her fever
Bobby Darin thinking of thing
Eddie Fisher wishing we were there
Frank Sinatra having one for his baby
And one more for the road.

Not all the songs were classics.
Sometimes they were about
chewing gum losing its flavour
on a bedpost overnight.
Sometimes they were about
holes in a bucket dear Henry,
dear Henry.
But when the singers of the fifties
sang torch songs
they broke your heart in two.
We felt we knew them

15

and that they knew us
even though they were
all those miles across the ocean.

Today everything is more diversified.
There are five million singers
all looking for that place on the ladder
as they dance to special effects
and lip-synch with better lighting.
It looks much more elaborate
but it makes me yawn.
Nobody is very going to be build a statue
to Olly Murs.

Films, like songs, were more important to us than books in those days. There were two cinemas within walking distance of us. The Estoria was just across the road. The Savoy was around the corner. My father knew the owner of the Estoria. He often got us free passes for it. People from the town wondered how "the Malones" were always going to films.

He liked gangster films or, as he put it, "Hitchcocks." He also went for "Edward Robinson." (For some reason he left out the "G".) Keith brought us all up on Humphrey Bogart: "Here's lookin' at you, kid." "The problems of three crazy people don't amount to a hill of beans in this crazy world." When we went to these films we became the characters.

Like most children of my age I loved cowboy films. Audie Murphy seemed to be in every second one:

Tearing down Garden Street
to the latest Audie Murphy film
slapping your thing
as if it was a horse
and saying 'Giddyup.'
You paid your one and six
to the girl
behind the desk
with your heart beating fast.

A big man
with a torch
and a cross face
led you to a seat
that smelt of Taytos.
You jumped across it
to join your friends
with guns
and rubber arrows
in the one behind you.
Then the cinema got dark.
Everyone went quiet
as Audie Murphy came out
with his six guns.

Shane was in a league of its own when it came to cowboy films. We analysed every scene in it time and again in the kitchen in Norfolk over the years.

Shane wasn't just a film
in our house.
It was more like a second religion.
I don't know how many times
I saw it.
Keith acted out the scenes from it
so often,
eventually we came to know
the script by heart.

'I've come to get your offer, Ryker.'
'I'm not dealing with you, Shane.
Where's Starrett?'
'You're dealing with me.'
That scene
became the soundtrack
of my youth.
The poster in the Savoy said,
'There never was a picture like Shane'

and there wasn't.
The scenery, the sadness,
Alan Ladd's gold fringed buckskin,
even the blue shirt he wore
that my cousin Grace loved so much.

The only writer in my family that I knew of was our cousin Paddy Dillon-Malone. He was the son of my father's brother Louis. Uncle Louis became a doctor and moved to England marrying another doctor there. He was the practical one of the family. That was in contrast to my father, the free spirit. Paddy wrote a book called *An Analysis of Marketing* which championed the virtues of a love of the open market. He called this "agoraphilia." Louis' daughter Mary became a journalist with the *Daily Mail*.

Would any of my own family ever become writers? I didn't know. Keith liked reading books about the cinema. Maybe he'd write one some day. The rest of us started to read more as the years went on.

Basil bought Joyce's *A Portrait of the Artist as a Young Man* in Keohane's one day. That was our local bookshop. Hugo bought Norman Mailer's *Advertisements for Myself*. I looked at these books with just a vague curiosity. The new covers were a novelty to me, a contrast to my father's dog-eared reprints of all those orange Penguin novels. I don't remember Ruth reading books. June was partial to chunky novels that she really got her teeth into.

Even though Hugo was reading *avant garde* books like Henry Miller's *Tropic of Cancer* as well as Mailer's *Advertisements for Myself* when we were in Ballina, he ended up going on to become a priest. Basil, on the contrary, read mystical writers like John Steinbeck and entered the world of business.

Nobody is simple. Basil became an engineer but read Joyce in his spare time. Hugo read radical literature in the seminary and eventually left it. Both of them sought worlds outside books. Hugo had ideas about going on the missions.

SHANE
Paramount's Classic Western

Aubrey Malone

He wanted to spread the word of God, like Clive in Africa, whereas Basil was more like my cousin Paddy. He sold engineering products with his own brand of "agoraphilia." Basil was talented at giving presentations for whatever company he worked for. He did the same with his books after he became a writer. Clive wrote books on religious topics relating to his lecturing career.

Keith and myself were more introverted. Keith didn't push himself as a writer. Hugo and Basil were "performance" writers. They liked acting out words in the same way my father did. Hugo was in various dramatic societies over the years and also liked reading his poems to friends and family. Basil carried on my father's practice of doing recitations.

Maybe we all have our theatres. Keith sang Jolson songs at parties. Clive lectured in universities. My "stage" was the rostrum after I became a teacher. Basil spoke from·rostrums all over the world at conferences. Keith occasionally sang songs in pubs.

Keith and Clive were gone from Ballina before I got to know them. So were Hugo and Basil. They left Muredach's the year I entered it, 1964. I was the first boy in the family to be on my own there. That probably gave me whatever independence I had growing up.

Hugo came home from the seminary on holidays. One year towards the end of the sixties he arrived with a man from our street, Frank McGrath, who'd just been ordained. I remember the bunting stretching across the road. Becoming a priest was a big deal in those days, the dream of most parents for their children.

Hugo wasn't your average seminarian. He talked about people like Brando, Bob Dylan, Ingmar Bergman. He loved Elvis as well and did a good impersonation of him. Elvis and Brando "owned" the fifties but it was the sixties before I was old enough to experience them. By then they'd passed their peaks.

Clive only came home once every seven years. The Jesuits was almost like a monastic order from that point of view. Keith was in Ballina every now and then and so were June and Ruth. I wrote a poem about their visits:

The family in the fifties

I used to meet them at the train station.
They talked nonstop
about people I didn't know.

Everything seemed strange
but when we got home
it was like it always was.

We sat around
the green seat
that was shaped
like a rectangle
before the fireplace
and we were children again.
If the doorbell rang
we ran under the stairs.

June and Ruth sang in harmony,
stealing our hearts away.
We played a tape recorder.
The spools were huge.

We listened to Roy Orbison
and Buddy Holly,
those incredible voices
singing incredible songs
about love and loss,
emotions that entered our souls.

We exchanged stories
about other worlds
other towns, other countries.
We played table tennis
in our father's office
on the mahogany table.

We played chasing
in our huge kitchen.
We played poker
for matchsticks.

And So to School

English was a drag at school. We learned poems by rote in
Muredach's: "The Assyrian came down like a wolf on the fold."
"Fair daffodils we weep to see you haste away so soon." You
were whacked if you didn't get the lines right. How could you
love literature at this level? There was no Seamus Heaney, no
Austin Clarke, no Paddy Kavanagh. The educational system of the
fifties and sixties even made you hate a beautiful poet like Yeats.
It took years to unhate him.

Lines like "Break, break, break on thy cold grey stones o
sea," appear musical to me now but when I had to learn them off
they were just meaningless words. They come back to me at
unusual times. I can appreciate them now that they're not being
rammed down my throat. We learned poetry like we learned
prayers, without having much of a clue of what they meant.
Maybe you're not supposed to know what poetry means but if the
learning of lines is predicated upon being beaten if you mess them
up it's hardly going to leave you with a devotion to them. There
was also the slavishness of analysis. I knew how to spell "iambic
pentameter" but hadn't a clue what it meant. We lay stagnated
back in a dark time, far from Seamus Heaney or Thomas Kinsella
or Austin If someone suggested a singer like Christy Moore be
placed on the curriculum (as he is now, they'd have been laughed
(or belted) out of the classroom.

One year our English teacher, Padraig Loftus, bought a set of
novels for us that weren't on the course: Graham Greene's *The
Heart of the Matter*, Evelyn Waugh's *The Loved One* and
Nicholas Monserrat's *The Cruel Sea*. It was a noble ambition. We
contributed to the cost. I think there were about a dozen copies of
each bought and circulated around the class. Sadly, his wish to
convert me to "good writing" (whatever that was) didn't really
work. *The Heart of the Matter* was full of Catholic guilt and I had
enough of that, thank you very much. (It was impossible not to at
the time). *The Loved One* was an easier read but I didn't "get" the
satire of the funeral industry, much as Fr. Padraig tried to convey
it to me. As for Mr Monserrat, I always hated sea novels and still
do.

24

My father and June at Enniscrone

Clive blessing our cousins the O'Gradys

We oscillated between the jollity of Wordsworth dancing with his daffodils and Gerald Manley Hopkins' "I wake and feel the fell of dark, not day" which is likely to have people reaching for their Xanex. Keats' "Ode to Autumn," which we were also called upon to learn off by heart, contains the phrase "half in love in easeful death." That's hardly likely to make you want to dance a jig of delight either. When we got to Yeats, we ran the gamut of "The Fiddler of Dooney" (a frivolity like Willie's daffs, to "An Irish Airman Foresees His Death." Did nobody hear of balance in those days? No wonder so many people of my generation ended up being bi-polar.

One day Fr Loftus started going on about things called gerunds. To this day I don't know what a gerund is. It reminds me of a rather unappetising part of the body. He talked a lot about grammar but what had grammar to do with life? Not any more than algebra had in the maths classes; We grew up being told that our lives wouldn't be worth living unless we mastered these areas of study but when we reached adulthood we realised they didn't matter at all, that the people who were "good" at them usually disappeared into black holes of anonymity, never to be heard of again. It was only when I read Joan Collins' autobiography that I understood what the "Past Imperfect" really meant.

I remember tiny oases in these deserts of pain, like another priest, Fr. Lynn, saying to us one day, "Isn't nostalgia a lovely word?" I learned later that the word came from two Greek ones, "nostos" for memory and "algos" for pain. His comment was out of sync with the drabness of the time. I liked unusual words – or names. One of our neighbours was called "Gildie." There was a teacher in Muredach's nicknamed "Gurks."

In Catechism class they told us the world was a vale of tears. Every Saturday we had confession. It seemed to be the main sacrament. There was, as the film director Martin Scorsese said of his Catholic upbringing in the U.S., "Too much Good Friday and not enough Easter Sunday."

Colm Toibin once said his life was comprised of two rooms, one for sleeping in and one for work I felt there were five buildings in Ballina that defined me. They were my house, the Estoria, the snooker hall, the college and the cathedral. The first

three represented pleasure, the last two pain. I tried to convey how
I juggled these parameters in a poem I wrote:

> *We had drill on Saturdays*
> *It was like being in the army*
> *In the afternoon, released,*
> *we watched Gary Cooper*
> *beat the Indians in the Savoy.*
> *At teatime there was television*
> *Get Smart, I Dream of Jeannie.*
> *Then confession, the long walk*
> *across the bridge to a grille*
> *through which a face peered:*
> *gaunt, serious,*
> *asking you to examine*
> *your conscience,*
> *to remember all the bad things*
> *you did during the week.*
> *That night, if you were luck,*
> *you got to watch more television -*
> *Arrest and Trial, The Virginian -*
> *the adult programmes*
> *that made you feel grown up.*
> *Before going to bed*
> *your mother defrosted the meat.*
> *She steeped the Sunday peas*
> *and made the jelly.*
> *She washed your hair*
> *in the sink. Waking*
> *up on Sunday*
> *you heard the church bells*
> *pealing like dirges.*
> *You followed them across the street*
> *across the Market Square*
> *and down past Wellworths*
> *to the Moy*
> *where the brown current*
> *curled towards the church.*

You waited outside it
for the celebrant to appear.
Women held their bonnet
against the wind.
Men stubbed out cigarettes
You blessed yourself
at the holy water font
as worshippers took their seats.
Your soul was clean
as the prayers began.
You could receive
the body of Christ,
could listen to the priest
talking about heaven,
the dear departed,
the resurrection of the body.

After the Mass ended
you went out to the sun.
It splashed itself over the Moy
like sanctifying grace.
The sun always shone on Sunday.
Your heart swelled
with the heat.
You kicked leaves into the river.
Fisherman lined the bridge
talking of the Moy Drainage,
of who married, who died.
Sometimes they gave you coppers.
A boy with curly hair sold newspapers.
You bought The People.
Your father liked Spot the Ball.

The crowds dispersed
towards Tyrawley Terrace,
Bachelor's Walk, Adrnaree.
Paddy Culkin
put on his bicycle clips

for the spin down the Sligo Road.
John Diamond guffawed
at some childish joke.
People were themselves again,
outside ritual, outside judgment.
You walked back to Norfolk.

Geography was another bogey subject for me. I had a blind spot at it. Not having any sense of direction didn't help. "Where are the Ox Mountains?" the teacher asked me one day. I didn't have a clue so tried to spot some peak out the window. I was unlucky. They may have been visible from another window. Not mine. So that drew a laugh, and a clout. "Do you not look at them every day?" he enquired. Maybe I did. Maybe I thought I was looking at Nephin. Was Nephin part of them? So what if it was?

I always felt my mind was elsewhere. Other people talked about things that were going on around them but I was rarely part of these conversations. I wasn't aware of the free days that were corning up or what football match we were about to play. I didn't know what my classmates' fathers did for a living or even where a lot of them came from.

It wasn't as if I was in some higher plane. I wasn't on any plane at all, going through my days in a kind of dream. I wasn't only that way at school but at home as well. I didn't know the names of people we were connected with, what cars they drove, when they might be coming to visit us. It was as if I was living in a kind of continuous present. Maybe people would call it mindfulness now. I think it's more like mindlessness.

I tried to convey the feeling in a poem:

I grew up in a bubble.
Nothing seemed to be happening
when it was happening.
There were parties,
sing-songs, football games,
poker.
I felt removed from it all.
It was outside me.

The beach, the church.
even the love.
It was happening to someone else.
It was too good, too perfect.
I didn't feel worthy of it
in that street
that house
where I was treated like a God
even though I did nothing
to deserve it.

I think I must have had a form of ADHD, although it wasn't called that then. It was just called being difficult, or bold. I daydreamed a lot. When we were asked to write notes on what the teacher was saying, I wrote them in notebooks rather than copies. Maybe I was subconsciously getting ready for life as a journalist. More often than not the teachers couldn't read what I wrote. My attitude was, they didn't have to. I was the one who would be reading them.

It was different when you had to hand something up, like an essay. I hated doing these because they required you to think and I didn't like thinking. It took up too much energy and it required a brain. Other people in the class knew things about current affairs, about organisations like Bord Bainne, about the Common Market. I couldn't even tell the difference between one car and another on the street.

My ADHD didn't just apply to school, it applied to everything. I zoned out with people if I wasn't interested in what they were saying. It would have been nice to have a "fast forward" button to press if this happened but they hadn't been invented then, not even for televisions. It wasn't a good way to be in school where teachers acted like they were splitting the atom every time they opened their mouths.

If someone asked me to do something I had to do it immediately or I'd forget. My brain couldn't work on two different channels. If I put on the kettle for a cup of tea and then went into another room to do something else I'd forget it was on. Today that's not a problem because kettles click off when they boil. In those days they didn't. You could burn the house down.

Even though I couldn't multi-task, my mind was still all over the place. That might sound like a contradiction but it wasn't. I focused on something for a few seconds then on something else for another few. There was no joined-up thinking. I tried to shrink reality to fit my brain. Other people tried to expand theirs to fit it. I wasn't versatile.

My father did my essays for me. He loved language so it was no bother to him. I'd just give him the title and off he'd go, walking up and down the floor with his hands behind his back as he declaimed. I took down everything he said religiously. I'm sure the teachers knew it wasn't my stuff. If I was cleverer I would have thrown in the odd mis-spelling to throw them off the track but I didn't think of that.

In another poem I wrote I tried to capture the manner in which the difficulty of school prepared me for life better than the world of Norfolk, or my imagination:

> *Brando telling us piningly*
> *that he could have been a contender*
> *or Shane squaring up to Wilson*
> *in the final reel in Grafton's saloon*
>
> *were heroes that shaped me*
> *much more than those of 1916, or 1798.*
> *Dolores Sheridan waltzing down Bury Street*
> *in her Convent of Mercy gabardine*
>
> *was an infinitely more enticing figure*
> *than our Blessed Lady or Joan of Arc,*
> *and Pythagoras' square on the hypotenuse*
> *was nothing beside our own Market Square*
>
> *where pitched battles were held nightly*
> *and we rattled Silvie McConn's gate*
> *with a thousand and one mis-taken penalties.*
> *We didn't have a Parthenon or an Acropolis*
> *but we had Moyne Abbey and St. Patrick's Well.*

My cousin Paddy Dillon-Malone (right) with former Taoiseach Sean Lemass (middle) and unidentified man

We were told that Jesus saved the world
but Audie Murphy looked more durable
from my velvet seat in the Estoria cinema

as he fended off Geronimo.
We read about the Pass of Thermopylae
and the brave 300 Spartans
but John Wayne at the Alamo

spoke more to us about bravado.
As we thrilled to Ben-Hur
the crucifixion was an anti-climax
to Charlton Heston's chariot forays.

When we read Paradise Lost·
we might have rooted for God to win
but our hearts lay with the doomed Lucifer.
The Estoria was our Bel Air,

the posters on the stairs
our gateway to the Gods
When we were beaten at school
we wanted to be Pretty Boy Floyd

or Babyface Nelson, anything
to challenge the old order.
At the Saturday matinees we told ourselves
we would create our own Dead End Kids

our own angels with dirty faces
to dethrone the cane-wielding life-deniers
holding court at the blackboards,
their canes like swords.

When I go back to that old college now
and walk through the deserted rooms
where once I felt terror
at the punishments dished out

for failing to memorize some history date
I feel strangely grateful.
The teachers gave me a rebel's cause
like Brando's dumb longshoreman

with the mobster bosses.
They woke me from a sleep
that could have lasted all my life
were it not for their scabbard strife.

My family life was too romantic
to blood me for the challenges
that lay down those mean streets
far from the bosom of cinema

where real Johnny Friendlys lurked,
in different Hobokens.
Education, they say, prepares us for life.
Not because of book learning, I think

but something more cerebral and dark.
What little academic lore
I took into this limp brain
has long deserted me,

replaced now by the sights and smells
of a past I cherish
every passing year
for its liberating negativity, and fears.

Dear Dirty Dublin

We left Ballina in 1969. My father was retiring. There was no point in staying on. We could join the rest of the family in Dublin. It made sense for everyone to be living together than paying rent in separate places. Now we could have a Dublin Norfolk.

My mother's nephew, Paddy Murphy, bought our house. Once it was decided we were leaving the town, everything moved fast, so fast I found it difficult to take in. I wrote a poem called "Phone Call" to describe that sudden brutality:

> *Like the stopping of a clock*
> *the middle of a sentence*
> *a footstep suspended on a stairs*
> *the life you knew*
> *taken away from you*
> *with that one call*
> *those final words*
> *from my cousin,*
> *'Goodbye Auntie Pat,*
> *Goodbye Uncle Hugh.'*
> *He hung up.*

I was the last of the family to leave the town. My mother and father were both unwell and had to go to hospital in Dublin. After the sale of the house took place I spent a few days with a man called Sean who was organising the move. He was the son of an auctioneer. One night he held an auction in the Town Hall. All of our furniture was put up for sale and so were my father's books. I didn't think he'd have allowed it if he was there but he went ahead of me to Dublin. They were flogged for £1 each, or less. I felt sentimental watching them go. Maybe that was the night I realised I did actually like books. We only appreciate something when we see it being taken away from us:

> *Everything my father*
> *spent his life amassing*
> *in his life*

went for a song
at an auction
in the Town Hall
in August 1969
as he lay in a hospital
in Dublin 8
being fed on a drip.
In another hospital at the same time
everything my mother held dear
threatened to fall away from her
as she fought cancer
of the breast,
suffering the after-effects
of an operation
she postponed for months
or maybe even years
because her life was too busy
to consider it.
Meanwhile I played snooker
on windswept nights
in a dusty hall
off King Street,
attending classes by day
in a college
I'd already left
in my mind.

I didn't get to say goodbye to my classmates. Before I knew it I was in Dublin.

When I got off the train I headed for Phibsboro. Keith was staying in a flat there with Ruth. Basil had been there up until recently. He was in Holland now on business.

It was the year of the moon landing. A new world was dawning, an old one ending. My head whirled with confusion as I wrote these words:

August nineteen sixty nine.
I've just got off the train

at Heuston station.

An American astronaut has stepped on the moon.
A woman has died in Edward Kennedy's car.
The words Chappaquiddick
and Mary Jo Kopechne
are on everybody's lips,
making tragedy almost exotic.

I'm about to go into a new college,
a new house.
Cars whirl around me
and I blink in the haze,
trying to dodge them like a merry-go-round.
I walk like a ghost
my footsteps barely touching the ground.
I've left Ballina for Dublin,
been whisked from it
much sooner than wanted,
the wet streets engrained in my mind.

I try to acclimatize to my surroundings
to a redbrick house in Cabra Park
that you reach through a lane.
My brother puts his arms around me,
welcomes me to his little empire.
He's wearing a crumpled suit
and an awkward smile.
On the window-sill is the statue
of a falcon.

Later in the night
I'm at a party
where I know nobody.
I can't see faces,
only shadows on the wall.
People talk to me and I respond
merry with a drink I've been given.

The things that are happening to me
seem to be happening to someone else.
I submit to them,
a willing victim.
Someone asks me if I feel disoriented
when I knock over a glass.

People are talking about the Sorbonne riots,
the murder of Sharon Tate.
It is the end of a decade,
or more than that.
I feel a part of some unnamed revolution,
sucking at sensations
like a character from a play
I've either written or performed in
but still don't feel a part of.

A woman puts her lips on mine
and I taste her lovely scent.
She seems to know who I am
but I don't know her.
Who are all these people
and why are they making for me?
I feel I'm at the still centre
of an avalanche.

I try to remember Ballina but I can't.
Already it's gone,
replaced by another illusion.
I watch the evening skyline,
the grey bricks of Belvedere College,
a picture of the new family home.

There's a mahogany table shining at me,
the placid smile of a priest.
This is where I'm going now.
I have a foot in both camps and neither,

my mind neutral.

My mother says, 'Are you minding yourself?'
She wants to know about food, clothing,
how things are going in the flat
in 66, Cabra Park.

I walk down a steel staircase
into the Cosmo snooker hall.
A man knocks over a fruit machine beside me.
Another man is sleeping
under one of the tables.
I leave the dark vault,
the night sky almost touching me as I emerge.

The Astor cinema is showing The Razor's Edge.
On O'Connell Bridge
a neon sign lights up the sky.
It shows a man flicking sausages
onto a pan
in glittering colour.
I watch the page of a newspaper
blowing over the Liffey,
drink in the coffee stench.

My past has abandoned me
I feel like I'm on a train track
that keeps narrowing but going nowhere.
The lights on the street go
green, yellow, red,
green, yellow, red.

A beggar approaches me.
He's telling me the story
of a woman who left him.
He tries to cry
I take my coat off, sit on a bench.
A blue light falls on the river.

I'm engulfed by the tall buildings around me,
engulfed by sadness.

There's an airlock in the radiator
of the hospital my mother is in.
It clacks like a drumbeat.
I bend down to kiss her,
her skin like folded parchment.
She's locked into a machine
that kills the bad cells
and the good ones.

The papers are full of the moon landing,
the safe return of the astronauts.
A journalist asks: 'Will science fact
spell the end of science fiction?'

Excavators are digging up the city.
I walk for the sake of walking.
The streets trap me, exhale their magic.
I hear the sound of Fairport Convention
from a doorway
like an invitation.
There's a palm tree in the garden
of the house we're going to.
It reminds me of American films I've seen.
There's no furniture in the rooms.
My footsteps resound on the wooden floors.

The phone rings
and a strange voice talks to me.
I can't remember what I say.
I hear static,
an engaged tone.
Images flicker on a television set,
it's a black and white programme
with Peter Lawford in it.
In slow motion the lights on the street still go

green, yellow, red
green, yellow, red
like a silent movie.

The leaves in the trees are fluttering.
In the distance a dog barks
like an incantation
as another one answers.
Green, yellow, red,
green, yellow, red.
Will it ever stop?.

A hippie waves at me.
The phone rings again.
My mother is getting better.
Where's my father?
Will he be all right?
I don't recognize him anymore,
don't recognize anybody,
not even my face in the mirror.
Will the night ever end?
Will any night?
And where will my future lie?

Nineteen sixty nine,
the year everything changed for me.
One life ending,
another beginning
and I'm not sure if I'm a boy or a man.

I couldn't settle in Dublin. Maybe I haven't settled there even yet, half a century on. When you leave somewhere too soon there's unfinished business. Each time I go back to Ballina I'm trying to tick some box but I know I'm never going to get closure on this. I need to go back there not as a tourist but as someone who's bored with its day-to-day routines. That's the only way to cure "nostalgia," to use Fr. Lynn's term.

After getting off the train I walked towards the city centre. I had a meal in The Luna restaurant in O'Connell Street. I'd never had a meal out before. The only hot food I ate outside the house before this would have been takeaway chips. The Luna was one of the fanciest places I'd ever seen. It was impeccably clean, with a polished wooden floor. There were all these Chinese waiters running around the place in white jackets ministering to your every need. I got to thinking: Had we just won the Sweepstakes?

I made my way out to the house in Cabra Park. Clive and Ruth were there. Keith was at work.

Ruth bustled around the kitchen making tea. Clive told me he'd just been over to Battersea. After all the years of the family being too enclosed together in Norfolk it was as if we were suddenly being splintered to the four corners of the globe.

He asked me if I liked Dublin. I told him I didn't know yet, that it was hard to tell. My head was spinning.

When I asked about my mother and father he went quiet. My mother was still having tests but she was fine. She'd probably be home in a few days.

When I asked what school I was going to, he told me he had some good news for me. Due to his being a Jesuit he'd managed to get me accepted into Belvedere College for my last year. It was run by Jesuits and carried a lot of prestige.

The next day he brought me in to be vetted by the President, Fr McGowran. I had nothing to wear so Keith loaned me a white mackintosh coat he had. It was a few sizes too big for me. I was brought into a big room with a mahogany table in it.

Fr McGowran came in and shook my hand. He started talking to Clive about me. Clive explained that school might be difficult for me seeing as I was breaking off from curriculum and starting off with a new one. Fr. McGowran said not to worry, that he understood perfectly.

I started in Belvedere the following week. It was an unfriendly school and nobody bothered with me much. I sat in rooms with people who'd known each other since the cradle, people who had no interest in making friends with a stranger from the country. I wasn't interested in making friends with them either.

One of the priests asked me if I'd play rugby. I said no. That would have infuriated my father if he knew. Another one asked me if I'd join the tennis club but again I refused. The only person who addressed a personal comment to me was the English teacher. He said he'd been in Ballina once. 'Nice town,' he remarked. Under the circumstances this seemed like a huge gesture of goodwill to me.

Over the next few weeks I sat in classes feeling a million miles away from everything that was being said. There was pupil involvement in Belvedere unlike in Muredach's where you were just fed notes but I was too used to being a sheep to want this. I wasn't used to being asked for my opinions and didn't seem to have any as a result.

There was also a lot of insolence tolerated. One day a priest told the pupil sitting beside me that he didn't like him very much. 'The feeling is mutual, Father,' he replied. If somebody said something like that to a priest in Ballina it would have been the talk of the town.

I went to a lot of films during my year in Belvedere. One day a classmate dragged me to see Fellini's *Satyricon*. I tried to act interested in it but it bored me. It was the film the "intellectuals" were going to but I didn't see it as a Fellini film. I thought he was losing his touch. I preferred *Love Story*. I'd bought Erich Segal's best-selling book before seeing it. I was interested in the fact that a university professor could write something that would enthuse the masses, this breed generally being better known for writing pedestrian theses about Restoration poetry that would be of interest only to people as dull as themselves.

I went to see the film afterwards and promptly fell in love with Ali MacGraw, the heroine. Girls who parted their hair in the middle always attracted me. I was so taken with her I kept going back to it again and again. Each time I saw it she got more beautiful, even though she's dying of cancer in it. Hollywood didn't care about such details. Maybe we should all get cancer, I thought, if it made us look as good as Ali. I even fell in love with her characters' name: Jennifer Cavalieri. The film became almost as successful as the book, thereby making Segal even richer. In later years I wondered if I could produce something equally junky and reach success with it. (Answer no - but I tried.)

In the year I was in Belvedere I found myself more drawn towards biographies of writers rather than what they wrote. I wanted to learn about their motivations, their work practices, their lives. A biography I read of John Steinbeck revealed that he slept beside the manuscript of *East of Eden* as he was writing it. He saw it almost as a human thing.

A book I read on Hemingway revealed that he always stopped writing for the day when he was, as he put it, "going good" because it meant he'd have an easy start the next morning. (That was particularly helpful to a man who often went into his study with a sore head after the previous night's imbibing).

I didn't have my father to write my essays for me in Belvedere. It was time for me to get the finger out. The first one we were given was "Escapism." I didn't even know what the word meant. You never forget the first time you hear a word. I eventually figured out, Einstein-style, that it had something to do with "escape." I don't think my essay qualified for any awards. Our teacher Jack Daly threw my copy back at me from about twenty feet after he read it. I managed to catch it. ''Well done," he said, "You'll make a good rugby player."

I didn't think so. Just like writers are readers before they become writers, so players of games usually watch them before playing them. I never watched rugby and hadn't the foggiest what the rules were. I still don't. All I know is that you can't pass the ball forward. After that it's just a lot of hefty men huffing and puffing and barging into one another, after which a referee blows his whistle for yet another stoppage. I liked watching people scoring tries but didn't feel you should have to suffer twenty minutes of boredom for ten seconds of excitement.

I think my father probably agreed with me, even if it was the "old school tie" game. He played it when he was at Castleknock but was never sporty. There was a story that he got a round of applause once for blocking a forward scoring a try for the other side. "I just closed my eyes and stood in his way," he said. I'd probably have done the same thing.

My main ambition in Belvedere was to get a piece of paper. I refused to play rugby. I didn't socialise. I kept my head down in class. Life began when the school day ended. Something similar took place in Muredach's but at least there I was with people I knew, and in my home town. Dublin was just bricks and mortar.

It was nice to have the family to go home to. I didn't envy people in boarding schools. That was like 24 hour education. After the official school day ended, they had study periods. Then they had to face running into the teachers all evening. Could a greater hell be envisaged?

The year passed in a fog of apathy for me. When it came to the Leaving Cert I learned off an essay about the modern world, a general one that took in everything. I then wrote it out in English, Irish and French. No matter what topic came up on the exam paper, I slotted it into it in some way. I did the same in the Matric. The person reading it must have thought I was some kind of genius. I just hoped the reader of the English one didn't see the same basic essay in the other two languages.

Though yet only seventeen, I was learning how to play the system.

Belfield

My results were enough to get into university but I didn't know what I wanted to do there. Ireland had just joined the Common Market and Keith felt accountancy would be a profitable career for me. He was an accountant himself in a firm in Finglas called Unidare but he hated it. He had an ulcer from the stress. It seemed like strange logic to me. 'Most people hate their jobs,' he reasoned, 'so you might as well pick one that pays you to be miserable.'

I applied to the Accountancy faculty without much conviction. I could have stuck a pin in any of the other ones on the noticeboard and felt as enthusiastic about it. With the exception of medicine. I'd sooner have put lighted matches under my fingernails than that.

For the next year I got the Number 10 bus out to Belfield every day. (The question of where to park Tina's bike didn't arise). Basil described the campus as an architectural monstrosity but I didn't mind that. Its blandness relaxed me He did his degree in Earlsfort Terrace where everything was more intimate and as a result thought moving the university out to the sticks was insane but that aspect of it I could take. I even put up with the mechanical lake on the edge of the campus.

The only thing that made UCD different from Belvedere was the number of pretty girls in the class. Chauvinist that I was, I was surprised to learn that women could actually be good at subjects like Maths and Economics. Or maybe it was just that my four sisters hated anything mathematical and I was generalising from that.

One day during a lecture I was chatting to a friend when the lecturer stopped talking and looked up at me. 'Silence!' he said, rapping his desk with a cane. I gasped in shock. It was like being back in school.

I boycotted his lectures afterwards in protest. They were mostly useless to me anyway. I worked better from books in the library rather than taking down notes from some self-satisfied talking head.

The year dragged on interminably.

Where are you going to park the bike when I go to University?

I had no social life to speak of, my head swimming with figures. I buried my head in books heavier than the telephone directory and memorised whatever data I thought I needed. If the subject matter interested me it might have been bearable but it didn't. I would have preferred to be at the dentist. When I was informed I'd passed all my exams I greeted the news passively. I couldn't see myself carrying on with this mental torture for two more years, let alone for life.

I spent the summer working in an Irish pub in London. It was called The Blackstock Hotel but it was more like a tip.

I went with a friend of Hugo's called Chris Griffin.

He was from Gort, not far from where Yeats had his tower in Galway. He seemed to know a lot of Yeats poems by heart and quoted them often to me. At this stage I wasn't reading literature. I had a book with me called *Rebels* which was about rebel heroes in films. That was more to my taste then.

Hugo came over to join us at the end of the summer. One night after the bar closed we had a heart-to-heart with him about my future. I told him how unhappy I was. He said he'd been unhappy in the seminary. We talked about existentialism, about the importance of living in the "here and now."

"Why don't you join me in the Arts faculty?" he suggested at one stage of the night. We were both fairly well on. It sounded so simple. Why hadn't I thought of it? Sometimes when you're in a situation you can't think straight. I couldn't see the wood for the trees in Ireland. Now that I was away from it I realised how miserable I was in the world of Commerce.

That was the night I made my first "existential" choice in life. As Sartre said, "Man is condemned to be free." When I got back to Ireland I registered for Arts, picking English and Philosophy as my subjects. I was walking on air for the first few weeks. I dipped into Sartre and was blown away by him. He was "the big guy" in the philosophy department. Albert Camus was big too. In some ways they were like two sides of the same coin.

Reading Camus' *The Outsider* – upon Hugo's recommendation – blew my mind in a different way. The second half didn't measure up to the first (except for the last page) but I can safely say it was a book that changed my life. Nothing else

Camus wrote even came close to equalling it, just as nothing Sartre wrote after *Iron in the Soul* came close to that book for me. The fact that philosophers could write novels amazed me, but then I thought back to Plato, who sort of did even then.

Other iconic texts followed, Heidegger's *Being and Time* being the most memorable, and some of Hegel and Husserl. Reading texts for pleasure, or even just browsing through them (life wasn't long enough to read some of them in total) was so much an antidote to the year in Commerce. There I was force-fed books that seemed to be written by automatons to be read by other automatons. When I started reading books for the English course, the pleasure was increased exponentially.

Lectures became minor inconveniences, especially if they were given by people like Maurice Harmon or Eva Thornley. They reminded me more of secondary school teachers. Some others, like Jim O'Malley, exuded energy. Their enthusiasm became infectious. Paddy Masterson, who would go on to become president of the college some years on, brought a book into Theatre L called *Atheism and Alienation* one day. He said atheism was now more prevalent than belief in the world. I tried to imagine someone saying something like that in Ballina, a town which seemed to be crowned by St. Muredach's Cathedral as its centrepiece. I felt myself outgrowing it, outgrowing everything in my past as I buried myself in radical texts.

After the lectures I usually went to the bar.

Was this supposed to be study? If it was I thought I could get used to it. At least if I didn't succumb to cirrhosis of the liver before graduation. We treated the lectures as preludes to the night's revelry.

Sometimes after a late night I wrote notes to my mother with messages like 'Wake me at two, I have a lecture.' Ballina had engrained this nocturnal lifestyle in me and university continued it. I hated going to bed early. It was as if you were letting the day away with something. My mind seemed to come alive after midnight There were no distractions then. You could commune with your real self.

Our most noteworthy lecturer was Denis Donoghue. He was an authority on literary classics. He swept into the room like a ghost, as tall as a basketball player and whip-thin. The lectures were like extended poems, delivered in his urbane rhetoric. Most of us didn't have a clue what he was talking about but his classes were always full. 'Mind-blowing,' we'd say, 'truly mind-blowing.' But our notepads were usually empty after he'd departed the rostrum. It was like *The Emperor's New Clothes*. He could have been the greatest fraud on earth and got away with it. None of us wanted to admit we were stumped by him.

One of the people in my class was Harry Clifton. In time he'd become a highly acclaimed poet. He was submitting his writing to David Marcus of the *Irish Press* when I knew him. 'The scrounger only gives me £2 a poem,' he complained, 'It's hardly the Guggenheim Fellowship.' But the thrill of seeing one's name in print couldn't be priced.

Harry and myself did night security work on the docks together at that time. We only earned pin money but a big perk was the fact that you could sleep on the job. We even brought our alarm clocks into the office with us. Anyone who tried to rob any of the premises we guarded would have had an easy time because we'd probably have been snoring like pigs as they made off with the loot.

One night when I was supposed to be minding a place I went off to the pictures instead on my bicycle. When I got back the boss of the premises was standing there waiting for me looking like thunder 'Did you have a good time?' he asked me

I once asked Harry where he got his inspiration. He said, "When I'm scraping out pots." I tried that but nothing came. On the credit side, the kitchen was cleaner.

In our first year in Arts we had to study Old English texts like *Beowulf*. This is the only book that makes Chaucer look good by comparison. He was next up for us, Old English giving way to Middle English. It was a bit more recognisable but you still had to sort of "translate" it before it meant anything. I couldn't understand the point of studying dead languages. Hadn't universities given up Latin to avoid this? Hadn't Greek been dropped from the curriculum in Muredach's to spare me such ridiculousness.

With Harry Clifton. He always reminded me of Kafka

The philosophy classes were fine but this felt like going backwards. Was it what I'd given up Commerce for? I went through a period of thinking I'd made a mistake. I was studying crap and not guaranteed to get a job from it. Commerce wasn't any better than watching paint dry but I knew if I persevered at it I'd have become filthy rich after graduating. Watching paint dry didn't seem too bad if you were living in a five-bedroom mansion and driving to work every day in a Maserati. All Arts grads got were woolly jumpers and Volkswagens and jobs tutoring spoiled kids from Stillorgan while Mummy went to her needlepoint class. When were we going to be allowed to read books that looked like the language we grew up speaking?

That happened in second year. It was as if we were being rewarded for serving our time in linguistic boot camp. I jumped for joy when we were given Arthur Miller's *Death of a Salesman* to study. Edward Albee's *Who's Afraid of Virginia Woolf?* followed. Hugo even did a reading of it in one of the lecture halls one day. A reading was where people acted out the parts with copies of the books their hands so they didn't have to learn off the lines. It enabled talent scouts from Dramsoc – the university dramatic society – to spot future Oliviers

Even though I liked a lot of the things about the English course, some of it annoyed me – like the tutorials we had to go to. At each of these we were presented with a poem by somebody like William Carlos Williams and people would go into ecstasies about it - because the writer was famous.

I felt if I brought a poem I'd written into one of our tutorials it would be laughed at even if it was better than the ones we were called on to study there. Every week a poem would be left on all our chairs. For the next hour or so we'd analyse every syllable of it like scientists dissecting frogs in a laboratory. That might have been justifiable if it was a masterpiece but often these poems were deadly dull, at least to me. They were also very obscure. Obscure poems lent themselves to varying interpretations. That didn't mean they were any good. Often as I watched my classmates trying to think up denser and denser theories I'd find myself wondering what was on television that night or if I'd have time for a coffee in the bar before getting the bus home.

Denis Donoghue told us poems didn't have to be apocalyptic. They could be about someone stumbling on a stairs. I couldn't have imagined Donoghue stumbling on a stairs, or indeed writing a poem. He told us once that he'd never felt inclined to write one despite having given over his life to studying them. I thought that shouldn't be allowed. Would we allow an electrician into our house who hadn't had experience working with electricity? Or a plumber who hadn't spent time plumbing? English seemed to be the one area people could drop into willy-nilly and pontificate without being adept at it themselves.

Donoghue undoubtedly loved poetry but sometimes I thought he loved poetry critics just as much. For every Marianne Moore there was an F.R. Leavis, for every Baudelaire there was a Frank Kermode. The people carving out the creativity were no better in his framework than the people talking about it in haughty tones. It was all part of the same machinery.

My tutor was a man from Derry called Seamus Deane. He had such a sonorous voice it almost hypnotised you.

In later years Deane would write some fine books of poetry and a highly-acclaimed memoir. He fell from grace when he compiled a Field Day anthology of poetry which left women out of it. (His excuse "I forgot" didn't really do him any favours.) It was a bit like staging *Macbeth* without Lady Macbeth because the director "forgot."

At UCD I learned there was a pecking order of scribes just as there was of everything else. There were some writers you were "allowed" to like and some you 'Weren't allowed to. Wordsworth had fallen out of favour by now. He was "infra dig."

Andrew Carpenter was another tutor I had. A bunch of us impressionable souls trudged into his little office every Tuesday for a weekly dose of culture. He was British, with a demeanour that reminded me of a cricket player. All he was missing was white shirt and flannel shorts. His voice was so mellifluous he could have been an actor. I imagined him in some Noel Coward play in the Gate.

"Do you like Wordsworth?" he asked me once. I was afraid to say I did. It was as if it was some kind of secret sin. "Maybe you could compose a sonnet for us," he continued. He looked out the window and went into a reverie. "You could be lolling in a hammock as the flowers shivered in the mid-day heat," he suggested. Poor Willie. He was being made fun of. How quickly reputations died. Maybe it was all those sermons under the stones, if not the famous daffodils. Later day I had a coffee with Harry and he told me how much he loved "The Prelude." Balance had been restored.

Maybe the negative feelings about Wordsworth went back further than this. James Stephens once described him as "a half-witted sheep who bleated articulate monotony." Harry obviously saw something in him that the rest of us didn't. "It's the sweep of The Prelude that sets it apart," he said to me. Sometimes it was the sound of a line that hooked you in rather than the imagery. I felt the same about Hemingway when I got into him.

I didn't know whether to go for the "top" writers or the more middlebrow ones. Hugo used to talk about a critic who didn't know whether he enjoyed a book or not until he read the reviews. The film critic Pauline Kael once said, "If we can't enjoy great trash we shouldn't go to the movies." I felt the same applied to books. Sometimes we needed roughage in our diet of reading just like in our food one. If I read a good paragraph of Maeve Binchy – not saying she was trash I could enjoy it as much, maybe more, than Shakespeare.

I read *Madame Bovary*, *Moby Dick*, *The Ballad of the Sad Cafe*. I picked up George Eliot's *Middlemarch*, the so-called "much admired but little read" classic...and decided to leave it that way.

Hugo loved Lee Dunne's *Goodbye to the Hill* and prevailed on me to read it. I was captivated by the directness of the style. When I finished it I went back to page 1 and read it again. I went from Dunne to the great writers of the past, - Gide, Gogol, Baudelaire. Harry referred me to Rilke's *Duino Elegies*.

If a writer took too long getting to the point, or if they wrote to impress rather than express, I lost interest in them. They had to draw me in fast. As I rambled between the shelves in the Belfield library I picked up books by people I'd never heard of before, people like Jorge Luis Borges and Gabriel Marcia Marquez. I was like a drug addict looking for a new fix. I'd open their books at a random page and read a few sentences. If I liked them I'd read on. If not, I wouldn't. Other people read the back covers to see if they might enjoy books. I never liked doing that. The back cover usually had some quotes from other writers about the style – usually too laudatory – which pre-empted your own response to it. Secondly it became a plot spoiler, telling you what a book was "about," and I never wanted to know that. Was it Ford Madox Ford or Henry James who said, "Ah yes, the plot," as if it was a necessary evil. I thought the same way. I had no interest in plots. That's why I was never a fan of crime fiction – unless it was by someone like Patricia Highsmith. She used plots as devices to carry her style around in.

Agatha Christie I found particularly insufferable. Ruth Rendell said calling her characters cardboard cut-outs was an insult to cardboard cut-outs. But then people didn't read her for her characters. They read her for what they did. And the Beeb did such wonderful adaptations of her work, didn't they?

I also found Russian novelists hard to read - or anyone else who spent twenty pages telling you they made a cup of tea - but it wasn't kosher to admit that. It looked impressive wandering around the campus carrying a beefy tome by someone from St. Petersburg with an unpronounceable name.

I started discussing books with anyone who was interested. They didn't have to be in my class. Chris was always on for a chat. He loved talking about books, continuing the fascination with Yeats that he'd shown in London. He had a friend called Dennis Cotter who was fond of Charles Dickens. Both Chris and Dennis started dating two American girls who were friends of one another. They married them some years later.

I gobbled up everything I could find in the library that year, pulling books from shelves at will. As I sat down to read them looking out at the lake, suddenly it didn't look so mechanical. They transported me into daydreams. Hours passed like minutes. Before I knew where I was it was dinner time then tea time. Harry might tap me on the shoulder, or Bill Cunningham, a person I'd known, from Belvedere. Over meals we talked more about books. In Bill's case it was Accountancy books. He'd been in my Commerce year as well.

Back in the library I'd see Harry scribbling poems in his spidery scrawl. I'm sure many of them ended up in his future collections. I wasn't doing anything creative at this stage, just soaking up other people's outpourings like a sponge. I thought of John McGahern's statement: "We become readers before we become writers." It wasn't like in Commerce where I read them out of duty. This was fun. I thought of Basil buying Joyce in Ballina and still having a career outside literature, the best of both worlds. He was in America now but loved coming home. You can see his devotion to June and Ruth in the picture opposite. Ruth would soon go to America to live too.

I liked reading forbidden books. *Lady Chatterley's Lover* was the first time I ever saw the "C" word in a book. Was that something to be lauded? It certainly stopped me in my tracks when I read it. "Bad" language is everywhere nowadays but we should remember a time when it wasn't. There's a famous story about Norman Mailer. He wasn't allowed to use the word "fuck" in *The Naked and the Dead* so he put in "fug" instead. At a party one time a fellow author came up to him. She said, "Oh, Mr Mailer, delighted to meet you. Aren't you the person who can't spell 'Fuck?'"

Many people read Philip Roth's *Portnoy's Complaint* at this time, maybe because they were told they weren't supposed to. In that sense it was like a modern day equivalent of what *Lady Chatterley's Lover* had been for a previous generation. The forbidden fruit always attracted. Someone once suggested that the best way to revive the Irish language was to ban all books written in Gaelic. It's a good theory.

I read *Lady Chatterley* and found it to be very well written. The erotic, or quasi-erotic, passages annoyed me because of Lawrence's tone of high seriousness. He sacramentalised sex. It took Roth to make it into a joke. That was also something Charles Bukowski (when I eventually discovered him) was also good at. And of course Woody Allen, though Woody is mainly known for his films.

Basil with June and Ruth in the sixties

There was a lot of talk about the unbanning of *Lady Chatterley's Lover* but it seemed to me that censorship wasn't really beaten by rulings like this any more than it was by allowing us to see films like *Red Dust* or *Lolita*. The best way to beat it was to write books like *Portnoy's Complaint* or make films like *Bob and Carol* and *Ted and Alice*. Placing sex on a pedestal, even a forbidden one, endorses the mindset that made it so. Better to put it on a vaudeville stage or a burlesque, I thought. In other words, give me Boccaccio's *Decameron* rather than *Last Tango in Paris*.

Seamus Deane told me I should read D.H. Lawrence's *Women in Love* and Norman Mailer's *Armies of the Night*.

I'd dabbled with Mailer's novels and found them wanting. Was there ever an author who strove after effect as much as he did? Sometimes it was intoxicating but after reading a few pages you were never sure what you had to show for it. More often than not it was a victory of style over substance. I didn't even rave about *The Naked and the Dead* like other people did. *Armies of the Night* was different. I was immediately hooked when he wrote about himself in the third person. For years after this I could only read his journalism instead of his fiction. I'd sampled this in Ballina with Hugo's copy of *Advertisements for Myself* but I was too young to appreciate it then. I now read it fully and convinced myself he was a genius. I thanked Deane for that.

A third book Deane recommended was William Faulkner's *A Light in August*. I'd always found Faulkner unfathomable up to this. *A Light in August* was only slightly unfathomable – an improvement. Deane also recommended Saul Bellow's *Herzog*. My friend Glenn was a Bellow nut, read all of his books and made sure I did too. My favourites were *Dangling Man* and *Henderson the Rain King*. When you've never heard of someone and then go into them full tilt it's a weird experience. I became obsessed with Bellow for a while but then the allure wore off. I didn't read any of his later books. It was like a love affair with a woman that went cold. There was no reason for it. What surprised me was that I was starting to think of books like I did people. I fell in and out of love with them as if they were living things.

Sampling people like this set me on a journey to other authors – people like Virginia Woolf, Herman Hesse, Flannery O'Connor,

Sylvia Plath, Kurt Vonnegut, Eudora Welty. I went through a
John Updike phase, a Richard Brautigan one. I read Rilke's
poems – Harry had a thing about him. Likewise Ezra Pound: My
concentration spell was poor for some of these, the old ADHD
still being alive and well. I was impatient with long-winded
scribes like Henry James. Studying *The Bostonians* "cured" me of
him. Some people I knew were into Proust. I felt life was too short
'to even start on him. Chris introduced me to the poetry of Paddy
Kavanagh and I never looked back. I re-read Yeats and found him
spell-binding. All we'd got of him in Muredachs was a few of the
trivial poems. We weren't regarded as "mature" enough for the
significant ones. But I often found these more accessible.

Basil exposed me to James Joyce. I loved *Dubliners*, mainly
for "The Dead." but I couldn't make head or tail of *Ulysses*, never
mind *Finnegans Wake*. I found Flann O'Brian hilarious but he
wasn't in especially good favour with my fellow academics.
Maybe that was because he wasn't on any of our courses. Not all
of them read "around" them like I did. Or maybe he was too
funny. Writers were supposed to be a miserable lot, weren't they?

There was a lot of "whataboutery" surrounding *Finnegans
Wake*. It bored me. The only mystery it threw up to me was why
such a genius would want to spend so many years of his life on
what Ezra Pound called "one long spelling mistake."

I didn't know why Joyce would want to follow the most
unread book of his time with the most unreadable one. For
mischief? It would have been a very time-consuming party trick,
even if the benefits were large.

I saw *Finnegans Wake* as his two-fingered salute to the
groves of academe. He once said, "The only demand I make of
my reader is that he should devote his life to reading my works,"
adding that *Finnegans Wake* would keep scholars in theses until
the end of the millennium. Maybe if they were sequestered away
in dusty libraries, the rest of us outside those groves would be
safe. I thought radar equipment should have been installed at the
exits of universities to warn us they were coming out. When
Flannery O'Connor was asked if universities stifled writers she
replied, "They don't stifle half enough of them." It would have
been better if they stifled the academics. This breed seemed to go

on forever – probably because they never had to break into a sweat thinking up something original.

I didn't think literature should be a crossword puzzle. If I wanted to do a crossword I'd do a crossword. When I took up a novel I expected something more.

Everyone knew Joyce painted himself into a corner after finishing the writings he did in Ireland. That was all right. He wanted to experiment. It was the degree of experimentation that bothered me, that and the degree of self-indulgence.: I was one of those people who thought *Ulysses* could have done with a hefty dose of editing. The fact that Joyce was effectively his own editor, having been "enabled" in this department by all the generous ladies he knew, meant he got away with murder in all his "big" books. What a pity that was. He was too good a writer to have to resort to the gimmickry of some of *Ulysses* and all of *Finnegans Wake*. And no, I didn't want to devote the rest of my life to unravelling that "long spelling mistake."

From the tutorials I deduced that the more "difficult" you were as a writer, the better you were as far as the academics were concerned. Hence the poor favour of Flann O'Brien vis-a-vis Joyce. If Joyce had written *At-Swim Two Birds* the same academics would never have stopped talking about it. Because it came from O'Brien it was dismissed as a curiosity piece.

Hemingway was another writer who was dismissed by the cognoscenti because he wasn't "difficult." It was easy to accuse him of bigging up the machismo thing but I never saw him that way. The first book of his that I read was *For Whom the Bell Tolls*. Hugo had a tattered copy that became even more tattered when I dived into it. It became a fixture in my jacket pocket on way to Belfield every day.

Some of my classmates quoted Zelda Fitzgerald's dictum about him wearing false hair on his chest as if that was all there was to him. I felt sorry for people like that. They were doing themselves out of so much. Others said things like, "He never quite matched up to the early stories." It was another cliche that made me want to throw up. Harry was the first person I heard praising *The Sun Also Rises*. Today it's regarded as one of his best novels but in the seventies people weren't saying things like that.

Seeking inspiration from the old artificer

61

A writer called Ellery Sedgewick made an interesting observation when she said books should begin with Chapter Two. Fitzgerald felt that about *The Sun Also Rises*. Hemingway had originally written an introductory chapter which Fitzgerald thought was unnecessary. How ironic that someone who often over-wrote saw Hemingway, the great under-writer, as being guilty of this. It was even more amazing that Hemingway, who didn't normally take other people's advice, realised he was right. (He never liked talking about this because he looked down on Fitzgerald).

Dennis Cotter liked *A Farewell to Arms*. Another person I knew talked about *Across the River and Into the Trees*, the "forgotten" Hemingway novel. It was written when he'd lost his famous "inbuilt crap detector" but it had its moments.

No matter where you stood on Hemingway, one thing most people agreed on was the brilliance of his short stories. There was an almost mathematical perfection to them. You felt if even a word was added or subtracted it would upset or destroy that. Nobody before him had been so conscious of the length, or sound, of a line – at least in prose. F. Scott Fitzgerald said the opening sentence of "*In Another Country*" was the most beautiful one he'd ever read: "In the fall the war was always there but we did not go to it anymore."

The girls in my class didn't like Hemingway, seeing him as a man's writer. I was aware some of the women in his books were poorly depicted but the women in the stories – again – were real.

I wasn't much good at talking to girls when I came to Dublin, seeing them almost like a foreign species. Dance halls meant fumbled conversations in dark corners, often with drink on board. In Belfield it was easier. You didn't have to shout cliches at someone and hope not to be drowned out by the music as you pretended to be able to dance. You could say "What do you think of *One Day in the Life of Ivan Denisovich*?" without them thinking it was a chat-up line.

There was a girl in our class called Moya Cannon. I remember her saying to me one day, "The problem with this country is too many men are going around wearing fáinnes, tricolours and Pioneer pins." I thought to myself: There's no way she's going to end up pregnant, barefoot and in the kitchen like so many of her predecessors in De Valera's Ireland. She went on to become a highly acclaimed poet.

Another girl in my class, I think her name was Barbara Allen – like in the song – loved *The Great Gatsby*. She was an unusual person. Every day she'd slip into Theatre L and go down to the front seat where she'd listen to the lecture without taking any notes. Then she'd slip out again. She rarely talked to anyone. I hadn't read *The Great Gatsby* until she recommended it to me but of course I was delighted she did. The first time you read a book like this you wonder how it's escaped you for so long. When I started to get into Hemingway I read that he told Fitzgerald that he needed to get "over" it so he could produce more great work. I don't know if that was true. Was he jealous of it?

In 1973 I met Mary, the woman who would eventually become my wife. She worked in a solicitor's office in Clare Street called O' Connors. Like me she was from the west and like me she'd been uprooted from it. My father came to Dublin because he was retiring but hers came because he was offered a promotion there. He was working in the Civil Service in Galway at the time and was happy there. His boss wanted him to take the promotion. He'd offered him similar promotions in previous years that he'd turned down. He was told this would be the last one. It was now or never. He decided to take it. The two of us often compared notes about how we'd failed to adjust to city life. Sometimes we went back to Ballina and sometimes to Galway. Each time we went back it left us with a wrench. We were feeding a desire that we couldn't fulfil because our homes were gone. Mine had been turned into a community centre now so I could never go back to it.

I wrote a poem about my feelings of displacement:

Trying to look intelligent at a literary function

Other people had homes to go back to.
I'd see them at Heuston and Connolly
bank clerks, student nurses
pupils at boarding schools
laughing and joking at kiosks
with satchels in their hands.
They were the lucky ones
the ones with two addresses
their lives intertwined in carriages
where they talked about what they'd done
since they hit the city
what they planned to do
on the long weekends home
sitting around the house
being spoiled by parents
going for walks
in villages
that surrounded Ballina
like satellites.

I couldn't be part of them.
I only had tourist places
to go to now
picturesque destinations
advertised by Bord Fáilte
for foreigners -
five star hotels
with all the best amenities,
renovated cottages
in places like Charlestown,
Newport, Castlebar.

I watched the villages whizzing by
as the train picked up speed
as commuters got off
carrying teddy bears
toys, footballs
for family members.

I imagined them playing with them
as I once played
with toys
and teddy bears
before I
became a city person
catapulted from
what I knew,
slotting myself
into a life
of apartments
where everything
was that more compact,
where your possessions
lay in compartments
and your neighbours waved to you
on cold Monday mornings
as they drove to work
on distant estates.

Mary liked coming out to Belfield with me. It was so different to her from the world of law that she inhabited with people who worked from nine to five and didn't talk about books, only letters to be typed and deals made. She'd written some great stories but hadn't confidence in herself.

If we were ever sitting in the restaurant with people from my class she'd go into a shell, feeling she couldn't compete with the conversations that were going on. I'd say to her, "Don't feel intimidated by these people. They know nothing. You're the one who's able to write." She looked up to them because they knew some big words. I told her they were just hiding their ignorance behind those words. If they talked down to her I got annoyed. She reminded me of Gelsomina in Fellini's *La Strada*, a pure spirit who wasn't wise in the ways of the world.

She was never academic. As a result she put bookish people on pedestals. After a while she realised they were more like her than she realised. She became friends with Harry and Chris.

Sometimes the three of us went down to a local Simon Community to help out. At twenty you think you can save the world. The three of us were also doing some night security work at this time.

Now and then she sat in on lectures. That was a different kind of buzz, watching Denis Donoghue breeze into Theatre L as if catapulted by a chariot from the gods.

Donoghue mentioned writers like Alain-Robbe Grillet and Nathalie Sarraute to us. They were hot at the time. He gave lectures about plotless novels that were supposed to entrance you with their style. At the end of them you were no wiser as regards what they were about than at the beginning but you weren't supposed to complain about this. You were meant to embrace the fact that you'd just read the intellectual equivalent of a whodunit without the who that dunit.

I could also start a conversation about Roland Barthes, another writer Donoghue liked boring us about. Barthes was a structuralist of the New Criticism school. New Criticism meant you analysed texts to within an inch of their lives. Barthes wrote a whole book about one of Balzac's short stories once. Worse still, I went out and bought it. I had Mary losing sleep over him.

After philosophy lectures I talked to her about George Berkeley's "Esse est percipi" dictum. "If a tree falls in the forest," I'd say, "and nobody hears it, it makes no sound." "That's nonsense," she'd say, "Of course it has to make a sound."

I'd say, "You don't get it. It's about duality, the confluence of subject and object." She'd say, "Does anyone agree with me?"

After a time she grew tired of these discussions. One night she said she wanted to see the latest Glenda Jackson film that was on in the Savoy. Instead I brought her to oblique monstrosities by Godard in the Irish Film Theatre. I'd stroke my cheek meaningfully as we came out into the foyer afterwards. "What a film," I'd say to her but inside myself I'd be thinking the same thing she was: "What the fuck was that all about?"

I got excited about Barthes' deconstruction of texts, putting him with Robbe-Grillet as the Great White Hope of literature. That was the thing about being in the English faculty. You now spoke with authority. Not for you the latest bonkbuster by Jolly

Super - that's Jilly Cooper to you, mate – or Shirley Conran. You were able to go to parties and say, "The thing about writing is that it's meant to elevate and depress you at the same time." Nobody could disagree with you because you were an Arts student. You were reading the Romantics, the Elizabethans, the Renaissance poets. You knew everything. Dammit, you even knew that A.S. Byatt was Margaret Drabble's sister. Put that in your pipe and smoke it, commoners.

Getting Published

The first time I started writing professionally, to use that horrible word, was in UCD. I wanted to do film reviews but they had no slot for that in the student magazine. A friend told me TCD had one. I rang the editor of TCD *Miscellany* and asked him if he'd be interested. He said he would. It didn't seem to matter that I was attending the "rival" university. I mentioned that my father had been a Trinity student. That might have helped. "There's no money in this, by the way," he said at the end of the call. I said I hadn't expected there would be.

The first film I reviewed for him was Liliana Cavani's *The Night Porter*. It was a sado-masochistic film starring Dirk Bogarde and Charlotte Rampling - ideal for students. I was up and running. There's nothing to compare to seeing your name in print for the first time. You've been bitten by the bug as they say. *The Night Porter* set me up for decades of film reviewing with perhaps a dozen different outlets. Even so, I never really liked doing it. Writing about films took the spontaneity out of going to them. In Ballina I'd had more excitement as the curtains parted. There was excitement even going up the stairs of the Estoria looking at the posters. Now it was a job. You were thinking about what you were going to say during every scene. There was an element of showing off in that. You got the idea you were somebody, an authority on the genre even at nineteen years of age. Nobody is as arrogant as a teenager.

I started doing book reviews at this time too. The same thing applied: you compromised your natural reaction to a book when you were writing about it. It became a question of saying something more sophisticated than the next guy, writing to impress rather than to express.

The more reviews I did, the more I developed a style of writing that was formulaic. It made things even worse. At a certain point I felt the reviews were almost writing themselves in a kind of identikit manner that negated any individuality the films or books possessed. Would the day come when they'd be inconveniences you had to undergo? When you'd judge them as good or bad depending on whether they lived up (or down) to what you intended to say about them before you started the first page?

I now started writing little books as well, study guides for Inter and Leaving Cert students. Again it deadened knowledge, fossilising it the way the university often did. Like the character in 1984 I had fallen in love with my chains. I'd come to love Big Brother.

I churned these books out on a treadmill of cliches, writing guides to plays and novels with quotable quotes for clever clogs pupils who'd parrot my polysyllabic words at exam time and get the grades they needed to bring them to the next stage of their "education." If I did it well enough, they'd probably be so sick of it all they'd never read another book in their lives.

I pulled George Eliot's *Silas Marner* asunder for one of my books. Mary typed it up for me. For Gill and Macmillan I did a treatment of Henry James' *Portrait of a Lady*. Gus Martin, one of my UCD lecturers was drafted in to hold my hand as I did it. Some of my classmates dismissed him as "a glorified secondary teacher," probably because he'd been one, and collaborated on drafting the English curriculum for the Leaving Cert.

Kevin Brophy was-my editor for another company I worked for, School and College Services. "You never use a small word where a big one will do, do you?" he chided. I pleaded guilty. "They'd eat this sooner than read it," he said of one of my books. He reminded me that some of the potential readers would hardly be able to write their names. That's why they needed study guides.

Hugo was teaching English in a posh secondary school in Blackrock now. I don't think he was too impressed with my books but he was too nice to say so. He knew what I was at, straitjacketing texts into pre-ordained formats. It made them closed. I was God and nobody could disagree with me. He went into his classroom 200 days a year and had a different perspective on texts for each of those days – and for each of his pupils. I just had one.

I hated pulverising texts in the way I did but I kept doing it. Why? I didn't know. Hugo told me about a pupil he had one year in his Inter Cert class when they were studying *The Merchant of*

Venice. A question on the Inter exam paper asked, "How do you feel about Shylock?" They were expected to give a 1,000 word answer but this girl just wrote, "I feel sorry for him." I would have given her an A.

Analysis led to paralysis. I stopped doing the study guides and tried to get back to, for want of a better word, creative writing. David Marcus was still editing the page in the *Irish Press*. He took short stories as well as poems so I decided to send him some.

There are hundreds of outlets for writers today but in the seventies in Ireland there weren't. The fact that Marcus gave people who'd never seen their name in print before a chance to be read in every living room in the country was huge. He lit a fuse in me that still hasn't gone out. I bombarded him submissions over the next few years. Mary started sending him stories now as well.

Marcus was a shrewd critic and an inspired developer of unknown writers. More than anyone else he was responsible for me becoming one. (To that extent he has a lot to answer for.) One of the first stories I sent him had a scene in a country railway station where a woman was about to throw herself under a train.

The way I wrote it, there were about a hundred people milling around her. He called me into his office in Burgh Quay and said, 'This is a railway station in the middle of nowhere. It's 8 a.m. What are all the people doing there? It reads like a scene from *Anna Karenina*.'

The first story I had in his page was called At Lourdes. It was a benchmark for me. One paragraph dealt with a man who threw away his crutches only to find he was still crippled. He'd got euphoric too soon in the story.

It was a satire of people who convinced themselves they were cured of their maladies by a kind of self-hypnosis. I'd never been to Lourdes but Mary had. I picked her brain for the practical details I needed to make the scenes I was depicting look real

Maybe I was too real. My aunt Florence, a deeply religious person, read the story and thought I was making fun of religion. She was my first literary critic. My mother was staying with her at the time in a boarding house she ran in Dun Laoghaire. She gave out to her about me. My mother didn't like what she was saying.

She thought the story was well written. I tried to explain to Aunt Florence that the story was a satire of people who suffered from delusions rather than of religion but she didn't want to hear this. She stuck to her guns. My mother ended up leaving the boarding house and coming back to the Villas. I admired her for that as she was deeply religious too. The experience made me aware that writing could be divisive. It was good to learn these things early. Attention was nice but it came with a price.

I showed her some of my other stories afterwards. As she was reading them she saw a side to me I hadn't exhibited in my day-to-day behaviour. I wasn't sure if she was impressed with that or not. She said to me one night, "Why are all your stories sad?" I said, "Because life is." She didn't want me to reflect that. Books for her were meant to be uplifting things. I tried to explain to her that I could be more uplifted by a sad story than a happy one if it was well written.

She couldn't understand that. The things that uplifted her were dramatic films with happy endings or playing piano. Or singing "Jerusalem." I wasn't able to facilitate her there. There was no way I could be Julie Andrews tripping through the edelweiss singing "Climb Every Mountain" like she did in *The Sound of Music*, or Cliff Richard in a bus with Una Stubbs pumping out "We're all going on a sum-mer hol-i-day" like a ten year old Public School toff.

Publication of the stories led to me having a go at writing poetry. I knew I could never be Harry Clifton but at least I could try. I immersed myself in some of the greats to see it even a flake of their genius would rub off on me. Muredach's hadn't given me a love of poetry like UCD had but I wasn't bitter about that. I didn't think it was any worse than any other college in the country. It was the curriculum that was the problem. UCD opened up other kinds of doors.

I went on a binge of reading poetry. When I took up Yeats I felt I was reading the Bible. He had an architectural style that reminded me of sculpture. It was so authoritative it made you feel like giving up even before you started. When Leonard Cohen started quoting him to me in the late eighties when I interviewed

A Ripe Old Age

Aubrey Dillon-Malone

Cohen it made his power all the more obvious. I didn't realise how much of a global figure he was until then.

Joe O'Connor once said that the most pleasing experience of his literary life was writing "Yeats" and "Fuck" in the same sentence. I knew how that would have felt. He was like the poetic equivalent of Eamon de Valera, the ubiquitous president of our country who represented "the way things were done." You had to drive a wedge through that to feel a part of your time.

Eoin O'Mahony was the first person I remember bringing Yeats down to earth. "My entire involvement with the Irish Literary Revival," he said once, "consisted of standing beside him once at a urinal during an interval at the Abbey, where I remember he was having great difficulty with his waterworks:" It might have surprised some people to know that the august tower dweller actually had to go to the bathroom on occasion.

When I started writing poetry my mother became lost. "What does that line mean?" she'd say if I wrote something obscure. I'd say, "It doesn't have to mean anything." She'd say, "Why write it so?" I'd say, "I thought it sounded good."

We'd natter on like this but the conversation would really go nowhere. She was too practical for poetry to mean anything to her unless it was straightforward. My father had no time for abstract poetry either. Sad stories he could take – like the ones he learned off to deliver his recitations: "Babette," "Lasca," "The Green Eye of the Little Yellow God." He became so emotional delivering these I'd often find my eyes welling up too.

He didn't like Hemingway. "Wasn't he a communist?" he said to me one day. I continued to write my stories like Hemingway, or at least like one hundredth of him. That would have been the apex of my ambition.

Every writer is influenced by someone. The thing is how we use it. When I wrote the story "The Process of Maturing" I tried to write it in a William Trevor style. When I wrote "Phases" I was looking for a Des Hogan vibe. "On the Quay Road" is my Hemingway story. I etch in the atmosphere, create some tension, explain what causes the tension later on, end on a dying fall. It's the idiom he used all the time. I wasn't trying to copy these writers, just think like them so I'd see how they got their effects.

Joe O'Connor said he once re-wrote a John McGahern story word for word to see if he could replicate it some way. Maybe that's taking things a bit far but I saw his point.

Anytime I left a book down and then picked up another one I tended to hear the voice of the previous writer through the lines. If I left a poetry book down and took up a novel I read the lines as poetry for a while.

Likewise the tone. Things carried over when you read as many books at the same time as I did. They were all like *Finnegans Wake* in a sense, continually revolving on invisible axes towards their envelope patterns. From this point of view, browsing was really a fulltime thing with me. There was nothing else. My short concentration span wouldn't allow it. I tried to turn this into an advantage, soaking up as many atmospheres as possible.

Erica Jong once said, "Writers stand on the shoulders of the dead." I certainly did. When I got Trevor's voice, or Hogan's, or anyone else, I felt the story had arrived. The characters made themselves fit that voice. The mood, in other words, created the music.

Sometimes I got more inspiration from bad writers than good ones. The good ones intimidated me because I knew I could never match them, whereas if I read someone like Mickey Spillane I thought it might trigger something in me that I could improve on. Which isn't to say Mickey Spillane is a bad writer. I took him up expecting him to be and was pleasantly surprised.

John Broderick believed that the two worst experiences for a writer were "to see books so good they dishearten him, and abysmal ones selling better than his own." That said it all for me.

I kept inflicting my stories on Marcus, sometimes sending him two or three in the one week. Most of them came back.

Mary had a better strike rate with him even though she only sent him stories now and again. She wrote them "on the hoof" between secretarial assignments in O'Connor's. If she got an idea she stuck a piece of paper in her typewriter and off with her. If her boss came into the room she had to pull it out and look busy. A novel she wrote years later was called *Trials of a Legal Secretary*. "As opposed to an illegal one," she explained.

Her stories were better than mine. They weren't laboured. Mine were. She wrote in a stream of consciousness style without even realising it. When I said to her, "I like your stream of consciousness," she said, "What's that?" That's what I loved about her. She was such a relief to the people I was meeting in Belfield who knew all the jargon but couldn't write their way out of a paper bag.

Marcus immediately spotted the spark and spontaneity in Mary that I admired so much. He accepted, I think, everything she sent him. She'd only had brief squibs printed before this, in a magazine she contributed to when she worked in the GPO. Her parents were proud of her.

Her father carefully cut the stories out of the paper and put them into his wallet. When he had a few jars on him he'd pull them out and show them to people in bars just like my father used to pull out photographs of our family in bars to show people.

Marcus became the victim of one too many of my Tortured Adolescent outpourings in time. He replied politely to my first few "Life is hell" diatribes but after the receipt of Armageddon Number 37 he'd had enough. He was usually meticulous in his dissemination of what was good and not so good about my stories but then came the killer rejection slip which had just one line written in his small, neat handwriting: "There's less to this than meets the eye."

What do you do with a response like that – put your head in the oven? Decide on another career? No, I went straight back to my study and composed another opus, this time a bit lighter. Less Ingmar Bergman, I told myself, and more Bob Hope. Try to be Mary. She had the right balance.

His barb – was it a Tallulah Bankhead one? – hit me where it hurt. Marcus was usually very constructive in his criticism. Putdowns like that seemed more like showing off. Was he getting cranky in his old age? Maybe a lifetime of reading other people's material instead of getting out work of your own wears you down. He was also editing anthologies of stories and judging competitions at this time. I'd also sent stories to these. Everywhere I went, it seemed, he was there before me. He was obviously suffering from an overdose of me.

I got my BA in 1974. Everyone was excited about the graduation ceremony but I failed to share the enthusiasm. All I did was read some books and regurgitate them. The people who deserved the mortarboards, I thought, were the writers of the books we read – or the parents who paid our university fees.

I had no idea what I wanted to do so I applied for the M.A. It was really just a way of postponing going out into the "real" world, whatever that was.

To get your M.A. you had to write a thesis of 18,000 words on some writer. Keith told me I should do it on F. Scott Fitzgerald. He wasn't much for reading novels but he loved the films made from them.

At the end of the day my taste ran to the leanness of Hemingway rather than Fitzgerald's more florid style. I argued with Keith over this. When I said I'd like to do a thesis on Hemingway he said, "Why not Fitzgerald?"

It was like the difference between two eras. In films I preferred Marlon Brando to his hero Humphrey Bogart. An article I once read on Brando said he brought "doubt into the locker room." I felt the same about Hemingway. That's why I was bored by all the talk about his machismo. If his life – and death – told us anything it was that a life of action in itself couldn't fulfil someone with his complexities.

Were people not aware of the emotional devastation of his last years? It was even evident in some of the early stories. You wouldn't see a more chilling depiction of depression than "A Clean, Well-Lighted Place."

The M.A. went on until August. That meant I couldn't get away for the summer unlike all my other years. I didn't realise how long a summer could be until that year. It was nightmarish strangling books you loved into intellectual debates but you had to do it to get the piece of paper.

In September I got on a plane to Paris and hitch-hiked to Athens. I think I had about £100 in my pocket. I slept on park benches, in all-night garages, on the beaches of Greece. By Christmas I was back home again. It was the most enjoyable three months of my life.

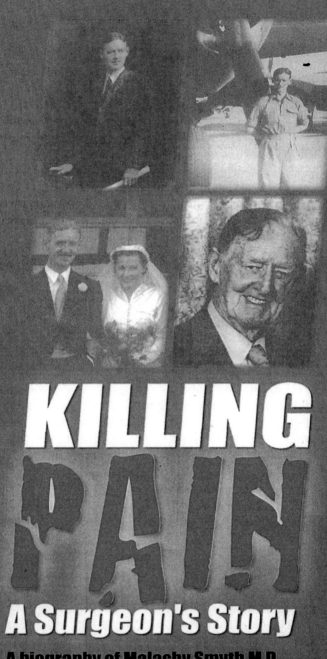

KILLING PAIN

A Surgeon's Story

A biography of Malachy Smyth M.D.,
F.A.C.S. F.R.C.S.

By Aubrey Malone

Floating

After I got back to Ireland I didn't know what I wanted to do. I was like the character in the book *The Graduate*, Benjamin Braddock. "Meet Benjamin," the blurb proclaimed, "He's a little worried about his future." So was I.

I never thought I'd become a writer, someone who answered an ad once to co-write a doctor's autobiography like in the book cover opposite. For two weeks before Christmas I became an auxiliary postman, helping out with the overload post offices always had at this time of the year. It was well paid. A lot of people I knew did it. One night I was at a party in Glenn Kiernan's flat on the Morehampton Road when one of the guys in our class – in an advanced state of inebriation – said, "I got tired delivering so I fucked all the cards into the canal."

I did some more night security work with Harry when the new year came in. The fact that we liked reading helped. We brought books with us along with our sleeping bags and alarm clocks to places in the middle of nowhere. The boss knew we spent most of our time sleeping. He didn't mind. We were employed so the places in question would qualify for insurance.

Every so often we had to go around the factories we were "guarding" with keys and turn them in what were called "clocking points." These were little machines affixed to walls in various rooms to prove you'd checked these places. In time we learned how to remove them from the walls and bring them back to the huts we slept in. Here we'd put the keys in every now and then – i.e. whenever we woke up. We took care to put them back on the walls before our relief arrived at dawn.

I signed on the dole for a while. Then I got a job on a building site. I was basically a messenger boy in a hard hat. My mother asked me what I planned to do for a living. She was more concerned about things like that than my father. He was as easy-going as he'd been when I was a child and wanted a day off school. I gathered it was the other way round in most families, the mother usually being more biddable. "I'll look up the Sits Vac if you want," I said. It was a column in the *Evening Herald*. I trussed myself up for a few interviews for dead end jobs but nothing came of them.

This was a period of pleasant idleness in my life. Maybe I could say the same about the whole three years since I'd done Commerce - after I'd had my "art attack." I wrote about it in a poem:

> *Crawling back from Alexandra Sheds*
> *on the red eye shift*
> *to Sherrie's*
> *for the injection of coffee*
> *that makes the day begin*
> *in earnest*
> *you survey the way your life has gone*
> *or not gone*
> *the degree that was to make you rich*
> *evaporated into nights shared with mice*
> *in a 12-by-4 hut*
> *where boneheads in uniforms*
> *examine your clocking points,*
> *your unironed trousers,*
> *your attitude problem.*
> *'You think you're somebody, don't you?'*
> *they accuse*
> *and you shake your head,*
> *hiding Anna Karenina under a lunchbox*
> *that smells of stale cheese.*
> *Girding your loins afterwards*
> *for the night ahead,*
> *and all the nights,*
> *you try conveniently to forget*
> *what your father had outlined for you*
> *in another life.*
> *Meanwhile you quoted Nietzsche*
> *in the Belfield bar,*
> *footloose and fiancé-free,*
> *gravitating afterwards to the library*
> *to rail against The System,*
> *a term you didn't understand*

but never stopped using, nonetheless
When you left college
you presented yourself to a society
you once reviled,
dolled up in your
one respectable suit
to confront an economy in disarray,
fudging the lines of revolt
against what was on offer,
hanging by the silken threads of narcissism
in a graduate factory
that was a home from home to you
before the dream dissipated
into the pyrotechnics of making do
on a building site,
the quotable quotes of dead Viennese poets
scant consolation to you
as you signed your autograph in a dole office
and your future, somewhere,
waited to present itself.

My mother thought I should do teaching. I didn't agree. I thought this was where all disgruntled graduates went to die. I felt it was the last refuge of a scoundrel, a return to the scene of the crime. Considering I'd been so miserable in Muredach's and Belvedere it could hardly work out. "Maybe you can make up for the mistakes made on you in these places by becoming a good teacher," she suggested. It was a good theory but I wasn't quite sure it would work. The mistakes that were made on me were more likely to make me want to murder the children rather than redeem them. I was too damaged.

I couldn't envisage myself back in a classroom to save my life but then something happened to change my mind. John Wilson was the Minister for Education. He spearheaded a scheme where university graduates could do a short course in primary teaching in St. Patrick's Training College. Full-time Pat's students did a three-year one. This got them a Bachelor of Education. We were being offered basically the same qualification for just one year's study. It was a good deal. I applied for it and was accepted.

My decision surprised a lot of people. They couldn't see me as a teacher. There was no chalk in my blood, as the expression went. Teachers were people who got hot and bothered about children's "development." I didn't really care about such things. If I saw a child I'd prefer to have a bit of fun with them rather than teach them the "three Rs."

Teachers I saw as people who dressed in duffel coats and drove cheap cars. They were pillars of the community. How could I be that? How could I even stand in front of forty children, never mind teach them anything? I'd be terrified. But where else was there to turn?

I had a piece of paper under my arm called a B.A. It stood for Bugger All. You couldn't use it for anything except teaching unless you went into advertising or RTE or something like that.

My father didn't want me to be a teacher either, especially a National one, but I felt myself backed into a corner after leaving UCD. There was nowhere left to turn except St. Pat's Training College. I contemplated the next year there as I neared the end of my night security "career."

A few months later I started in Pat's. I felt like I was going into the jaws of a lion. As soon as I entered the building I felt I was back in Muredach's.

There were stained glass windows and meticulously scrubbed floors, a far cry from the plexiglass of Belfield and the litter strewn all over the corridors. People had a look of having had a good night's sleep the night before; they looked ready for the challenge of work. Everyone looked too focussed, too tidy.

I was given a list of lecture times. I doubted I would be asking my mother to call me at 2 p.m. here. It would be more like 7 a.m. We wouldn't be studying for the love of it but for the expectation of a job.

There was a big emphasis on Irish. We studied the language at university level to teach children how to say things like 'John likes Mary.'

At one point of the year we were all given a grant and sent down to a Gaelic school in Kerry to brush up on our command of the language. Most of us just used the opportunity to lash into pints of Smithwicks.

We started to skip lectures and head to the local pub for fun. One day while we were in there playing snooker the lecturer got wind of our location and followed us. We hid in the back of the bar and the barmaid covered for us but he spotted the cue of one of my friends and followed us into the back room. When he saw the four of us cowering there he said 'Caillfidh sibh an deontas." That meant 'You'll lose the grant.' As it happened we didn't lose it but that was the end of my pool-playing career in Kerry.

When I got back to Dublin I made a more genuine attempt to learn Irish. Many nights after the lectures were finished I went io the Conradh na Gaeilge club off Stephen's Green. Irish was spoken there by all the customers.

The icing on the cake was the fact that you could get drink served up to you into the small hours. Before the bar closed I'd stock up on about half a dozen pints, standing them like soldiers on the counter. You had to speak Irish as you drank them or you'd be told to leave but that wasn't a problem for me. In those days if somebody offered me a pint after midnight I'd have been happy to converse with them in Swahili.

The year I spent in Pat's was enjoyable in its way but after the freewheeling atmosphere of UCD I felt like a fish out of water. I also suspected the full-time B. Ed. students believed that us 'Wilsons' thought we were superior to them. Or maybe they just resented the fact that we got to do in one year what they were doing in three.

They seemed more committed to what they were doing than we were. Many of the people I knew from UCD were suffering from a sense of displacement. We were in Pat's as a last resort.

This led to some problems when we went out on teaching practice. A cartoon of the time had a straggly-haired teacher going into the Principal's office with a cigarette in his mouth and drawling, 'Sixth want to know who won World War Two.' He was like a Trotskyite version of a Wilson.

I knew the feeling. I'd never stood in front of a classroom of thirty children before and tried to impart knowledge to them. I asked myself why I was doing it now. Was it because I was the youngest of a family and had some kind of subconscious craving to have a younger brother or sister to take care of? I was asked to give my first lesson to Third Class on religion at Easter time. I chose the crucifixion as my theme but became carried away talking about Judas one day. I told the children the biggest sin he committed wasn't betraying Jesus but thinking that Jesus wouldn't forgive him for betraying him. The class teacher called me aside after I said that. He looked tense.

'That might be a bit advanced for them to take in,' he said, 'They're only nine after all.' I saw his point. He handed me a Catechism with questions like 'Who made the world?' on it. The answer, 'God made the world', had a big ring around it made with a felt marker. That was the end of my sermons about Judas Iscariot. The teacher was probably afraid I'd come in the next day and give a diatribe on the existential nuances of Marcel Gabriel's theology.

I tended to lecture pupils instead of teach them, a fault shared by many 'Wilsons'. In secondary school you taught subjects, it was said, whereas in primary you taught children. In one project I undertook, the inspector told me my work cards were so elaborate they would have been more suited to university students. I hadn't quite given them the binomial theorem to learn off but I wasn't far off that. 'You don't need a degree in Nuclear Physics,' he informed me, 'to tell children the cat sat on the mat.'

One of the people in my class as called Dermot Dunne. He was fiercely intelligent and also very entertaining. His mind was on fire all the time. He lit a fuse in me, giving me the inspiration to write more stories.

I spent a lot of time hanging round Dermot. Sometimes he came out to the house in Glasnevin. He talked almost non-stop there. Everything Dermot said was like a quotation. He reminded me of a character in a play or a novel. He could put people down with a phrase like a Dublinesque Bazarov. I couldn't see him staying at teaching for too long. There was too much going on in his head. Like me he'd droplanded into the teaching college. We both felt we were made for something better.

The exams took place in June. They weren't like the B.A. or the M.A. where the words flowed from me. They were more like Muredach's, or Belvedere. What did I know, or care, about people like Jean Piaget or Maria Montessori?

I got through them but didn't relish the prospect of looking around for a teaching post. Some of my classmates had already got jobs without even applying for them. They were heading off to small schools in the country where their parents might have taught – two or three teacher schools where they'd almost immediately walk into a principalship and be set up for life. Nice work if you could get it.

I didn't know if I'd be any good at teaching. English and Maths I thought I could hack, but I wasn't looking. forward to teaching subjects like art or music that I hadn't studied at Muredach's. I couldn't imagine trying to convince a Board of Management at an interview that I'd be an asset to their school.

God help the children, I thought, that would be entrusted to my care.

Twilight of the Gods

My father never really settled in Dublin any more than I did. Before we left Ballina he said all he wanted was a back room somewhere to live out his retirement but the day we arrived in Iona Villas he expressed disgust at the small size of the house. It was only small if you compared it to Norfolk. Despite our new status, he still wanted to dwell in Marble Hall. He was always an aristocrat in his heart, even when he was dressed in his pyjamas.

That became his preferred mode of dress in his last years. Now and then he put on the old Trinity gear to go into town to, as his friend Mido Cooligan said, "give the people a thrill."

He generally travelled by taxi in Ballina whenever he had anywhere to go. I think he owned a car once for about five minutes but he crashed it. It was a big deal if he sat in the front with the driver. He only did that if he knew him really well.

In Dublin sometimes, to my amazement, he'd take the bus to town. It seemed so incongruous for him. I associated him more with taxis. He liked to tell a joke about a man of fallen grandeur who found himself on a bus to the centre of London once. He said to the driver, "Do you stop at the Ritz?" The driver replied, "What – on my salary?" ("Stop" is sometimes another term for "stay" in England).

He still carried an air of elegance about him even if he was only dressed in his pyjamas. "Authority forgets a dying king," he'd say but to us he was always a king: a lion in winter.

No matter what went wrong in his life he was able to make a joke about it. "Money talks," he'd say, "Mine said goodbye." If we told him he looked distinguished he'd say, "No, I'm extinguished." Everything became fodder for a oneliner.

Ballina retreated further and further back into the recesses of his mind. The people he drank with there had never been "bosom" friends, he assured us, they were just "boozing" ones. I doubted that. Anyone I met who knew him spoke of him with great affection.

I wrote a poem about a typical sortie he might make into town when he tried to turn back the clock and act like "the old days" were still there:

The rituals of dress begin –
the waistcoat, pinstriped suit,
the precious pin
of old school tie
mislaid once more.
Frustratedly he scours the floor.

Outside he hails the bus,
remembers as it lumbers
when these fingers summoned chauffeurs
Gresham waiters. Now he carries,
for the nouveaux riches to see,
his pension card, free travel voucher,
paltry national recompense
for his insolvency.

In lounges with the parvenus
he stands apart.
At closing time – no bearhugs now,
no feus de joie – he exits
nonchalant, with simulacra
of lost dignity.
At home
in cobwebbed rooms he lies alone
a pale frame stretched across a bed
his reminiscences at random edited
by alcohol's dull moan.

Consciousness begins to wane.
Unsummoned,
vague illusions
pacify his brain.

My cousin Paddy Dillon-Malone died when he was only in his forties. His widow, Anne, later edited a magazine called *Image*.

I told my father I'd like to write film reviews for it. He said he'd ask her if this was on the cards. They met for lunch in the Shelbourne Hotel at the end of 1976. He always got on well with her. She was now married to a man called John Reihill, a coal manufacturer. He made his fortune importing coal from Poland and selling it at competitive rates here. They lived in a huge house called Deepwell in Blackrock and threw lavish parties. Their children – there were some from both marriages – remembered picking their way through bodies on the mornings after as they made their way to the breakfast table. There would be ash and whiskey in their cornflakes.

Towards the end of the lunch, my father told Anne I was interested in writing for *Image*. Would there be a slot for me? She said she was sure that would be fine. I don't know if she'd seen anything I'd written up to that point. Whether she had or not, I felt sure my father would have "bigged" me up.

I was looking forward to taking up my new job. Cinemas had been like homes from home for me ever since childhood. The fact that there were two within a few hundred yards of Norfolk helped. We talked of film stars the way people in other houses talked about people they knew personally. As someone said, "We couldn't accept the fact that Joe Louis was being talked about as the toughest man in the world when we knew it was Humphrey Bogart. That certainly applied to Keith. I saw Audie Murphy in that vein, despite his small stature. When I heard years later that he was America's most decorated was hero it only fortified the union of films and life.

I didn't only think of films when I was in cinemas. They became part of my life. After I saw *Psycho* I could never go into a shower again without thinking of someone being on the other side of the curtain. After I saw *Jaws* I could never look at a still sea without seeing a fin sticking out of it in my mind's eye.

Reviewing films, I thought, would be like getting paid for something I wanted to do anyway. I envied people who spent their lives at the activity. I didn't see the downside of it until years later when it threatened to suck the sap out of the film-going experience.

The first film I reviewed for her was Sidney Lumet's *Network*. What a way to start. It paved the way for a biography of him decades later. I didn't realise how good the film was when I saw it. Maybe I was thinking too much of my review – the old sin. Little did I know that people would still be talking about it as an iconic work fifty years later.

My father died at the beginning of 1977. I was at a film at the time, significantly called *The Omen*. He'd given me my breakfast in bed that day. As I was eating it he asked me if I'd buy a book on Hitler for him in Eason's.

He had a heart attack while I was in town. As soon as I walked in the door I knew something was wrong. My mother was crying. He'd got a massive coronary while I was at the film. I was shocked but even in my shock I was relieved for him. He'd never really been sick a day in his life. In his last few years he'd suffered from depression. "The world is in such a state," he'd say, "I think it's a crime to bring a child into it." "You can talk!" I'd say back.

"He sucked on the pap of life," as Basil said. Now he was, as they said, gone to a better place. I'd had a great relationship with him; the memory of that sustained me in the days and weeks following.

My thoughts went to my mother. How would she be without him? I knew how strong she was but also how emotional. She said she was relieved too. In some ways she had a motherly attitude to him.

When he died I lost a friend as well as a father. I remembered all the days I sat lying on the bed with him in the back room beside the glasshouse, talking about everything from the way the world was going to the last bet he put on a horse.

He never told me to do anything, never gave out to me, never ordered me about, never told me what time to go to bed or what time to get up. Neither did my mother but fathers usually did those kinds of things at that time. There was a lot of talk about "growing up with your children" in the hippie era. He was there before them.

The immediate cause of his heart attack was an argument with a coalman. He'd had a number of bags delivered to the house that day. The exact amount was queried. He became distressed. It was a trivial incident with a tragic result. I wrote about it in a poem:

A bag of coal
killed my father.
There was some confusion
about the order.
He got worked up
and wen out like a light.
In a way it seemed apt.
Everything about his life was fast
Including the way he left it.

With others it's more dramatic.
There are earthquakes, hurricanes,
global disasters.
And then there are the absurd deaths.
The man who sops to tie his shoelace
as a car races towards him.
The man who walks into
an empty elevator shaft.

Death doesn't discriminate
between what's deserved
and what isn't.
Did Hitler suffer
more than Mother Teresa
in 1945?
Is he suffering more now?

In the midst of such conundrums
we live our lives,
not knowing why
we do what we do,
fighting wars
against unseen enemies,
crossing bridges that break,
reaching planets
that explode into the ether,

falling into traps
set by others
or ourselves as we lurch
from day to day.

He donated his body to charity. "You can see me in the medical department of Trinity anytime you want," he used to joke. My mother was very sad in the following months. She didn't want to let any of us see this as she wasn't the type to look for sympathy but she couldn't hide it as much as she wanted to. I asked her if I should leave Pat's for a while to be with her but she said not to. She wasn't the type to want to be treated as a patient. Doing things like making sandwiches for me kept her going just like all her other household chores did, or worrying about her children now that her "tenth" one had passed away.

Elvis Presley, another hero of mine, died later that year. I would always remember 1977 as the year I lost two members of my family, my father and my "surrogate brother," Elvis.

I'd grown up on Elvis' music. It was hard to think of a world without him. I wrote a tribute to him that was published in the *Western People*. They gave it a whole page. I called it "The Day the Music Died" after the Don MacLean song. It was the first article I ever had in that paper. I later wrote a poem about him:

I always associated Elvis
with Ballina.
It was there
I first heard
the haunting strains of
'Are You Lonesome Tonight.'
It was there
I first heard
the power and tenderness
of 'It's Now or Never.'
It was there
I first heard
the pugnacity
of 'Jailhouse Rock.'
I was too young

to have witnessed
his explosion into music in 1956,
the year he changed the world.
In the sixties
he was tame.
The mothers
I knew
loved him.
The juvenile delinquents
I knew
disowned him.
At the end of the decade
he returned to live performing
the thing
he started out with
and should have stayed with.
Paul Brady said he threw it all away.
If he did,
he got it back before he died.

Our house was sold
the year he opened in Vegas.
Paradise would have been going there.
Ballina was my Tupelo
and Dublin my Memphis.
When he died
we mourned him
like a member of the family.
They gave me a full page
in the Western
to write a tribute to him.
He was my brother,
my father,
my son.
He formed my childhood
from 3,000 miles away.
I never met him.
I was another small town boy

who felt misunderstood
until the world listened.
Music was his liberation.
He was mine.

The
ELVIS
Diaries
WRITTEN BY AUBREY MALONE

A GLIMPSE INTO THE LIFE OF A ROCK AND ROLL KING!

Teacher Man

After I finished the course in Pat's I started applying for jobs and after a few weeks got one in a small school in Clonsilla. I was given fifth class which felt a bit like being thrown in at the deep end but the pupils were high achievers and it was easy enough to get them to work. My, classroom was a prefab that the Principal called 'The Horsebox because of its small size but in time I grew attached to it. I felt the wind could have blown it over but even that gave it a kind of cosiness.

I often came in early to prepare classes and stayed late after school cleaning up when the children had gone home. The other teachers were friendly and the community closely-knit. The downside was that you felt on display all the time because everyone knew everyone.

Not having had experience of people younger than myself in my family, I didn't know much about children. They were a novelty to me. I liked being asked to peel oranges and tie shoelaces. It gave me a kind of role.

A lot of the other teachers were married with kids. Nothing in the classroom was new to them. As a result, they were sterner with their pupils. I was soft. Maybe I would have been anyway, even if I had children of my own.

My attitude to the pupils was too lax. If someone came in without their homework done I didn't blow a fuse. In time I learned you had to pretend to blow one even if you didn't mind. Misbehaviour tended to snowball. If one child got away with something, ten more would want that same leverage the next day. Sometimes I felt they were playing me like a violin. I tried to create myself as a Mr Chips figure but it didn't work.

One day I asked a child to go down to the local shop to get me a Kit-Kat. When he came back I told him to keep the change. I was sitting in the staff-room at the time. A teacher beside me said, "What did you just give him?" I didn't even know. She almost exploded. "There's no way I'd give a child anything like that!" she said.

I wondered if I'd have a problem combining teaching with writing. I thought of people like Frank O'Connor, John

McGahern, Bryan McMahon, even Joyce. One of the first things the principal said to me after getting the job was, "I hope I don't see you writing your stories behind the rostrum." There was little danger of that with forty pupils running around me. It would be like trying to write something as you were minding mice at a crossroads. The other classrooms in the school were quiet. Mine wasn't. I don't know if I got bored by silence or couldn't get it but it was never there whatever the reason. The Department of Education recommended a "steady hum" in classrooms to facilitate learning. My hum was more like cacophony.

Some of the pupils saw my class as being like Butlin's Holiday Camp. I felt life was hard enough outside school and didn't want to continue that. Who wanted a continuation of Dickens' Gradgrind from *Hard Times*? But if you didn't give that you got flak from parents. They wanted their children marshalled.

Taking my foot off the pedal gave them too much freedom at a time when freedom was coming in anyway. Eventually it rebounded on me. When I tried to get tough they didn't accept it, knowing it wasn't the "real" me. It was like letting a horse out of a stable and then trying to tether it as it roamed free. When I tried to backtrack, to become like the teachers who'd taught me in primary school, it was too late. The toothpaste was out of the tube. I tried to become mechanical with them but they weren't having it. Children are good psychologists. They know when you're pretending to be someone you're not.

Many of the pupils' parents knew I wrote in my spare time. They often asked me what I thought their little darlings should read. I knew they expected me to suggest books like *Animal Farm* or *Little Women* but I didn't oblige. I usually said something like, "Let them start with a Cornflakes packet." I remembered Ulick O'Connor saying about Brendan Behan in his biography of him that one day his father saw him picking a tram ticket off the floor and reading the back of it. Some of these parents reminded me of the kinds of people I saw in Waterstones on Sunday mornings trying to find "stimulating" books for their children. I thought a tram ticket would be preferable.

I pitied children like these. They usually looked as if they'd be happier kicking a ball down the street. And why shouldn't

With one of my teaching classes

they? Their parents weren't impressed by my philistinism in suggesting Cornflakes packets as preferable to Louisa May Alcott, I didn't care. If I had to be a responsible adult in front of a blackboard by day that was one thing. I didn't want to sabotage· my life – or theirs – in our after-hours pursuits.

I started writing for a newspaper called *Hibernia* now. It was run by a man called John Mulcahy. His wife Nuala O'Farrell was the books editor. Every few weeks she gave me about twenty of them to review. How do you review twenty books in a page? The answer to that one is, "With great difficulty." I only had about 2,000 words to play with, in other words 100 words per book. Some of them were over 500 pages in length. It didn't make sense.

Sometimes I felt Nuala should have given me a wheelbarrow to carry them home. There were that many. How could I do justice to them in a single page? I imagined some godforsaken writer spending his life on a labyrinthine novel and me dismissing it with something like David Marcus' line, "There's less to this than meets the eye." What if he was thin-skinned? Would my barb cause him to put his head in the oven? I knew how hard writing was so I shouldn't have been disparaging but few writers can resist the urge to show off.

Logistically, there was no way I could read even a twentieth of the books Nuala gave me. After browsing through a few pages to get a flavour of the style and then checking the blurb to find out what the hell they were about, I was usually able to come up with some oneliners to make myself sound impressive, and the writers of the books somewhat less so. It wasn't fair but it was the only way it could be done. A part of me was thinking there's no such thing as bad publicity. Another part was mindful of Sydney Smith's dictum, "I never read a book before reviewing it. It prejudices a man so."

I was given a book about Dylan Thomas to cover once. In my introduction to it I referred to him as "Mr Once Below a Time." Harry wasn't impressed. "You bastard!" he glowered the next time I met him. I didn't think Dylan would have minded. There was no way of finding out. He died the year I was born.

I wanted to say wise things in *Hibernia* so people would

think I was a bright button. I wanted to be as clever as someone like Hugh Kenner, who famously wrote of *Waiting for Godot*: "This is a play in which nothing happens twice." How long would I have to be writing before I came up with something like that?

The person I sent most of my articles to at this time was Damien Corless, the former editor of *In Dublin*. Damien never published anything I wrote, despite me sending about thirty articles to him during his tenure.

A subsequent editor of *In Dublin*, John Waters, published me quite frequently and had a much more pleasant manner. He was from Roscommon, my mother's county. I always felt a kinship for anyone west of the Shannon. It was a kind of brotherhood.

I also worked for the magazine *Books Ireland*. Bernard Share was the editor. Getting my name known gave me a buzz, and a thought that another kind of life might be available to me at some stage outside teaching.

Sinead O'Connor said an interesting thing once: "When you become famous, you don't change. It's other people who do." I never got to be famous but when I started writing I noticed people related to me differently. I started being listened to even if I was talking nonsense. I was reminded of something Marlon Brando said about his own experience of being in the public eye: "I get asked for my views not just about acting but about everything from plumbing to astrophysics."

I was viewed differently in the staff-room too. Instead of people asking me if I'd put on the kettle for a cup of tea now, they wanted to know how I felt about everything from parking charges to politics, two subjects of which I was profoundly ignorant.

The parish priest came into my classroom one day brandishing a page of a newspaper. "You had a review in the *Evening Herald*!" he beamed. It was as if I wouldn't have seen it or even been aware I wrote it.

A school inspector said to me one day, "Do you sell the books you review to second-hand shops?" I felt almost embarrassed telling him I owned this phenomenal piece of furniture called a bookshelf where they could be stored.

Globetrotting

In the summer of 1979 I went on a fly-drive with Dermot Dunne, the livewire from Pat's as well as two other lads from the class, John Moynihan and Don Conway. All three of us were installed in schools but none of us too enthralled by our jobs. Dermot was out in Drimnagh. He said he was thinking of going into an insurance job. John wanted to be a solicitor. Don worked with underprivileged children in a St. John of Gods school in Chapelizod and seemed happy enough at it.

Italy is the country I remembered most from the trip. I saw the pomp and ceremony of the church in St. Peter's Square. It was a long way from "the shoes of the fisherman."

We also visited Milan, Florence, Naples and Livomo. Everywhere I went I wanted to write about. 1 thought they'd inspire me but often they didn't. I came to the conclusion that there wasn't much difference between having a cup of coffee in Dubai or one in Dublin.

My father used to talk about people who had "travelled bodies but untravelled minds." When I was growing up I was envious of those who had jet-setting lifestyles. The 1979 trip cured me of that. In later years I met many high-fliers who were only marginally more interesting than toads. It wasn't where you went that mattered, I concluded, it was who you were. People like Carson McCullers and Emily Dickinson hardly went anywhere. Likewise for Sherwood Anderson and God knows how many others. Maybe there was more diversity in his street in Winesburg, Ohio, than all the American states put together. Maybe there was more diversity in Arthur Street, Ballina, than all of Dublin. Or Ireland. Or the world. I put that concept into another poem:

> *Like a woman you couldn't forget*
> *a hangover from a party*
> *that lasted two decades*
> *you trekked across Europe*
> *seeing sights more spectacular*
> *than any you could have dreamt about*
> *in Ballina,*

At St. Peter's Square

Crossing a border a day
You drove past fields
that looked like Rembrandt paintings
wheat waving in the breeze
as you arced towards a new life.
More than Seven Wonders beckoned you:
the dazzle of strangers,.
psychedelic streets
that had no end.
nights promising everything
except reality.

Italy became your Eden,
then France and Spain.
You fell in love with details
a shadow on a mountain side, ripples on a lake.
You became as one with the universe,
sinking into its embrace.
The seasons
morphed into one another,
making you a party to them.

What about the Prussian fisherman
who brought you out on the lake
that looked like blue steel?
Or the Swedish girl
who wore angora
and talked to you
as if she knew you all her life?
You held your breath
as these people brought you
into their worlds.
Were they better or worse
than the ones you grew up with?
Would you have missed something
if you didn't know them,
if you'd lived like Emily Dickinson
or Carson McCullers

in their enclosed spaces,
if you'd been like Sherwood Anderson
in Winesburg, Ohio,
or William Faulkner in Yoknapatawaha?
Did they need to live
like Ernest Hemingway in the Abruzzi,
bringing food to troops
on the frontline
during World War I?
Maybe they could be bounded in nutshells,
like Hamlet
and still count themselves
kings of infinite spaces.

Rivers broke their banks.
Waves slashed over the horizon.
You watched them
like a disembodied creature
a stranger to your life.

On other days you trailed
the map of the heart,
your contours invisible.
People asked you where you'd been
and you couldn't tell them.
Grey skies, white fields,
your heart palpitating
as trains sped through tunnels.
When they emerged,
different people looked at you:
a child in a strange hat.
his father gazing out the window
at some other dream.

At the Acropolis

I tried to write a poem on a gondola in Venice but realised it was stopping my enjoyment of the experience. First you lived, then you wrote. That was what I had to keep telling myself. If you tried to write too soon you destroyed both experiences, becoming like an elephant rolling a pea.

I was glad to get to Greece. It had been on my radar for years. We did all the touristy things like visiting the Parthenon and the Acropolis. I had a photo taken of myself at the Acropolis with my arm raised in a kind of victory salute but in truth I wasn't really interested in being there. A place is its inhabitants. As much as we could we tried to veer off the more well-travelled paths and meet the real people. They brought you to places the tourist guides didn't know about. An article I read once in a paper said, "If you want to find the best cafes, follow a local." That certainly proved true for us in Athens.

I found it difficult to settle back in Ireland after coming home. It was always the way with me. My mind was still abroad - whether it was a "travelled" one or not.

I became more and more disenchanted with teaching as the eighties came in. Dermot and John had conveyed their restlessness to me on the fly-drive and maybe I got infected with that. I found myself giving less to the pupils as the years went on and as a result they became harder to contain. As their boisterousness increased, my health started to suffer. I came down with a lot of bugs.

The summers recharged my batteries the way they did for every teacher. In the summer of 1980 I went to America again, this time staying with a relative of June's husband, Pat. He owned a bar in a rundown area of New York. There were bullet holes in the wall. A lot of fights took place there but I had fun as well. Some nights the bar it became a dance hall as various people took one another round the floor – often strangers – for no apparent reason.

I got to know the customers well even in the short time I worked there. I'll never forget the man who came in at the same time every night and drank whiskey without talking to anyone. All he'd say was "Hit me again" after each refill. Then he'd disappear into the night. There was

no such thing as closing time in the bar. We only pulled
down the shutters when the last customer left. It was they
who decided. I was writing poetry about everything now. The
bar was no exception:

> It's midnight in the Bronx
> as I serve beer to dissolutes
> like myself, with nowhere better
> or worse to go.
> Before me is a Mexican
> in need of a frankfurter;
> beside him a Puerto Rican lass
> asking coquettishly
> for a condom.
> The latter is more easily arranged.
>
> At closing time I sit surrounded
> by the night's predictable remnants,
> some of them vaguely human,
> others having given up that ambition
> too many years ago to be an issue.
> We bathe ourselves in the cocoon
> the night affords
> as a couple takes the floor,
> doing a slow set to the backdrop
> of Frank Sinatra
> having One For The Road
> while we have twenty one ...
>
> The male is an insurance salesman
> taking a night off
> from his suicidal wife;
> the female a Hungarian refugee
> who belly-dances in the strip-club
> down the block.
> Together they are discussing
> how they will make a baby
> later in the night.

They are both looking for release
from a tragic liaison;
they will both replace
a former tragic liaison
with the present one.

I was writing some more stories now as well. After I got back to Ireland I sent them around to a few publishers but none of them were interested. I wasn't well enough known and they probably weren't good enough. In the end I tracked down a fellow teacher, a man called Uinsin O Donobháin, (pictured overleaf) who said he'd bring them out. He lived just up the road from me in Raheny. Uinsin was a writer too, and also from the west. He gave me a good feeling about the book.

I went down to Listowel that year to launch it at Writer's Week. It was where all the major writers congregated.

I found myself sitting beside Bryan McMahon in a pub one night. He was the man who said, "The true artist is a madman who tries to appear sane. The phoney one is a sane man trying to appear mad." It was a bit like Michael Caine saying the main problem with people playing drunks in films was that they tried to act drunk, unlike drunk people in real life who did their best to appear sober. The secret of writing was to let the reader fill in the blanks. That's what Hemingway was so good at. The danger, he said, was that if the blanks weren't significant they just looked like holes in the page. They had to be significant ones to make them work.

I didn't find McMahon particularly friendly. He was launching a book too and that was foremost on his mind, not the debutante scribblings of a nobody like myself. His fellow county man John B. Keane was much more amenable. He chatted to me about how he wrote his plays, how so many colourful people came into his pub and basically gave him the plots for them.

I had to give a talk about the book one day, which I stumbled through with the help of Arthur Guinness. I can't remember what I said.

After I got back to Dublin I was interviewed about it by John Feeney for the *Evening Herald*. He was also very supportive. Tragically, John died soon afterwards when a plane he was on

I

crashed. Another journalist, Kevin Marron, was also on board. They were on their way to France to launch a wine product from Beaujolais.

Shortly after the interview I decided to join a dramatic society. Maybe talking with John B. had moved me in this direction. I suggested to the director, Maureen Kavanagh, that we do one of his plays and she agreed. It was *The Buds of Ballybunion*. Her other selections went back to the dark ages of stage-Irishry. We rehearsed in pubs and drank a lot as a result – or maybe we would have anyway. None of us were much as actors but that didn't really matter. For a lot of the time, the society doubled as a dating facility.

We mainly played in pubs and nursing homes, at least for the early performances (I use that word advisedly) of our plays. Everything was done on a strict budget. We had no money for costumes so wardrobes were raided for anything suitably "period" in style. All we had to pay for was a copy of texts in Eason's, at least if they still carried such antediluvian tomes. If they did they were often mildewed after spending decades on a draughty shelf.

The sets were hardly made by ace carpenters. Every time I opened a door I'd hear creaking noises and expect the whole fortification to come crashing down on my head.

I'd never acted in Murdeach's. I never did anything in Muredach's. A guy a few classes ahead of me, Gerry Walsh, made it to the Abbey. That was a big deal. I saw him once or twice and he wasn't half bad. Meanwhile I malingered in Delta-K, doing runs of poppycock in pubs out in the sticks. It helped if the audiences were blotto. They often were. How else would they be expected to suffer us? So, unfortunately, were many members of the casts, especially me. I tried my best to stay upright after one too many ciders in the Green Room, or what passed for it.

In the nursing homes I hoped the audiences would be doolally. If they were they wouldn't notice me fluffing my lines, or "corpsing" as the expression went, while an overworked prompter whispered (or, on occasions, shouted) them at me from the wings. After inflicting our pastorals on these people for a week or two the chances were that we could now, whisper it, appear in "regular" theatres to audiences who were compos mentis.

110

Dammit, we might even survive the brickbats of the critics who gave them thumbnail reviews in the national dailies if we were lucky. Or should I say unlucky. We rarely got positive ones. "Yer man is in tonight," Maureen would say, peering through the curtains at some curmudgeonly-looking eminence in the front seat, making me feel I was almost expected to genuflect.

Sometimes I heard audience members snoring. I didn't mind. It was better than being pelted with rotten tomatoes. The people who stayed awake were usually family members and friends. These were co-opted to swell the numbers. "Spread out and make yourself look like a crowd," we admonished. The reviewers might damn us with their poison pens but you could always count on your parents or siblings to tell you that you were great. They were good liars. Sometimes I saw people I knew grinning up at me with the expression of a proud parent gawping at their child in a kindergarten panto, playing one of the Three Wise Men in a nativity play. The expression said, "That's my little Johnny up there, taking his first steps in theatre." All for Hecuba. Or maybe Arthur Guinness.

I was just there for the craic. No Robert de Niro me, nor Des Cave nor Peadar Lamb nor any other Abbey icons. The idea was to wind down from a day's labours at the school and recharge the batteries for another dash into the valley of death in Clonsilla the following day. Forty impressionable youths would once again be delivered to my care in a rundown prefab but I'd be able to deal with them now, even with a hangover.

I alternated the acting and teaching with reviewing. Having got the stories out of my system meant I was freed of them for a while. The cool reception accorded to them brought me down to earth with a thud. I felt I hadn't lived enough to be able to write well.

Maybe it was time to explore other writers again, I thought, like I'd done in UCD. I went on a binge of reading Norman Mailer, especially the non-fiction. *The Executioner's Song* had just come out and it blew my mind. Mailer was so good on real people, why did he let his discipline desert him in his fiction?

I felt he reached his nadir with *Ancient Evenings*, a study of Egypt that came out a few years later. It was sent to me for review. As I struggled to read the first few chapters of this mammoth tome I felt there should have been a law to stop people writing books as long – or as boring – as this. It should have come with a government health warning. There were interesting flourishes as was always the case with this man but ultimately it was a book about himself as much as his subject.

Mailer once said, "When you're writing a historical novel, the secret is not to know too much about the period." This was as interesting a concept as his one about God being on a learning curve. I knew what he meant. Novelists are often paralysed by facts. You can get all that kind of thing later, when you've done the creative bit.

Sometimes when I was reviewing books I developed a reaction to them that had little or nothing to do with what they were about. Such a reaction then became the guts of the review. Not knowing the plot of a book, as was the case with *Ancient Evenings*, didn't really matter. I left reading the blurb until I'd done the review. Today the equivalent would be going to Google or Wikipedia to beef up your knowledge.

Mailer invented the word "factoid" to describe playing around with reality. It was when he was writing his book on Marilyn Monroe that he coined it. People gave out to 'him about this, claiming the book was outrageous in some of its assertions. It was, but nobody can be as deliciously outrageous as Mailer. Let's not under-estimate factoids, or "fake news" as we would say today. (Thank you, Donald). *Ancient Evenings* ended my attempts to read Mailer's fiction but I kept gobbling up his journalism.

I found it increasingly more difficult to write at home as the years went on.

There was always chaos round the house in Iona Villas, people continually coming in to the house to chat about anything and everything going on into the wee hours. Shakespeare could never have written his forty or so plays if he lived in our house. One night I locked myself into the toilet with a six pack and my typewriter. I sat on the seat and put in on my knees, opening a can of beer and starting to tap. An hour later I felt I'd be able to give J.D. Salinger a run for his money. I emerged drunk and fulfilled but when I looked at my pages the next morning I realised they were like the products of a bad trip. Where was my discipline? I'd wasted a night.

The booze didn't work as well for me as opium did for Coleridge when he wrote "Kubla Khan."

Partings

My mother died in 1985. Her death affected me a lot. In many ways I took her for granted in all the years I'd been with her. After my father died I put her into the background. After she died she became centre stage again, and a focus for my guilt.

I tried to assuage my feelings in a poem.

> Her life was taken from her.
> I couldn't accept it.
> How could she die?
> She was so perfect
> she couldn't be mortal.
> She was the Blessed Virgin,
> immaculate, impervious,
> but cancer took her down
> to where the rest of us live.
>
> I visited her in a hospital
> that smelt of cleaning agents.
> I asked her to forgive me
> for past transgressions
> but she saw none.
> She gave me no attention.
> She was already elsewhere.
>
> I thought back to talks we'd had,
> mainly about myself.
> She lived in my shadow
> and I pretended to live in hers.
> What could she tell me?
> Nothing very much
> because I knew it all.
>
> And yet I kept running to her
> like an acolyte with a lover
> or a reluctant idol.
> And then her life ended,

dismally, like a bad movie.
There was unfinished business.
She had no right to leave me
without sorting out my madness.
She'd promised me this.
Why had she reneged?

At the funeral
everyone was a friend.
They pressed the flesh,
bearhugged hollowly
in the silence.

I sidled up to a drunk
who was blessedly removed
from this incestuous frenzy.
His indifference relaxed me.
I drank so much
I blanked out.
Afterwards I had a vision
of white walls, charcoal voices:
I bowed to stasis,
sunk into a shell.

After three days
I came out of my room
to re-connect with the universe.
I got a bus to town
on the advice of people
who said they cared for me.
I did the normal things.
Everyone said,
'He's let go.'
That night I had a nightmare.
She became my guardian angel,
my terror.
Now she owns me.

All nine of the family get together the year my mother died 1985

I took her death much worse than that of my father. Even though his one was a shock, I felt he'd lived his life. He also died suddenly. My mother had a lingering death with cancer. Basil asked a priest once why my father, who indulged all his appetites, was granted a quick death whereas she, a "saint," had such a painful one.

The priest just said, "God works in mysterious ways." My mother used to say, "There are causes for everything and raisins for cakes." She had so many sayings: "I'll have it for you in two shakes of a lamb's tail," or "Before you can say Jack Robinson." Now I'd never hear them anymore.

I didn't know what I wanted to do with my life now. I felt guilty for having neglected her over the years, being out most nights drinking or playing snooker when she could have done with the company at home. What good were all those nights to me now?

I felt as if I was floating on ether. The rest of the family had had experience of moving away from home and then coming back for holidays.

With me it was the other way round. I went away for holidays instead of coming home for them. The fact that my holidays were for two months rather than two weeks, my siblings' average times, gave me the illusion that I could fly the nest cavalierly without sentiment. I now knew that not to be the case.

I spent a year in Iona Villas after my mother died. Then I moved into a flat nearby, commuting to the school on the back road to Finglas. I wrote a story about my mother now, one I called "Loyalty." It was different to my other ones, harder maybe because of what I'd been through.

I sent it to David Marcus. He hadn't been accepting anything I'd sent him for some years now but he took this immediately. I felt I'd matured as a writer with it. He said something like that too in his acceptance letter. I thought my grief helped me outgrow some of the bad habits I'd picked up in the writing of the earlier ones.

Teaching became even more difficult now. The days passed by in a blur. I looked out the window of the classroom and envied the birds pecking at the breadcrumbs on the tarmac. I even envied the caretaker picking up the leaves that fell on it.

I taught Irish verbs to the beat of a metre stick that sat on my desk, desperately trying to whip up the kind of enthusiasm in the children that I myself had lost. 'Chuaigh mé,' I'd say, 'chuaigh tú, chuaigh sé, chuaigh sí,'

They'd chant in unison, their shrill voices puncturing the air, only one of us realising the absurdity of trying to drum boring verbs into the heads of children who'd have preferred to be out playing hopscotch on the tarmac.

Afterwards we wrote it all down, me on the blackboard and them in their copies. And then we went on to other conundrums: the mysteries of mathematical equations, the rigours of English grammar, the civic pride we should take in our lives.

I had them for five hours a day, their tiny faces gazing up at me curiously as their lives were about to begin while I wondered if mine had already ended. Each passing year I'd see these same faces walking along the road to the nearby secondary school and feel left behind, as if I was the one pupil who failed to graduate.

One day a pupil said baldly to me, 'You're not as good a teacher as the one I had last year.' When I asked him why he said, 'Because you're not hard enough on us.' What saddened me wasn't the criticism but rather the fact that an eight-year-old child would have such a yearning for being disciplined.

After the fun went out of the job I was reduced to thinking of my night life, of my writing and any other things I did. I became the thing they warned us against in Pat's: becoming a clock-watcher.

The routine got to me. Despite my best intentions, I became a robot like all the other robots. It was like Muredach's all over again-with one exception. Children weren't afraid of teachers anymore. At times it seemed the other way round.

I felt I was losing my grip on the job, even on myself. Classes I once almost did in my sleep became momentous chores. I once told Dermot Dunne I felt the job wasn't good enough for me. Now I felt I wasn't good enough for it. I used drink to try and escape my problems but it only made them worse.

I wrote a poem about my torpor:

Ramshackle prefabs jut out
like gothic edifices
on the desultory plateau.
Treading worn-out floorboards
to a worn-out theme,
I inhale chalk-dust
into my poisoned lungs,
exhale gravitas about the sacred cow
of academic prowess
to their unhearing ears.
The clockface crawls to noon.
Outdoors, crows peck
at discarded breadcrumbs.
I watch autodidacts knuckle down
to rotational symmetry,
hardchaws fritter like eels
over the workdead benches.
"Three threes is six,"
he says pontifically,
this latest Einstein of my troupe,
and I smile
as I turn the tables for him.
In my own day
we would have been leathered
for the error;
today we smile.

The morning cools.
They mute themselves
as I unleash my trivia,
or denigrate their gods
of rock and roll, or video,
or silver screen.
But when the bell rings
they'll be kings
of lands I am exempt from
by my trade.
"Pick up your pens."

"Remember this."

My words drone onwards
like a disembodied rage
emulating its own intransigence.
I feel a distance from myself,
the madness
of this solidly pragmatic day.
Their paradise, I know,
would be a world
of no curricula,
where adults faced the lash
of teenage wrath,
and mortarboards were strewn
along the playing fields
as evenings stretched
to their infinities ...
I may be of their camp myself,
but I can give no empathy,
can only offer formulas,
equations, rules of thumb
they will forget
the day they enter jobs
their fathers left
which they will leave
to their own stock
as history repeats its sins...

Come nightfall I too
will abnegate the lunacy,
retreating,
like a jungle beast,
into a netherworld
that gives some brief relief
from what it is I do
assuming for a time
that new identity, or liberty,
or greed for reckless play,

until the daylight
calls me back again to recitations of old verities
in words that render moribund
each feeling I have had
since first I drew a breath in life.

What would I give
to be their age again
I ask myself
ground down by my irrelevance
in a world that has their future
as its quidditas.
I'd give the earth
to share their microchips,
that bland posterity
where each bald need
each crude proclivity
is entertained,.
indulgence as the new tin god
for Rousseauites,
each fulsome passing thought
unfurled as gospel
in our brave new
children-centred World.

I married Mary in 1989 and left my teaching job the year afterwards. There was now the question of what I'd do with the rest of my life. I wasn't yet forty and I was effectively retired. How was I going to fill the days? Writing was all very well when things were happening but when they weren't it became a drudge.

Mary suggested I do part time teaching but I felt that would have been disastrous, a busman's holiday with all the old tensions. I did a few weeks in a posh school in Stillorgan one year to see if I was right and I was. I nearly ran out of it screaming.

Wedding Day

I did some courier work to pay a few bills.   It was demanding physically but easier on the mind than teaching. The hours were longer but there was no preparation and no corrections. Neither was there any worry about what parents might say to you about how you were doing your job. It ended when it ended. Some of the packages I was given were for newspapers I wrote for. I didn't like going in to these offices in my courier gear. It looked as if I'd fallen on hard times. I often stayed outside the offices until another courier arrived. I'd give them a few quid to go in with my package. They never knew what my problem was. Sometimes I'd say I had an argument with the editor in question to "explain" it.

The courier work didn't pay much. After I moved from a motorbike to a van it paid even less. The stress was also much worse in the van. It was impossible to get anywhere fast in traffic. Even if you did, you'd often be asked to do a U-turn if a new job came in. For a lot of the time I felt I was chasing my tail. If I got a ticket, as happened often, it ate up a whole day's earnings.

When I left the courier job I felt at a loose end again. It was transient work but at least it filled in the time. I scratched my head as I contemplated my next move. I was no clearer on what career I wanted than I was twenty years before when I left UCD. What did I want to be when I grew up? Or if I did?

Keith left his accounting job around the same time as I left teaching. He was as unfulfilled in his work as I'd been in mine. The difference was that he was 16 years older than me. Was my stress comparable to his? I wasn't sure.

Retirement made me selfish. When you're working for someone else you have to think of what they want even if you do it grudgingly. When you're on your own time you don't.

The moment I left the courier job I had 24 hours a day to think of what I wanted to do. No more delivering packages, no more taking heat from irate bosses or customers over the air. In theory it was the formula for nirvana but I knew it wouldn't be like that for me.

Many people wilted in retirement as they didn't prepare for it. I was lucky that I didn't like my job so there was no heartache in

With Mary

leaving it. I was also lucky to have writing as a hobby. Could I turn it into a fulltime "second" job? That was the 64-dollar question.

Jean-Paul Sartre and Simone de Beauvoir

In Search of a Muse

I sent a second collection of stories to Poolbeg Press now, not realising that David Marcus was their editor. He rejected it and they sent me his report. I'm sure this was included by accident with their rejection letter to me. I was shocked by some of his comments. He criticised some of the stories he himself published in the *Irish Press*. Was that not a case of second-guessing himself? If he had a problem with them, why didn't he mention it to me before printing them? God knows I edited them enough to satisfy him. This seemed more like retroactive criticism.

"This writer is obsessed with drifters," he wrote in his report. I didn't know why he said that. Weren't all writers consumed in some way with this theme?

He even made some disparaging comments on "Loyalty," the story I wrote about losing my mother a few years before. He'd praised it highly after I sent it to him and said he'd be delighted to publish it. Now he said "Mr Malone should have ended this differently." I saw this as a trivial remark. Was that his only problem? At times in the report it looked as if he was looking for reasons to find fault with things. I lost a lot of respect for him over it. I felt he did more of a disservice to himself with it than to me.

I brooded about his comments. Mary said not to let them bother me, that he probably had to accommodate better known writers and I was collateral damage. She said not to take it personally.

I decided to try and forget books for a time and concentrate on making the most of my life. My health had improved since leaving the teaching and we were able to survive financially. Was that not more important than books?

Mary became disgruntled with her own job now and went on part time. She'd always wanted to work in creches and started to do that now. Every so often we went away, to Ballina now and again and Galway at other times. We talked about moving to either or both places instead of remaining as "dulchies" (i.e. culchies in Dublin.)

We generally spent a fortnight overseas during the summers. One year we flew to Jersey on a plane (from a private airline. It developed problems en route, making me wonder if I was going to end up like John Feeney and Kevin Marron. I don't think I ever prayed as hard as on that flight. (Yes, I promised God I was never going to do anything wrong for the rest of my whole life if he got me to the airport safely).

When we landed, eventually – wobbling to a halt on the runway as I surveyed my white knuckles and my even whiter face – I said to Mary, "I'll never fly again" – and I didn't. It wasn't just the safety angle (made worse after 9/11, of course) but my claustrophobia, which I even got on buses.

I always hoped the summers would summon my muse and brought my typewriter on holiday with me in case it did. Unfortunately it wasn't used as much as I expected it to be. As soon as I unpacked and fell under the glare of the sun I became a vegetable, eating too much by day and drinking too much at night. After the late night movie (horror preferred) I'd sink into a slumber and wake up at noon the next day, at which time I'd continue my decadent lifestyle. Walking to the beach – or the off-licence – was often the only exercise I got.

I asked Leonard Cohen where he got his inspiration from when I interviewed him in 1989. He said, "I wish I knew. If I did, I'd visit there more often." I asked him if he ever thought a song pre-existed him, if it was there waiting to be discovered. He said, "That's a nice way to put it." I was thinking about the idea of a statue being already inside a block of stone that someone like Henry Moore might carve.

Sometimes I sought inspiration by visiting literary places. Basil said he was inspired by writing on a blackboard once used by his hero Albert Einstein. Could I find such catalysts anywhere? Going to Graceland had been helpful to me in writing my biography of Elvis, even though we weren't allowed inside the house. I roamed around the grounds and felt his spirit was still there. Years later Marc Cohn would write the wonderful song "Walking in Memphis" where he talks about seeing the ghost of Elvis on Union Avenue before following him up to the gates of Graceland. I felt that too.

The home of Nora Barnacle in Nun's Island didn't do much for me when I went there once. Neither did being in Sean

O'Casey's house in Taunton. Another year Mary and myself visited Wordsworth's house. That wasn't very uplifting either. There was something bland about it. It made me think the UCD professor was right about him being too straightforward. Another year we wandered around Tintern Abbey but again there was nothing there to get me going.

Maybe I needed to go to the homes of wilder writers - 5 Cymdonkin Drive in Swansea, or the Boathouse in Laugharne to see if the spirit of Dylan Thomas was still roaming about. Or how about putting on my bicycle clips and cycling up to some haunts beloved of my old friend Philip Larkin, the hermit of Hull. Maybe that wouldn't be a good idea. I got shivers down my spine every time I read "Aubade."

Mary's favourite book was *Jane Eyre*. We went to Haworth one summer. It was fascinating seeing the parsonage, and a museum devoted to all the Brontes, but at the end of the day they were more in Mary's area of interest than mine. I loved *Wuthering Heights* when I read it in UCD but afterwards felt there was something overwritten about it. Mary liked the ordinariness of Charlotte more than the gothic excesses of Emily. In later years I started to feel Anne Bronte had gifts that could equal both of them, gifts that were ignored by the establishment.

I had no excuse for not being able to write good books considering I had so much time on my hands. Hugo's friend Liam Hogan said to me once, "I could be Denis Donoghue if I was able to afford to give up my job." Liam was also a bachelor with no kids to worry about raising. I wasn't a bachelor but I didn't have children. I think it was Cyril Connolly who said, "The greatest impediment for a writer is the pram in the hallway." Having said that, Mary would have been a great mother. She loved children. Keith's wife, Jacqueline, sent her a text every Mother's Day because, she said, she'd been as good as a mother to the children in the creches she worked in. It was a sweet gesture on her part.

I decided to do something practical to help my writing now, employing a carpenter to transform the spare bedroom into an office. We took out the bed that was in it to make space for him to put in bookshelves and some cabinets and drawers. He also installed a desk which I subsequently demolished. Instead I put

*In search of some Wordsworthian inspiration
but so far no sign of daffodils*

my typewriter on top of the set of drawers.

This became my working environment. I bought a little transistor and plonked it on top of the cabinets, turning it up as loud as possible every morning to try and get my brain working. There was a station that played country music all day long. If that proved too relaxing, I tried one that played heavy metal. Noise gave me energy but at a certain point it made me tense so I had to turn it off.

I sat on a chair with crooked legs. At night I turned on a lamp with a loose, lopsided shade. All that was preventing it from falling off was my resting it on a shelf.

One of my sisters gave me a convector heater. I turned it up high on the cold days, tilting it towards me at an angle on top of *The Collected Letters of Dylan Thomas*. It crackled as it blew out the heat, always threatening to give up but never doing so. I tried not to either, even when I started to run out of ideas for publishers and they started to run out of enthusiasm for the ones I'd already submitted to them.

Most of the journalism I was doing at this time was for the *Evening Press*. One day I got a call from John Boland, the features editor. He said he needed a photo of me for a new column he wanted me to be a part of called At Wit's End. I told him that could be awkward for me because many of my friends knew me as Peter and I didn't fancy the idea of my identity being revealed. I told him I hated the name Aubrey and rarely used it with people I knew. 'Why the fuck do you use it for writing then?' he asked.

I tried to explain my predicament to him. 'Engelbert Humperdinck's real name is Gerry Dorsey,' I said. 'That's fine for him but I'm different. I'm not looking for attention. If I was born with a name like Engelbert Humperdinck I'd want to change it to something like Gerry Dorsey.' That sounds like inverted snobbery,' he said, 'If you weren't looking for attention you wouldn't want a byline. You'd have a pen name.'

The column couldn't be sacrificed so I knew I was going to have to disguise myself in some way for the photo. The next day I went into a theatrical accessory shop and bought myself a wig and a fake moustache. When I got home I tried them on. Then I added a hat and an old pair of glasses that had belonged to my mother.

I sent the photo in to Boland. He wasn't over the moon about it but accepted it grudgingly. The day my first article appeared with the photo I showed it to Mary. She said I looked like an Iranian terrorist. I didn't mind that if I was unrecognisable. Later that day I called into my snooker club. I was chatting to the owner for a few minutes when I noticed he had the *Evening Press* open on the counter before him on the page where my article and photo were.

As we finished talking he started reading my article. I felt like someone in a movie under the Witness Protection Scheme in the scene where the hero infiltrates the hoodlum's gang under an assumed identity and then one day they find a photograph of him with his real name under it. When I said this to Mary she said, 'That's a bit dramatic. You're not in a James Cagney film. You're in *The Evening Press*.'

A few months later *The Star* newspaper interviewed me about one of my books. I was again faced with the old problem: They wanted a photo of me for the article. This led to another minor panic. I raided the biscuit box where I kept all my photos and tried to find one where I didn't look like myself. Mary said, 'Are you still going for the Iranian terrorist image?'

I chose a photo Basil had taken of me a few years before. I was in a group of about ten people in it. We were standing near the statue of James Joyce in the city centre. My head was about the size of a pea in it so I felt safe. What I didn't realise was that the picture department would blow the photograph up and cut everyone else out. The result was that my face looked like I had the worst case of acne in recorded time. The even worse part was that I was still recognisable. I didn't leave the house until it got dark for days after this for fear of someone asking me about it.

To avoid further problems I decided to write for places that would have little or no interest in what I looked like. In some ways I felt as if I was under house arrest. I thought I might need to consult with someone like Salman Rushdie for advice. He obviously had a more sophisticated set of disguises than I had.

I went through a brief period of sending articles to the *Irish Times* in the following months. They used to take book reviews from me in the old days and I also had a feature printed there once commemorating Walt Whitman's centenary but after that I could have wallpapered my room with their rejection slips. The Whitman piece must have been read widely because for ages afterwards people came up to me telling me they liked it. Had it become a collector's item, I wondered? People who hadn't even seen my books, or the hundreds of articles I wrote for *The Evening Press*, came up to me in the street and said, 'I liked your Walt Whitman article.' Maybe Walt himself even got reincarnated to read it.

One night during a radio interview for a book I was promoting a few years later the interviewer said, 'Are you still writing for *The Times*?' I told him I hadn't had anything in that newspaper for about eight years, a comment that floored him.

It was the paper everyone seemed to want to get into. I didn't know why.

I often found it dull. Charlie Haughey put it well when he said about the *Times* editorials, "Who writes these things anyway? They read like they've been done by an old woman sitting in a bath with the water getting cold around her fanny."

Aubrey Malone

You Can Quote Me on That!

'We shouldn't upset the apple tart'
(Bertie Ahern)

'If you pee standing up, you're worth an extra fifth in the salary department'
(Eddie Hobbs)

'The one thing men could do with a little helpful advice on is apologising'
(Terry Prone)

'The only thing worse than a rock star is a rock star with a conscience'
(Bono)

Different Genres

I continued writing books, many of them quotation anthologies like the one pictured opposite. Sometimes my life as an author and a reviewer clashed. There were occasions when I'd get a snooty rejection letter from a publisher and in the same post, in a different envelope, a "heads up" about a book they wanted me to review, often including it with the letter. I doubt they intended this double-up of missives. Most departments in publishers' offices didn't interact in matters like this. My name was on file as a reviewer and that was it. If I gave a positive review to the last book they sent me they'd keep me in mind for the next one, using (and, as the case may be, abusing) me any which way they could. On such occasions I felt as if I'd received the literary equivalent of a "Dear John" from a girlfriend alongside a letter asking me if I'd like to go out with her.

I never knew how to react. Should I ring up and give out to them, telling them that they were missing out on the opportunity of having a best-seller by rejecting my book? Or would I not mention my book, instead just telling them to put their review book where the sun didn't shine. If I decided on a more subtle approach I could give a damning review to the book even if I liked it, just so the author could suffer like I did. I think the Germans call this schadenfreude, which is a fancy way of saying you're being a right bastard.

I never did that, not so much out of sympathy for said author as me thinking I might wish to try the publisher with my next masterpiece (it had to be only a matter of time). If I said caustic things about one of their authors in the interim they probably wouldn't even read such a proposal. I knew one author who told me a company had a "thing" against him on account of a poor review he gave one of their books. As a result, he could never get one of his own ones accepted by them.

"They don't even read what I send them now," he told me. When I asked him how he knew that, he said he had a practice of sellotaping two pages of his work together. If the sellotape was still in place when the MS came back it would prove his point. When I said to him, "Maybe they didn't get that far," he replied,

"It was pages 4 and 5." I agreed that sounded bad all right. Even when I'm reading George Eliot I get beyond page 5 before I lose the will to live.

I continued churning stuff out for my "Wit's End" column in the *Evening Press*. In August 1992 I had 17 articles in that paper. Bearing in mind it didn't come out on Sundays, that was 17 in 27 days. I never quite reached those levels before or since but I kept swamping Boland with submissions.

They probably drove him mad. He told Mary once that he had an Aubrey Malone drawer. Presumably he just threw them in there when they arrived and dug one out whenever he had a space to fill. I used to post one to him every other night. That's one thing I miss in this computer age of ours where everything is submitted online. Walking to the letterbox was often my exercise for the day. I never posted more than one at a time so I'd have to make more journeys. I sat the envelopes on top of one another on a tallboy and watched the mountain get smaller as each day went by.

My cousin Polly Sheil, Aunt Florence's daughter, told me one day that I should stop writing features and become a roving reporter like Charlie Bird. Poor Charlie would go on to develop motor neurone disease some years later. I told her I wouldn't have the confidence to stick microphones in people's faces and ask them about how they felt about the rising cost of milk.

"He does much more than that," she said. Of course she was right. The point I was trying to make was that I didn't like the world of facts. I once rang a newspaper asking for a desk job – the first and last time I ever did that – and the editor said to me, "Are you good on hard news?" I had to admit I preferred the soft variety. The conversation ended there because he hung up on me. Maybe he thought I was trying to be smart. I wasn't really. It was just that it was hard to go from reading novels by Dostoevsky to writing about a cat being rescued from a tree by a fireman, or ghosting the obit of a TD from Ballyslapdashmuckery.

The thing I had to keep drumming into myself was that I was writing for a readership, not for myself. That meant trying to be (horrible word) "relevant." It meant ditching the tortured Adolescent persona I mainlined in my stories and trying to become Steve Martin instead.

Herman Melville was dead before he became famous. So was John Kennedy Toole. I didn't want to have to shoot myself like Van Gogh, or cut off an ear, because my work wasn't being read by the public. Vincent only sold one painting in his lifetime. If I was Theo, his long-suffering brother, I'd have told him, "It's not happening, Vince. Maybe it's time to stop dabbling on canvases for a while and go down into the marketplace to see what's cooking." Put bluntly, I'd prefer to have my journalism printed in a third-rate rag tomorrow than have my before-its-time *meisterwork* novel propping up a table in a cold water flat.

The comedy writer Pat Ingoldsby contributed to "Wit's End" too. He once wrote to me saying, "Stop copying me." I wrote back to say he didn't have the copyright on eccentricity, that if I was modelling my style on anyone it was Groucho Marx.

I didn't want to hurt his feelings as I always liked Pat but nobody can claim exclusive rights to a genre. Most of the writers in "Wit's End" (there were five of us altogether) put slightly different spins on the wackiness of life. We were all at the same lark. Pat gave his life to comedy and I respected that but it was just one aspect of what I did.

After I finished writing the column I might have been doing a profile of Boy George or reviewing a biography of Ken Russell. I wore a lot of hats in those days. The "Wit's End" column meant putting on a persona. I always saw myself as a chameleon, an actor with words. Maybe that's what annoyed Pat, the fact that I did other stuff as well for the same paper. I was disappointed to see him being so possessive about his work. It made me wonder if he was as beautifully insane as he presented himself in his writings, which took the edge off them for me afterwards.

Pat sold his books in College Green and on the Howth pier, refusing to give them to traditional publishers. I often used to see him at a bus stop near me with a bin bag, waiting for it to transport him to one of his bailiwicks. He loved when tourists stopped to talk to him even when they weren't buying. I'd never have had the courage to stand in the centre of town with my books in front of me. I'd have felt like a beggar, as if the literary world had washed its hands of me. Maybe it had but I didn't want to advertise that fact, or to advertise the fact that I couldn't get a publisher. If you wanted to read Pat's books – I always did – you had to buy them off the man himself. I was slow to do this in case he'd say something like, "I suppose you're only buying that to pilfer some more of my ideas."

Other things Pat didn't give a stuff about were literary competitions, or prizes, or being included in anthologies or joining the Arts Council or any writer's groups. He stood magnificently alone in his assault on the industry. It made me feel good to know that such mavericks still existed in a world increasingly being overtaken by consumerism.

Speaking of prizes, I once wrote an article for the *Evening Press* outlining the best way to win the Booker. Here were my stipulations:

1. Try not to be born in Ireland.
2. Be unknown to the general public and overwhelmingly snobby about those who aren't.
3. Have a name that's hard to pronounce so that when critics are talking about you, even if they're only saying dum-di-dum, you'll sound devoutly impressive.
4. Write books that have to he read 2 or 3 times, or more, to be understood – if at all.
5. Never relate anything you write to your actual experience or the real world.
6. In interviews, don't say anything vaguely relevant to anything people might know about.
7. Try not to smile, as that will only lower the intelligentsia's general estimation of you. Just give the odd smirk when you're being bitchy about your rivals.
8. If a sentence comes to you that's straightforward, dump it in favour of one that's arcane, obscurantist and preferably polysyllabic.

One of my favourite articles for the "Evening Press" was on the film "Shane."
This photograph shows Alan Ladd and Van Heflin getting ready to present a
birthday cake to Brandon De Wilde, who's licking cream from it. He'd just turned
ten.

9. On your life, don't admit that you actually want to win the thing, even if you've been fantasising about what it would do to your reputation and/or bank account for the past 20 years. Because, as you know, All Good Writers aren't supposed to have either.

10. At cocktail parties, impress your friends by saying things like, "The only kind of writing that should make money is a ransom note."

I wrote a similar guide to how to spot a writer. It was from a series I was doing at the time called "Endangered Species." In such a group, "Writerus Latterdayibus" was recognisable by the following features:

Can be heard saying at cocktail parties: "I preferred *commedia dell'arte* to *nouvelle vague* until I got into Nuri Bilge Ceylan."
Hygiene: Suffers from halitosis.
Dresses: In polo-necked jumpers containing various forms of wild life.
Nests: Inner city penthouse with crumbling floorboards.
Drives: Bockety bicycle with crooked tyres.
Fave women: Spindly types who stutter a lot.
Speaks: With a lisp.
Reads: Kazuo Ishiguro, Michael Ondaatje, Pablo Neruda.
Listens to: Bartok, Metallica.
Pet hates: Ursula Von Der Leyen, Subo, Benny Hill.
Politics: The Greens.
Sex fantasies: Sylvia Plath, Marilyn Manson, John Wayne Gacey.
Vices: Enjoying Arthur Hailey behind closed doors.
Fave saying: 'Free verse is like playing tennis with the net down."
Can be spotted: In dusty second-hand bookshops off Exchequer Street.
Hobbies: Brooding about the meaninglessness of life while reading Nietzsche.

Socialises: Garden parties in Glasthule with Goths.
Chat-up line: "If Bacon wrote Shakespeare, who wrote Bacon?"
Is called: Gyles, Jeremy, Gareth.
Habits: Downing vast amounts of bad hootch when meditating.
Summer Habits: Lying in dark dungeons to escape the sun.
Biggest Fear: Dangling participles.
Mating call: "There goes another novel!"
Reached peak: During the Bishop Casey sex scandal.
Best Before: The "Bridget Jones" ballyhoo.
Projected extinction date: 2027.

In similar vein I did a piece on literary criticism which probably owed something to my time in UCD. It went like this:

The first law of 'litcrit' is that you should always strive to say the opposite of what everyone else is saying – even (or especially) if you agree with them. This confers you with instant notoriety and is an ideal way to make your initial mark. The second law is never say you liked a book, even (or especially) if it caused you endless hours of pleasure. This is, of course, presuming you read it, which few reviewers do.

If somebody asks you verbally what you thought about a book, a sneer is worth a thousand words, and much less time-consuming.

If pressed, you could say, something throwaway like "This book does for literature what myxomatosis did for rabbits."

Let's say you're called on to review an author you know absolutely zilch about, an eminently foreseeable prospect considering that you could safely put the sum total of your literary knowledge on the back of a stamp and still have room for a haiku.

The best approach here is to compare him/her to other writers. If it's a thriller you're reviewing – it doesn't matter if it's any good or not - say it's "Chandleresque". If it's a novel that totally flummoxes you, say it's "Kafkaesque". "Kafkaesque", as you probably know, is the most overworked word in the English language. It comes from an oddball writer called Franz Kafka who had about as many identity crises as the rest of us had chocolate sundaes. He also had a Persecution Complex, by the way – probably to keep the Identity Crises company – which means that most of his books end horrifically. And he was a guy who could never seem to get an answer to any question he ever asked. You'll know how he must have felt if you ever ring Eircom.

So if you pick up a book that's weird and/or horrific and/or querulous, have no hesitation in splurging out your trusty "Kafkaesque" to beat the band. It never fails. In fact the term has been so bandied about in the last few decades (Kafka was "re-discovered" in the sixties) that now I'm afraid not even Kafka is Kafkaeseque.

My articles in the *Evening Press* eventually came to the notice of the NUJ. I had to join the union to be allowed continue. I'd always been waiting for a phone call from them when I was writing for *Image* but they didn't mind the occasional column. In the *Evening Press* I had too big a profile for them to ignore.

To join the union you had to prove that two-thirds of your earnings were coming from journalism. About a tenth of mine were so I had to dummy up receipts to get in. Most people who dummy up receipts are trying to pretend they earned less than they did so I was in an unusual situation.

After I was accepted, the inevitable happened: I started to get less work in the *Evening Press* so I really didn't need to be in the union at all now. In future years I paid back to the union everything I'd ever earned from that paper in my monthly subs. It was Sod's Law. Then the *Evening Press* closed down. Brilliant.

I looked around for other work. A young journalist called Barry Egan was editing a celebrity magazine so I started writing for that. I did profiles of actors and sporting stars. He gave my pieces nice spreads. I didn't get any money for them but it was good exposure for me. John Waters started writing for it as well. By now he'd stepped down from editing *In Dublin*.

Barry and John went on to bigger things afterwards. I don't think any of us ever saw a penny from the people who owned the celebrity magazine. I heard from someone that it was run by a terrorist organisation and that if you asked to be paid you'd get kneecapped. That stopped me asking. In the succeeding months I sent out articles to other magazines that were like letters in a bottle. Most of them went unanswered. I was lucky if I even got a rejection letter. It seemed to be the way everywhere.

I started doing book reviews anywhere I saw openings – uni mags, freesheets, off-the-wall chapbooks. Most of the time I didn't get paid. I made for places where I felt there would be openings. That meant I ruled out the national newspapers. I felt I'd have to know somebody to get accepted in any of these.

The book reviews were like an extension of my *Hibernia* days. I'd be presented with joynormous tomes and asked to write 500 words on them. It wasn't a very good return on your time. Part of the 500 words would be quotes from the book. It meant there was precious little space left to say anything creative. I only did them because I had a history of doing them.

Jeremy Addis had long taken over from Bernard Share at *Books Ireland* by now. He sent me lots of books to review. I was given more space than in most of the other publications but the books he sent me were often dense. I was bored to tears with a lot of them but I didn't want to say that. It would offend Jeremy and also the writers in question.

If you panned their book you were making an enemy of someone you could pass on the street the next day. Jeremy would know a lot of these writers personally. I didn't want to hurt their feelings, especially if they were just starting out, but if you praised a bad book it put a question mark over your judgment. I tried to be fair but it was a hard balance to get.

I once got a book of Alice Taylor's to review in *Books Ireland*. In the course of it I described her as "literature's answer to Daniel O'Donnell." The book was published by Brandon, a company in Kerry.

The editor, a man called Steve Donleavy, rang Jeremy in an apoplectic state. I think he wanted me fired. Jeremy explained to him that the views of his writers didn't necessarily reflect his own ones. He had to say this as Donleavy was advertising in the magazine. "Maybe go a bit easier next time," Jeremy advised me.

Needless to say, I cut my throat with Brandon with that review. If I sent them a proposal of my own at any future date, I was likely to get a Molotov cocktail in reply. As Ulick O'Connor once put it, "Irish Alzheimer's means you forget everything but the grudges."

I was aware my views were personal and that they weren't going to be agreed with by all the readers of a given publication. Maybe they wouldn't even be shared by a small fraction of them. Every writer had their comfort zones and their blind spots.

In my own case, I never liked reading long books no matter how good they were. As a result I tended to give better reviews to short ones. I had similar kinds of problems with long films. My threshold of patience was so low I'd be jigging around in my seat after ten or fifteen minutes elapsed. I'd want to go out to the shop for a mineral or go to the bathroom just to pass time.

When I was young you could go into a cinema when a film was half way through and watch it to the end, then watch the beginning afterwards. That became possible again when video rentals came onstream in the eighties. With books you could always start wherever you wanted. Even better, you didn't have to rewind them before giving them back to the shop.

I always started reading books in the last half. People would say to me, "You'll miss the story." The point was, I didn't care about that. If I liked the book I'd read it again for the story. Starting in the middle, or two-thirds of the way through, you avoided what J.D. Salinger called "all that David Copperfield stuff."

In real life we have to suffer bores who spend an eternity introducing an anecdote. I like people to cut to the chase. If I like what I'm reading in the latter stages of a book I might "save up" the ending and go backwards to the first half. I chop it up into segments in my mind. That keeps my concentration keen.

Sometimes I literally chop books up with knives, like for instance the Philip Larkin letters. These run to a marathon length. Who wants to hold a book that's so heavy you feel you're carrying a bale of briquettes around with you? If you cut it in half and put a back cover from another book at the back of the first half and a front cover of another book at the beginning of the second half you have two nicely-sized books. All you have to be careful of is getting the same size covers

Aubrey Malone

Over golf
gesproken

Onvergetelijke citaten
uit de golfwereld

DELTAS

If you have any kind of an extensive library that's not a problem. Just rip up a book you don't like and save the covers. What could be easier?

One of the main problems with book reviewing was trying to get hold of editors. They seemed to be permanently "in meetings." All you'd get was their voicemail. If you left a message, it was unlikely they'd get back to you. I was reminded of Woody Allen's, "It's not just dog-eat-dog in this world. It's dog won't return dog's phone calls."

Sometimes the excuse for such laxity was inspired. One editor apologised for not returning my phone call because he had to go to Australia the previous day. 'I'm not talking just about yesterday,' I said, I'm talking about the way you've been ignoring me for the past ten years. (That caused an interesting pause on the line).

Sometimes the ignoring was simply from people being busy, other times it was personal. It always amazed me how people were always too busy to tell you how busy they were. A simple phone call to say "Busy" would have sufficed. How long would that take? In a future era, it could have been done by email in even less time. But people weren't inclined to do it. Silence was often used as a weapon by people in a higher position than you were. It was, as Mark Twain once said "The ultimate rhetoric."

Silence could also come from old-fashioned jealousy. Or to use the Irish version of this, begrudgery. "Was Joyce a great writer?" "How could he be? Sure I knew him when he had the arse out of his trousers."

Lee Dunne was well aware of Irish begrudgers, especially after he became famous on what they saw as false credentials. "Dublin critics know everything about everything," he remarked, "You can't stand for five minutes sheltering from the rain without being told you made a bollox of your last book."

George Moore once described an Irish literary movement as "Half a dozen writers who cordially detest one another." It was close enough to the reality of the situation.

David Kenny put it a slightly different way when he said, "If you're intent on becoming a real Irish writer it's important to make an enemy as soon as you can or nobody will take you seriously."

I first became aware of this when I started to publish books; Many people seemed to derive great satisfaction from not mentioning them when they were talking to me. They probably thought this would have upset me.

They couldn't have been further wrong. I hated talking about my books so they were actually doing me a favour by pretending not to know about them.

I put these anti-writer thoughts into a poem:

> *The only thing people*
> *Can't forgive you for*
> *Is being a writer.*
> *Tell them you're a rapist,*
> *a serial killer,*
> *someone who chops people into pieces*
> *and they'll find a way to exonerate you,*
> *to blame someone other than you*
> *or something other than you*
> *for the crime.*
> *They will put it down*
> *to a bad upbringing,*
> *a crisis in your life,*
> *a genetic imbalance.*
> *They will show you*
> *the latest psychological studies*
> *about the problem of evil*
> *and all our misconceptions about it.*
> *They will tell you*
> *how nobody really understands it,*
> *how you can be treated for it.*
> *But show them a book you wrote*
> *or something that was said about you in the media*
> *and everything changes.*
> *They look at you*
> *as if you've murdered someone close to them.*
> *as if a beast inside you*
> *is weighing them up,*

using them for raw material,
even stealing their souls.
They can't be natural with you now.
They can't talk about the things
you used to talk about.
You've ruined it.
You've become a writer,
one of those people who profess
to know it all,
self-satisfied souls
who mentally rape
their old compadres
to further inflate
their already inflated egos.
They may tolerate you
for brief periods afterwards if you talk
about other things like their children
or their jobs in the bank
but if you return to the subject of books
the expression of hatred
will come back again,
as they denounce you
before re-cultivating the lost art
of doing the 100-yard dash
the other way.

Editors didn't seem to like writers much either. I found it increasingly difficult to contact them with my submissions as the years went on. They were usually "in meetings" when I rang – in other words, hiding under the filing cabinet. My conversations with their secretaries usually went something like this:

"Hello. Could I speak to the editor please?"
"I'm afraid he's not here at the moment. Can I take a message?"
"I sent him a collection of stories. I was wondering if he was interested in them".
"Could you hold, please."

148

This was when the "Greensleeves" music usually came on. Ten minutes later she's back on the line.

"Yes, we received your manuscript but we have no word back on it yet".

"You mean it's in the hands of a reader."

"I would imagine so, yes."

"Could you tell me when I might know?"

"I'm sorry, sir, I have no way of coming by that sort of information. Could you call back in a week or so"?

"That's what you said last week. And the week before."

"You must have been talking to someone else. I've been out sick for the past month."

"What's the difference – someone said it."

"Look – ring back next week and I'm sure we'll have some word for you·. Okay?"

"This is my fifth phone call for a simple request. Is somebody reading my stories or aren't they?"

"If they've been received they're being read. That's all I can say."

"So who's reading them?"

"I'm afraid I'm not at liberty to give out that sort of information."

"Is the editor?"

"He would be but I can't disturb him now. He's in a meeting."

"The last time I called he was in a meeting as well. And the time before. Does he do anything else but be in meetings?"

"There's no need to be sarcastic, sir. He's a busy man."

"I understand that. I'm a busy man myself. All I'm asking you is to ask him that little question. It couldn't take more than 30 seconds."

"Under no circumstances can he be disturbed. He left instructions to that effect."

"Okay. Just for curiosity's sake, can you tell me the name of my collection?"

"May I ask why?"

"Oh just so's I can be assured you got them."

"Oh I'm sure we got them all right. The postal system isn't

quite that inefficient."

"I'm glad to hear that."

"Rest assured."

"What were they called, by the way?"

"I beg your pardon?"

"What were they called?"

After a lengthy pause she asks me could I hold again, please. Of course I could. It's all I know now. Then it's another ten minutes of "Greensleeves". Just when I'm contemplating indulging in a bout of Russian Roulette, another voice comes on.

"Hello?"

"I believe you're enquiring about a manuscript.''

"That's right?

"Could you tell me the title, please)?"

I say "It's a book about the film *Ryan's Daughter.*" Actually it isn't. But by now such minor details don't matter.

"Oh yes. We received that all right. Did you not get a letter saying so?"

"No."

"Well we have it all right. In fact it's being read at the moment."

"Might I ask by whom?"

"Hold on a moment, please."

It's Pass the Razor Blades time. Tap desk with finger. Check heartbeat. Another blast of our old friend "Greensleeves". By now you find yourself humming along with it. Dum dum de dum de de dum de dum de de dum de dum de de dum de dum. To keep your sanity, you understand.

But the darkest hour comes before the dawn. Because when it finishes a rather authoritative voice is speaking to you.

"Hello. This is the editor. I believe you were looking for me. Sorry for the delay. It's been septic here today. You know yourself."

"Indeed. I sent you a collection of stories."

"So I believe;'

At this point your heart begins to flutter. "I've been enquiring if you received them."

"We did."

At this point your heart begins to flutter.

"Ah. So someone is reading them."

"Well someone was reading them."

"And did he like them?"

"As far as I can gather, yes."

Check heartbeat again. Palpitations.

"Does this mean you'll be publishing them?"

Lengthy pause.

"Well there is a slight problem with the manuscript."

Sharp intake of breath.

"A problem?"

"Yes. I'm afraid we can't locate it at the moment."

"Are you trying to tell me you've lost it?"

"In a manner of speaking."

"What do you mean 'in a manner of speaking'? Either it's lost or it isn't."

"It's more complicated than that. Listen, sir. The best thing I can suggest is you send us in another copy of your manuscript and we'll consider it."

"That isn't possible."

"Well surely you've kept an original."

"What I sent you was the original."

He clears his throat.

"Oh dear. I'm afraid that's not recommended practice."

"I'm sure it's not. I'm sure it's also not recommended practice for publishing companies to lose material an author has been sweating over for 4½ years."

"I can understand your frustration, sir."

"Look – what chance has this of turning up?"

"It's more complicated than that. You'll appreciate an enormous number of submissions appear on my desk every morning."

"Do you lose them too?"

Ryan's Daughter
A David Lean Film

By Aubrey Dillon-Malone

"I don't appreciate your tone. We're a respectable company with an enviable track record. You would know that, of course."

"Is there a cause for legal action?"

"I beg your pardon?"

"I said is there a cause for legal action?"

"You're joking, surely. Nobody asked you to send us your stories."

You find your blood pressure rising. A sweat is breaking out on your forehead. You don't believe you're having this conversation. Four and a half years down the toilet.

Wait a minute. Keep a cool head. Pessimism will get you nowhere. They're probably buried under a pile somewhere. Have patience. Ring back next week like the lady said. Or next month. Or even next year. What's a year when you're talking about a book that contains every profound thought you've ever had since you left the cradle.

There's a long silence. Then he speaks again. "Hello?"

"Yes?"

"Ah, you're still there. I thought you'd gone."

"Look, let me just ask you one question. What chance has this of turning up? When will we know for sure?"

He clears his throat again. There seems to be delight in his voice when he speaks.

"I'm afraid we know already."

"How is that?"

"Because the reader's house burned down last week."

The World of Books

I tried my hand at book-writing now as well. I thought it might have more longevity than the journalism. Journalism was too uncertain. I sent many articles off to newspapers that weren't even acknowledged, never mind rejected. If I did something and it wasn't used, I had to throw it away. I thought things might be different with books. There were hundreds of publishers out there in all comers of the globe. If one of them didn't want what you offered them, another one might.

I had my first "real" book published in 1995. It was called *Hollyweird*.

The cover had sketches of a number of stars that resembled either negatives or poorly produced silkscreen images from Andy Warhol's factory; Did someone leave the dark room when the images were only half developed? It's bad enough when something like this happens. When you fail to rectify it, it's even worse.

Hollyweird was a compilation of a set of columns I'd been doing for the *Evening Press* called "Lowdown." It consisted of about twenty odd facts associated with a star of my choice. I'd done about thirty of these so there were enough of them to lump together and call it a book. Some of the facts were so "weird" I had to double check (and sometimes even triple check) my sources in case someone sued us for libel. The publishers were worried about this.

Even after I'd provided such sources they were leery about using some of them. "Surely if the people in question have a problem," I protested, "they'll go after the magazines or books who first printed these items, most of whom are much richer than us." They didn't agree. Sometimes it was the "small guy" who was singled out to make an example of.

It got more publicity in England than in Ireland. The researcher of a show Gerry Ryan was hosting asked me to go on it to promote it but I refused, having a horror of television. I knew I was cutting my throat in PR terms but I couldn't face the idea of the nation gawking at me as I outlined the stars' various peccadilloes. Instead I confined myself to the print media.

One editor I sent a copy to said to me on my follow-up phone call asking him if he received it, "Is that the book that was printed on toilet paper?" He was close to the truth - they'd skimped on paper quality just as they did on graphic designers – but I didn't appreciate him saying it. Don't ever expect sweetness and light from Irish editors.

The publishers flew me over to London for a series of interviews about it.

Being asked to go to London for over twenty interviews for my first book, even if most of them were for out-of-the-way radio stations in places I never heard of, was something of a culture shock for me. It was the BBC after all, and one of them (a joint interview conducted by Derek Jameson and his wife – a kind of early "Richard and Judy") went out live at prime time.

Every day there was some publicity person talking to me about it. I stationed myself in a booth in the offices of the BBC for some of the interviews. In the evenings little pieces of paper were slipped under the door of my hotel room naming places where I had to present myself at different times. I duly turned up and gave them the patter they wanted.

The procedure was that you sat at this microphone, donned a pair of headphones, closed the door (which was about as heavy as the one in fort Knox) and sat there waiting for a plummy Brit to come on and say, "Hi Aubrey! Over from Ireland are we? Great place Ireland, eh? Really take care of you over there. Lots of Guinness too, Ho ho.

After being asked for the 19th time if Robert Redford really had his face on his toilet paper I began to suspect the horrible truth that is the nightmare of most writers: 90% of the interviewers hadn't read the book at all and were just mouthing questions from the press release. A rather frantic phone call to my publisher after the 9th or 10th Redford inquiry confirmed indeed that that particular item featured on all the press releases sent out to the radio stations.

When one interview ended, another one began. By the end of the week I felt like a has-been actor on his last movie doing the cattle call routine with seventh rate outlets to flog his dead horse. Would these interviews result in sales or were they mainly to divert drivers on the M1 from the fact that there was gridlock and they needed some idiot like me to pass twenty minutes for them as they waited for it to thin out?

The good news is that the British press were kind to the book, unlike the Irish, who tended to adopt an intellectual snobbery about it. Some reviewers commented that it wouldn't change their lives. This reassured me somewhat. I'd be terrified of ever attempting such a thing, The Brits seemed to twig immediately that *Hollyweird* was nothing more than nonsense.

There was one man who accused me of 'digging the dirt' on the stars, but strangely enough he was a fellow countryman of mine (from Belfast actually) working in the Beeb. "Is this how you treat your own?" I asked him after I tried to convince him that Kitty Kelley and myself were somewhat less than kindred souls. I wouldn't be your average candidate for skulking in a bush spying on Liz Taylor with a long range lens to see who she was bonking.

There was only one show I refused to do. It was an "After Dark" style thing that ran for three hours. I would have been seated amongst po-faced gents like Auberon Waugh and Jonathan Miller being fiercely witty and worldly wise about all the luvvies in my book and anything else that came up.

Before one interview I met Joe O'Connor. I was flattered when he asked me to autograph my book for him. I had imagined the converse would be the scenario. As we parted, the woman who was to interview him (apropos the paperback release of *Desperadoes*) looked at my name on the book and said, "You're not the Aubrey Dillon Malone from Ballina, are you? 'Cos if you are. I knew your father." At this stage I told Joe I thought it was time to go.

Things got even stranger later that evening when I called in on a pub I worked in in 1970, A man came up to me and said, "I know you from somewhere." I told him I was a barman in this very pub once upon a halcyon time. He reminded me that I wore a green shirt with a matching tie and flared trousers. I kid you not.

Funny things happen when you're launching books in London. The same man had contracted epilepsy as a result of a mate hitting him on the top of the head with a pick-axe. He was now permanently disabled. which gave him a lot of time for spending in pubs remembering rookie Paddies over from Dublin on slave labour. (I was earning £11 a week for a 66-hour shift). I won't tell you what my friend did to the guy who hit him with the pick-axe. Suffice to say he no longer inhabits the planet Earth.

The highlight of the week was being on the Derek Jameson show. Derek was one of those Old World, salt-of-the-earth types who made me feel really at home, chatting away merrily to me during the songs that were slotted in between our chatty bits. 'I believe Ulick O'Connor is old and crabby now' he said to me at one juncture, 'When I knew him he was young and crabby.''

Himself and his wife had this kind of schooly thing going on between them whereby if one of them wanted to interrupt the other with a question, they raised their hand. It made me feel I was being cross-examined. Which of course I was.

The day after the show I was informed I'd be on a BBC World Network Station that went out to no less than 35 million listeners. Understandably enough, the interviewer here was rather picky and didn't let me away with much. On the credit side, he didn't say anything at all about Robert Redford's toilet paper.

I felt famous after it was all over. Fame at forty? Hell, that was young. I looked at Frank McCourt, who became a sensation at 66 with *Angela's Ashes* soon afterwards.

Frank became an overnight sensation after it came out. He'd spent most of his life up to this as a quiet teacher but was now sought out by interviewers as the Great White Hope of popular literature.

He followed *Angela's Ashes* with a book entitled "'*Tis*" (the last word of *Angela's Ashes*) and also one about "the day job" which he called *Teacher Man*. "If that kind of success came earlier," he said, "I'd have gone off the deep end." I knew how he felt. The attention I was getting for *Hollyweird* didn't turn my head because of my age. I was able to handle it. At forty you know you're going to be stale news in a few weeks. At twenty you mightn't.

Having said that, Frank was still subject to begrudgery. Some critics dismissed his book as "Misery Lit," a ridiculous term as there was as much fun in it as sadness. One sourpuss, a fellow Limerick man, almost made his disapproval of Frank into a cause, dissing him in various interviews and penning a "corrective" to *'Tis* called *'Tisn't.*

I followed *Hollyweird* with a book called *It's an Awful World Thank God*. With apologies to Dylan Thomas for the title, it was a collection of my "Wit's End" columns in the *Evening Press*. I tried to come across as outrageous in it but often the attempts were contrived. I wanted the publisher to have one page cut in half with a message beside it saying, "This was me last night – half cut" (i.e. drunk.)

Another page had nothing on it except some tiny writing in the bottom left hand corner saying, "If you're reading this bit you must be really hard up." The appendix had a drawing of an actual appendix, like the ones we had in our body, rather than a literary one. I thought all these things were ferociously funny when I was making them up. Later they just looked like the desperate attempts of an unfunny person to be cute. "Cleverosity" was the expression Dubs used for such an individual.

I sent *It's An Awful World* to the *Cork Examiner* for review. I'd been doing some features for the paper for some years and felt they might give it a plug. Instead of that I got a damning review. It was trivialised by the reviewer in a manner I saw as juvenile. I was on the phone to the features editor some time afterwards and mentioned my disappointment at the review. Her reaction was almost hysterical. "Are you saying you expected preferential treatment just because you're one of our writers?" she barked at me. I said that wasn't the point. Criticism was either fair or it wasn't. She didn't give me any more work after that.

I shouldn't have been so sensitive about the review. I think the reason I took it badly was because it was my first attempt at humour. In my innocence I thought people were buying the *Evening Press* over the years to read me. It was more likely they bought it for the news, or the racing page, or to find out what was on the telly that night. Publishing can be humbling from this point of view. It can also be a good reality check.

Iris Murdoch once remarked, "A bad review is less important than whether it's raining in Patagonia." When some people were stung by a bad review of one of their books they consoled themselves by saying, "That will be wrapping someone's fish and chips tomorrow." You needed to think like that to stop yourself going spare. There were a lot of people out there who'd never write a book but seemed to be determined to stop the rest of us doing so. It was like people who tore plays asunder from the comfort of their velvet seats. Try writing one, sunshine. It ain't easy. I rubbished books myself so I couldn't be a baby when someone rubbished my ones. I just hoped it would be for the right reasons.

A woman in Newbridge said she'd help distribute the book for me. She was editing a magazine down there that I contributed some articles to. She said my book could be sent to the same outlets One of them was about dating. I think she got the idea I was interested in dating her too.

Some of her phone calls to me were quite suggestive. At one stage she even said she was thinking of sending me a photo of herself in the nude. That gave me a bit of a fright. When I explained that I was married she seemed to lose interest in the book. At this point a large number of copies were on a palette outside a company called Newspread waiting to be. sent down to Newbridge. This company distributed her magazine as well but now the deal was off. I blamed myself. Some of the articles I sent her were naughty. Her magazine had box numbers in it for people wanting to meet other people for "interacting." I don't think they meant going for moonlight walks together or playing Scrabble. She put two and two together and got five.

I got some work from the *Sunday Independent* now. They asked me to interview the actor Tony Curtis. He was in Dublin to promote his autobiography. I was nervous meeting him but he turned out to be one of the most natural people I ever met. The interview I did with him became the genesis of a biography of him that I wrote some years later. The day after the interview, Mary and myself went into Easons to meet him at a book signing he was doing.

Both of us had copies of books of his. Mary had the book he was launching and I had a novel he once wrote. He took Mary's book and autographed it. Then he drew a sketch of a flowerpot with some flowers sticking out of it. He just put his name on my book. I felt a bit deflated. Surely the novel showed dedication on my part. Was there some kind of sexual chemistry going on?

With Tony, you felt he'd always do more for a woman even if I was the person who interviewed him. I couldn't see him having as much time for Jack Lemmon as Marilyn Monroe on the set of *Some Like It Hot*, for instance. He told me he impregnated Marilyn on the set of that movie under Arthur Miller's nose. I said, "Didn't you say kissing her was like kissing Hitler?" He said, "That was just to grab a headline. "She drove me crazy with her tantrums on the set but who could resist Marilyn?" She miscarried the baby which was probably for the best. I don't think she was sleeping with Arthur at the time. He mightn't have taken too kindly to it. (When a future wife, Inge Morath, had a disabled child by him he disowned it so just imagine how he'd have been to one that wasn't his own.)

The next book I wrote was *The Guinness Book of Humorous Irish Anecdotes*. It came about through an agent I had in London called Chelsey Fox - a good name for an agent. (I'd met her when I was promoting *Hollyweird*).

When I was researching it I wrote to about a hundred people in Irish public life asking them if they'd like to contribute an anecdote. About six replied, all in the negative. Ireland's future Taoiseach John Bruton (whom I would interview when he attained that office) wrote to say that the only anecdote he had was that he had no anecdote. This amused me slightly so I decided to put it in – especially since most of my other leads were being deafeningly silent.

The book sold well. That was mainly because Guinness employed a PR lady, Margaret Daly, to get it reviewed over here. She was so dedicated she sat outside Gay Byrne's studio for hours on successive days as he was doing his daily radio show in the hope of nabbing him and thrusting it into his hands. One day she got lucky. He mentioned it on the show. It was one of the most listened to shows in the country. The couple of minutes he gave it probably sold 1,000 copies or more.

Chelsey got me another contract, one with Pan Macmillan for a quotation anthology, Women on women. No, it wasn't a lesbian book about sex. Because of the title, they didn't want readers to know I was a man so I was only allowed use the initial

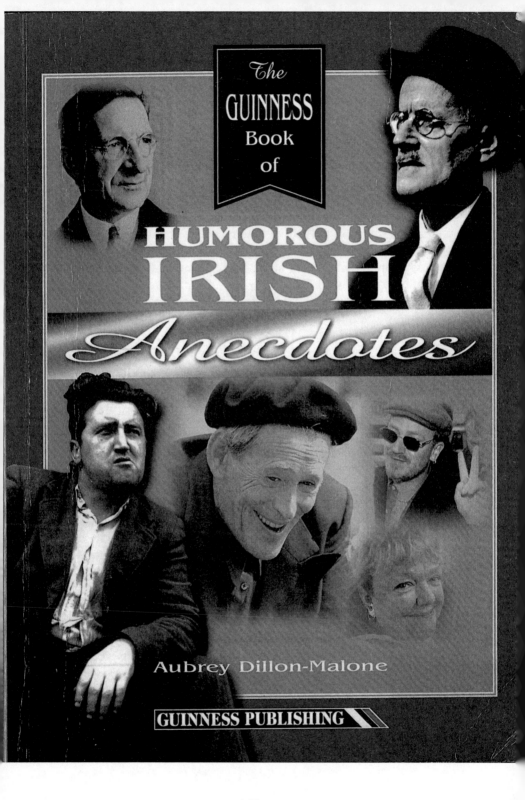

The GUINNESS Book of

HUMOROUS IRISH
Anecdotes

Aubrey Dillon-Malone

GUINNESS PUBLISHING

"A" for my Christian name.

Chelsey got me another contract, one with Pan Macmillan for a quotation anthology, Women on women. No, it wasn't a lesbian book about sex. Because of the title, they didn't want readers to know I was a man so I was only allowed use the initial "A" for my Christian name.

I said, "Didn't you say kissing her was like kissing Hitler?" He said, "That was just to grab a headline. "She drove me crazy with her tantrums on the set but who could resist Marilyn?" She miscarried the baby which was probably for the best. I don't think she was sleeping with Arthur at the time. He mightn't have taken too kindly to it. (When a future wife, Inge Morath, had a disabled child by him he disowned it so just imagine how he'd have been to one that wasn't his own.)

The book sold well. That was mainly because Guinness employed a PR lady, Margaret Daly, to get it reviewed over here. She was so dedicated she sat outside Gay Byrne's studio for hours on successive days as he was doing his daily radio show in the hope of nabbing him and thrusting it into his hands. One day she got lucky. He mentioned it on the show. It was one of the most listened to shows in the country. The couple of minutes he gave it probably sold 1,000 copies or more.

I was anonymous for my next book, a collection of wacky findings for a book called *I Don't Believe It*. This was Victor Meldrew's catchphrase in the show "One Foot in the Grave. Nice idea but the book didn't really take off. Neither did Michael O'Mara's next offer to me of a book of politically incorrect jokes. I guess I got too politically incorrect and W.S. Smith refused to take it. But O'Mara plc let me keep their generous £1,000 advance.

The following year I offered Duckworth Publishing another book I was working on, a collection of quotations from Brendan Behan. The Tessa Sayle Agency represented the people who held the rights to Behan's estate and they dug in their heels about releasing copyright. I secured the services of an octogenarian Russian agent, Vernon Futerman, to liaise with the Italian woman who worked in the agency to get the permission to use the quotes. So a Russian met an Italian in England to release rights for an

Irishman. I felt quite important. (But I didn't make a penny from the book).

Vernon had a really hard time getting the permissions. I don't know why they dug in their heels so much. Would the book not be publicity for Brendan? But Vernon was as dogged as Margaret Daly and he hung in there. Eventually they hammered out a deal.

I was beginning to learn an important lesson. Books weren't so much about writing as business.

The Life of Brian

My interest in Behan increased following this. A few months later I suggested collecting a bunch of funny stories about him to a publishing friend of mine called Gus Smith. Gus said he liked the idea but it was dependent on Sean Penn taking on the role of Behan for a forthcoming movie of *Borstal Boy*. Penn was spending a lot of time in Dublin at the time with his new love Robin Wright. He became so immersed in the Behan project he even had some of his teeth removed in order to feel more like him. (It gave the expression getting one's teeth into a role' a whole new meaning).

Penn also spent a fair amount of time drinking in Muiligan's pub that year to try and feel more like Behan. (I'd have liked that part of the research myself). I felt he'd take the part but he jumped ship at the last minute, leaving me with a book that now looked to be a dead duck. I decided that if he ever came back to Dublin I'd gladly remove the rest of his teeth for him, with or without the Behan project in mind.

A few months later 1 was watching Pat Kenny's talk show on the television when Brendan's brother Brian came on it as a guest. After the show was over I rang the TV station and asked them what hotel he was staying at. I was surprised when they told me. It turned out to be on Stephen's Green so the next morning I went there and ambushed Brian over breakfast. 'How would you like to work on a book with me about your brother?' I asked him. He jumped at the idea.

For the next year or so Brian and myself collaborated on a book that came to be called *The Brothers Behan*. It was partly a biography of Brian and partly a collection of the anecdotes I'd amassed for Gus Smith from the aborted Sean Penn project. It fell between a lot of stools but somehow came together.

Brian came over to Dublin with his wife Sally. Mary and myself brought them down to Glendalough one day. As he sat munching sandwiches he told us about his time in the Artane Boys School, a kind of reformatory run by the Christian Brothers. It was where children were put even if they had committed tiny offences. It left a horrible mark on him.

THE BROTHERS BEHAN

Brian Behan with Aubrey Dillon-Malone

The Sayings of

BRENDAN BEHAN

One day he saw a boy being slapped so hard on a staircase he fell over it and died. There was no inquiry into the death.

Every now and then a wadge of pages would come from him in the post. Some of it was handwritten and some typed. I had a job trying to wade through it for usable material. Occasionally there'd be a phone call from him. If Mary answered it he'd say, "Is His Lordship there?" He was usually in powerful form. The book was the last thing on his mind. I never knew what he was going to come out with. One day he said, "I'm beginning to feel upset that I wasn't sexually abused in the Artane place. Everyone else I know was. Was I not attractive enough?"

If he got onto a roll about Brendan he was difficult to stop. I'd be hard put to write down everything he said. I never learned how to tape calls or to affix a device onto the phone that would record them. All I had was my peculiar brand of shorthand, i.e. my illegible Muredach's scrawl – which I seemed to have inherited from my father.

He had some great oneliners: "I was thrown out of the Anarchy Society." "Brendan wasn't ambidextrous, he was ambisextrous." "I'm not a has-been, I'm a has-Behan." When I asked him if he ever thought about dying he said, "I don't like funerals. In fact I may not even go to my own one." He wanted the book done fast. I said, "Rome wasn't built in a day." He said, "I wasn't on that job."

"Books don't matter," he said to me once, "What matters is getting the bins collected. If a writer dies, nobody notices, but if the refuse collectors go on strike, society collapses." It was an unusual thing for a writer to say but then Brian was never predictable. When I asked him if he saw himself as different to Irish writers who stayed in this country – a subject I was interested in – he said, "I'm a plastic Paddy. We're all pissing in the same pot."

A champion of the worker's struggle in Brighton, where he spent most of his life he was an eccentric to the core. He once set up a society for distressed women on a boat. 'If they're not distressed going in,' his mother warned, 'they will be coming out!'

He came over to Dublin again for the launch of the book. It

was in McDaid's pub, a great haunt of Brendan's. Niall Toibin, who did a one-man show about Brendan, had been invited to give a speech. He liked the book and made some jokes about it. Niall's jokes went down very well with the crowd. At one point he said I wrote that Brendan's friend Paddy Kavanagh was pushed into the canal after coming out of a pub. "It must have been some push," he reflected, "because the canal was thirty yards away."

A man called Tony Mason, who edited the book, was also at the launch. As we were having a drink together he started asking me what my writing routines were. "What times do you start working," he said, "How many hours a day do you write?" I said, "You make it sound like Accountancy. I left that behind me in 1971."

The short answer to his question was, "I don't know." Some days I woke up and started clattering away even before I dressed. Other times I'd go for weeks or even months without going near the typewriter. If I was working on something that mattered to me it became more real than life itself but after a while I tended to lose interest in it. *The Brothers Behan* consumed me for a while and then I dropped it. Brian never minded that. As far as he was concerned, it didn't matter if it came out or not. He'd had his day in the sun with his plays in England and the few other books he brought out, like one on his mother, and some novels. He was coasting now.

I didn't have too much contact with Brian after the launch. Then one day out of the blue I got a call from him to say Sally had died. I couldn't believe it. She was so much younger than him. It was on a Christmas Day that it happened. My heart went out to him. I don't think he ever got over it. The life seemed to be gone out of him afterwards whenever I talked to him on the phone. He only outlived her by a few years.

Winding Down

I went into a period of seclusion after *The Brothers Behan*. Most of my books I wrote alone. That one had involved a lot of people and I needed a break from them. When I worked with people I felt my writing suffered, just like when I socialised with them my personality did. I felt I had a condition called People-itis. The only cure for it was solitude.

The process of writing always appealed to me more than writers themselves. Maybe I knew too many of them who wrote like angels and lived like devils. Reading their material I'd imagine they were the very souls of sensitivity and then at a function or some trendy party I'd see them shafting a colleague and think: Could this really be the same person who wrote that wonderful tribute to Goethe in yesterday's paper? Basically I agreed with e.e. cummings, who said once that he preferred the company of ice cream salesman to that of writers. (I would have agreed with that even if I didn't like ice cream as much as I do).

I also lacked ambition as a writer. Jack London said he'd rather win a water-fight in a swimming pool than write the Great American novel. I always thought I'd prefer to win the World Snooker Championship than write the Great Irish one. (I realised at this stage of my life that neither of these eventualities were very likely.)

I often had my articles bowdlerised at this time, or even pulled from publications at the last minute for little or no reason. Family members told me I was great but it was as dangerous to believe this as it was to believe the Dublin 4 critics who were lining up to take pot shots at me every time I put pen to paper. As Ernest Hemingway put it, 'If you listen to the good stuff about yourself you have to listen to the bad stuff too.'

One day the editor of a magazine I'd sent something to informed me that my submission was winging its way to the waste paper basket as we spoke. Other disgruntled souls seemed to relish telling me that I was a substandard clod who really should never have given up the day job. Sometimes I took these comments to heart but more often I felt they were being made by people who were either jealous of me or resentful.

My interview with Tony Curtis led eventually to a biography

There were times when I thought that even if I got an interview with God they'd say something like, 'Nice piece but I think we did Him last week. And isn't He a bit dated?'

Once again I felt a book could come to my rescue. I thought it might save me from the indignities I was going through with my journalism. At times it seemed to me as if my books were my wives and my journalistic articles my mistresses. I decided to compile an anthology of political anecdotes, calling it *Soundbites*. I sent it to a man called Richard Corcoran who was editing a small press called Leopold in Ranelagh. He said he'd publish it.

I can't remember getting an advance for it. I was always so delighted to get a contract for a book I rarely read the small print. It could have had a codicil stating, "You will be required to donate a kidney with your manuscript" and I wouldn't have noticed.

I started writing for other publications now, like *The Irish Catholic*, *Senior Times* and a newspaper called *Modern Woman*. It was a supplement to the *Meath Chronicle*. The editor, Margot Davis, became a great friend. So did her sister Carmel. Carmel did the social column for the paper. She thought I was a woman myself when I wrote to her first. It was that damn name again. I was writing for it for months before I talked to her. Her first words to me were, "You're a man!" I said, "How did you guess?"

I did every sort of thing for "*The Woman*" as she called it - film reviews, book reviews, features, funny pages. In some editions I'd have up to seven or eight pages.

A man called Tom Locklin did the music page for it. He was generally very positive in his reviews of CDs. "If I slate something," he told me once, "I don't get any more CDs from that company." I felt the same thing applied with my films. Sometimes I felt like saying something really nasty and held myself back. It wasn't like having a chat about a film in a pub. Your words were going to the whole 32 counties. I later learned that his real name was Loughlin. He changed it to make it similar to Hank Locklin. It was a nice touch.

Margot lived in Navan. She made her way up to Dublin every now and then. We spent most of our time gatecrashing parties and occasionally writing about them.

The features I did for *Senior Times* were skimpier than the ones I did for *Modern Woman* but no less enjoyable on that account. The central focus of this publication was the elderly but it cast a wide net. Des Duggan, the publishing director, was helpful to me with articles and also with getting publicity for my books through the magazine. He became a good friend too. He was always telling me I needed to be more technological in my approach to writing. He threw up his hands in horror the day I told him I was still doing most of my work on an electronic typewriter rather than a computer.

Des was also unable to get his head around the fact that I was probably the last man in Ireland who didn't have a mobile phone. 'We're the new elite,' I informed him. He couldn't understand how I could survive without one. He did PR for the magazine and was forever calling people and being called by them. I rarely had a conversation with him when a call didn't come through for him on his mobile. It was like an extension of his arm.

At this time I also went through a phase of writing letters to people. I became like Saul Bellow's *Herzog*. If Mayo lost a football match I'd write to the manager of the team telling him what the problems were, and even expecting a reply (which never came). I wrote to politicians telling them how to run the country and got quite peeved not to hear back. I even wrote to Arsene Wenger, the manager or Arsenal, telling him I sympathised with him whenever Arsenal played Manchester United because the United players were always diving in the box.

The most famous person I wrote a letter to was Bill Clinton. I offered my sympathy to him at the height of the Monica Lewinsky affair when he was being witch-hunted by Kenneth Starr. I got a reply that seemed to be signed by the man himself but someone told me it was probably just a stamped signature. When he came to Eason's years later to sign his autobiography I queued up to see him with the letter in my pocket. For some strange reason, however, the security men wouldn't let me through.

It gets frustrating when people try to stop you seeing the President of America when you're carrying all-important missives to him.

Issue 91 January - February 2018 **NOW** **€3.00/£2.75**

Senior*Times*

The magazine for people who don't act their age

And the loser is..

Aubrey Malone on the history of Oscar snubs, curses and scams

ISSN 1649-2056

02>

9 771649 205088

John Giles

Dylan Thomas

Legacies

Novel

I decided to write a novel. It was time. Stories were fine but they didn't stretch you. I thought of Hemingway's comment before he wrote his first one, "I felt like the last girl on the street to get married."

I was nervous as I contemplated the prospect. Somerset Maugham once said, "There are three rules for writing a novel. Unfortunately, no one knows what they are. Thanks, Somerset.

Did I have anything to say about myself, or about life? What was the plot going to be? How was I going to create characters that weren't me? I wasn't a Charles Dickens. I couldn't bring twenty people into a room like he could, all with their own personalities and quirks.

I'd always been minimalist. Maybe I should try a dystopian book about a man thinking he was turning into a spider. It might have got the critics to describe it as "Kafkaesque."

Every journey begins with a first step. The hardest sentence any writer has to write is usually the first one. When I sat down to write my novel, beads of sweat broke out on my forehead. How was I going to begin it?

Certainly not with what J.D. Salinger called "all that David Copperfield stuff." In the end I went for simplicity: "I grew up on a farm that swept all the way down to the sea." Okay, so it wasn't up there with "On they went" (*Dr Zhivago*) or "The clock struck thirteen" (*1984*) but at least it was simple. I felt Ernest would have approved.

When I finished the book I wasn't sure if it was any good or not. I knew it was too personal but how could I stop that? Every first novel was a thinly-disguised autobiography. We all knew that. But if I wrote from the heart it would be more real. As D.H. Lawrence said, "No tears in the writer, none in the reader." G. K. Chesterton countered that with his comment, "A good novel tells us the truth about its hero. A bad one tells us the truth about its author." How could I get the happy medium?

I told myself to stop analysing it and just fill the pages. At the end of the day I could cut out anything I didn't like. At least if I could avoid the possessiveness most writers had with their words.

Editors said asking some of them to trim down paragraphs was like asking a mother to kill one of her children.

I remembered Beckett saying to an actor in one of his plays once, "I wrote three dots. You only gave me two." He wasn't even talking about language then but rather a pause. It reminded me of the story of Harold Pinter faxing a comma from Berlin to London once. How might the skeletal souls of Hitler's concentration camps feel about such indulgences?

Benedict Kiely and Frank McGuinness gave me puffs for it. I was cheeky to ask them. They probably felt, "Who is this nobody expecting us to big him up?" but they complied, being the gentlemen they were.

I sent it down to Ballina for review. Mistake.

I knew I was asking for trouble by putting a photograph of myself with my father on the cover but I couldn't resist it. It was one of my favourite photos of the two of us together, taken on Enniscrone beach.

The problem was that his appearance was known to people in Ballina, especially older people, so it was going to make them think it was all drawn from life. That's exactly what happened with the features editor of the *Western People*, a man called Jim McGuire, who reviewed it. My main character was a farmer and there was no way Jim was going to accept my father as that. How could he? The man on the cover of my book had a monocle and a pin-striped suit, a waistcoat and an old school tie.

Jim wrote of "the almost legendary luminary" that was my father. He said he picked up the book hoping to discover "the relationships that existed behind that door in Teeling Street where the D-Ms resided before the transfer to Dublin." (It was Arthur Street during most of my youth. The name was changed to Teeling in 1966, the 50th anniversary of the 1916 Uprising).

Jim was discombobulated to read that, while I retained my father's monocle for the pic, the character inside the covers was a more rustic character by far, and not, as he expected, "the trademark Hugh Dillon-Malone with his double-breasted waistcoat and bulging briefcase." Jim didn't miss much, did he? Was it possible that he was even "Sean Bocht"?)

THE THINGS THAT WERE

AUBREY DILLON-MALONE

He concluded his review by saying that most people reading the book would not be aware of the "trick" being perpetrated on them. Was this not a little harsh? I was only using a photo because I liked it, for God's sake. "Gentlemen" farmers could well have monocles, couldn't they? Even if they weren't "legendary luminaries" like my father?

J.P. Donleavy, take a bow.

Elvis

An agent told me humour books had better chances of being accepted than anything else so for the next few years I concentrated on these. I compiled quotation anthologies on every subject I could think of – drink, sex, politics, sex, sport, sex, and, er, sex. I also decided to re-work Ambrose Bierce's *Devil's Dictionary* into a modern context, calling it *The Cynic's Dictionary*.

It went on to become my best-selling book, going from hardback into paperback in both Britain and the United States and even coming out in a Spanish edition called *El Dictionario de Los Cinicos*. This was the first time I ever saw one of my books in a foreign language. Whenever I went to parties now and people asked me what I was working on, I was able to draw myself up to my full height and say in my most self-important voice, '*El Dictionario de Los Cinicos*.' That was usually enough to make them depart the room in record time.

I now felt I was ready to attempt something a bit more ambitious. The twentieth anniversary of Elvis Presley's death was coming up so I decided to write a biography of him to tie in with that.

The book was originally supposed to have been published by a man in Bray called Terry Rowan, but Rowan led me a merry dance, dropping out of the deal just a few months before publication. It was just a verbal one but I trusted him so I wasn't too fussed about not having a contract.

Coming up to publication, though, I got a bit nervous when the contract still hadn't arrived. It was like the proverbial 'cheque in the post', always on the way to you but never quite there. On the eve of publication he said he'd had some problems and was sadly waving goodbye to my manuscript.

By this stage I'd had numerous meetings with him and had also employed a man to format the book. When I asked Rowan for compensation for these expenses his reaction was simply to say, 'This conversation is now over.' I couldn't take this lying down so I went to a solicitor for legal advice. He told me I was on shaky ground seeing as I had no contract.

The RISE and FALL and RISE of
ELVIS

Aubrey Malone

This was true but I had other documentation to make him sympathetic to my plight. He agreed to employ a barrister and we went to court. I was only looking for £700, a mere fraction of my overall costs. I told the barrister it was a question of principle with me rather than anything else, that what I was seeking was a moral victory rather than a financial one. My father had often told me of cases where plaintiffs were awarded a penny as a token. I thought I'd even be happy with that.

Rowan didn't show up when I appeared at the District Court on the appointed day so I was awarded damages. I thought that was the end of it but then he appealed the case to the Circuit Court. I now realised he was trying to make himself into something of a nuisance.

When we got to the Circuit Court I saw that he'd employed a solicitor. He looked very imposing. My star witness was my typesetter, Jimmy Lundberg. Jimmy had been in touch with Rowan about the book and felt he could shake him with his testimony but he was less gung-ho when he saw the solicitor dressed up in his finery. As the solicitor took the stand, Jimmy tapped me on the shoulder and whispered, 'Do you mind if I say something to you, Aubrey?' I said 'Go ahead.' He said, 'In my opinion, we're fucked.' I thanked him for his vote of confidence.

The solicitor tried to give me the third degree when I took the stand but I kept my cool. Jimmy was next up and he testified well, letting the courtroom know just how deep we were into the project before it was called off. John Kavanagh also wrote a letter for me that we gave to the judge. It testified to the fact that he'd spoken to Rowan on the phone and was assured by him that he going to publish a significant print run of the book.

A part of me felt the whole business was absurd. Six months of my life and two court cases for a few measly pounds. How Elvis would have laughed. Or would he? I suddenly remembered the fact that a book had probably caused his death. It was the one written by his bodyguards, spilling the beans on his excesses. Two weeks after it came out Elvis was in his grave. John Lennon put it well when he said, 'It's always the courtiers who kill the King.'

Despite my doubts I won the case and was awarded the compensation I asked for. It was pittance in comparison to what I would have made if the book had actually been published but as I told the barrister it was never about that for me. Outside the court he said to me, 'Well, you've got your moral victory.'

A few minutes later a photographer from the *Irish Independent* approached me and a crowd began to gather. Before I knew where I was I found a media circus around me. Microphones were thrust in my face and I was asked for my reaction to what had gone on. I couldn't believe it. I thought this was a trivial case nobody would have been bothered about.

'Let's get a shot of you,' the photographer said, raising his camera. 'If you click that,' I said, 'there'll be another court case here with you in the dock. Either that or I'll break your jaw.' Suddenly I felt like Frank Sinatra.

My father would have been amused. It was the twentieth anniversary of his death, just as it had been of Elvis'. In one sense I felt I'd done it for him.

I was standing there savouring my victory when Rowan passed. I was tempted to say, 'Now the conversation is over,' but I didn't.

A journalist came up to me and said, 'Could I have a few words from you about what just happened?' 'No comment,' I replied, 'This isn't for the papers.' 'Really?' he said, 'Did you not know it's already in the *Evening Herald*?' I was stunned. They'd obviously heard about it in advance and had the piece pre-set.

The next day the story was everywhere – in the broadsheets, the tabloids, you name it. The headline in the *Independent* read, 'One for the Money', making me feel totally misrepresented. These were the very papers that had pointedly ignored me over the years when I was looking for reviews of my books. Now they were putting me on their front pages with all of the wrong kind of publicity. Suddenly I knew how film-stars felt when interviewers didn't want to talk about their work as much as some trivial titbit in their private lives.

I now found myself looking for another publisher for the book. Where would I go? The answer to that question was actually staring me in the face.

I did it in conjunction with the Elvis Social Club, a spin-off from the official fan club. We used to meet in a pub on the Quays and under the influence of too many pints of Smithwick's dance around the place like idiots to karaoke versions of songs like 'Mystery Train' and 'The Wonder of You'. It was run by John Kavanagh, a very nice guy who was also an Elvis impersonator. His girlfriend at the time was Dee Maher, an equally friendly lady who'd seen Elvis live over twenty times. Dee actually got a letter from Elvis once thanking her for all her work on behalf of the club. She allowed me to reproduce it in the book.

We launched it in a pub on Thomas Street and everyone got suitably sozzled. At the end of the night Mary and myself tried to sing 'I Can't Help Falling in Love With You' from a rostrum John set up for the night. By that stage I could hardly stand never mind sing. Some sadist captured the moment on video and presented it to me afterwards. It cured me of any desire to be an Elvis impersonator. Maybe that was his intention.

On the anniversary of the night itself, August 16th 1997, I rang up a bar in Camden Street where an Elvis impersonator was doing a show. I asked the manager if he'd let me set up a stand with my books on it. He said he thought it was a good idea but he wanted 10% of my earnings for giving me the stand. I had no problem with that. Later in the evening I brought a few hundred books into the bar and set them up at the top of the stairs, just outside the room where the Elvis impersonator was doing his show. I had posters of Elvis all around the stand and the books were displayed prominently but I didn't sell even one copy that night. Everybody just wanted to hear the music and get drunk.

The night was a sobering experience for me, if that's not the wrong expression.

The book was well reviewed but some of the people in the fan club didn't like me saying Elvis had a drug problem, despite the fact that twelve different substances were found in his body after he died. Or that all his films weren't masterpieces.

One night at a function I'd been asked to attend to donate some copies to the Friedreich's Ataxia Society a woman came up to me with a growl on her face and said, 'So you're the horrible man who the book on Elvis. Well let me tell you this: I burned it.' 'Good for you,' I said. I felt strangely complimented that someone would have such strong feelings about something I wrote. As my father used to say, 'Love me or hate me but don't ignore me.' I learned afterwards that she was the wife of the man who ran the Elvis fan club that was in competition with our social club. Once again politics had raised its ugly head. When a radio programme devoted specifically to Elvis failed to mention it and I learned that the same man was behind this I realised what a cauldron I'd fallen into.

Whether out of masochism or some other reason I now started another book on Elvis, a spoof where I pretended to have found Elvis' hidden diaries in a disused shed near Tupelo.

I sent it to a publisher in London, Simon Mitchell of Quince Books. He said he was interested in it but he needed a sugar daddy to fund its publication. He got in touch with a man he knew called Ray Santilli. Ray had become famous - or infamous - for a spoof he'd done some years before. He pretended to have performed an autopsy on an extra-terrestrial being – as you would. This went on to become the subject of an Ant 'n Dec movie, *Alien Autopsy*.

Ray also had hundreds of rare photographs of Elvis, and a letter he wrote the day he died – about, of all things, American football. Simon and Ray flew over from London one day to show me all their stuff. They brought me for lunch and we discussed publishing the diaries with a big media splash. Ray said he had connections in Japan that he hoped could fund it.

Hugo was doing Elvis impersonations in bars for free pints at this time. I thought it would be good if he could launch it dressed up in Elvis gear. We could go into a theatrical shop and buy him a jumpsuit with a high collar and a rhinestone belt.

My idea was that as Elvis Hugo would say he hadn't died at all in 1977. Instead he flew to Dublin from Memphis in 1977 and got work stacking shelves incognito in a supermarket in Donnybrook. Hugo could do interviews where he said my discovery of the diaries blew Elvis' cover and made him come out of hiding to declare who he really was. I knew all about double identities from my years using the name Peter. Often I took Murphy as my surname instead of Malone. I don't know why.

Ray told me to put all my ideas on hold as he tried to get the book off the ground. The first thing that had to be done was to get it "legalled.". He gave it to a lawyer he knew in Los Angeles and he went through it with a fine toothcomb. Then he showed it to Joe Esposito, the best man at Elvis' wedding.

Esposito liked it but he thought there were some parts of it that might be sensitive to living people, like for instance Elvis' widow Priscilla, or some members of the so-called Memphis Mafia, Elvis' entourage.

When he showed it to Priscilla she insisted on a number of cuts. The lawyer also told Ray it couldn't be endorsed by Graceland so we'd have to plough a lonely furrow. Ray said he'd have to take a raincheck on it at this point because there were too many complications.,

The book stayed in dry dock until he sold it to a company called One Media along with some other musical properties he had for, I believe, £100,000. All I saw of this was £1,000. That's what Ray gave me for all my work. The contract I signed with him meant he held the rights to the book. I hadn't read it.

Moral of the story? Read your contracts. And always have, as Elvis might have said, a suspicious mind.

Thighland

Errol's hand crept up her thigh to the part of it where the sun didn't shine.

"Stop, Errol," Samantha cried, "you're venturing into dangerous territory." "I can't," Errol replied, "My brain is telling me to go all the way."

"Well my brain," snapped Samantha, "is telling me to give you a firm slap on the wrist."

When she did that, he stopped. Errol cried in guilt and pain. Samantha also cried. She didn't want to hurt her lover. But she had to maintain her modesty. Besides, didn't they say that if a man "had" a woman, he then lost interest in her? She didn't want to be the one to test that hypothesis.

"Love me for me," she pleaded.

"I will," he conceded, "but on the wedding night I want all of you."

"That you shall have," she promised, which made Errol's hand fell suddenly less sore.

****

Emboldened by my Elvis book I thought I'd try my hand at a Mills & Boon novel. Everyone was telling me that was where the money was. "You could write it before your breakfast" they said "and get as rich as Croesus."

I bought a tape telling me what they wanted. Entitled, appropriately enough, "And Then He Kissed Her," it was narrated by a lady with a sweet voice. She started by saying that Mills & Boon had 200 writers. All of them, she added, wrote to a "high standard." Of course I knew that already, having had numerous copies of their titles on my bookshelves beside Gide, Hesse and Nabokov.

M&B, the tape went on to say, didn't take thrillers, stories, poetry, westerns or adventure books. What they took were books with a hero, a heroine, a quarrel and a reconciliation. The story had to be written from the heroine's point of view – and also in the third person. It had to be upbeat in tone. As regards

189

the quarrel, it had to convey "the magic, wonder and tension of finding out if they can settle their differences by the end." The male had to be "tall, handsome and powerful." The female should be "young, spirited and vulnerable."

It was at this point of the tape that the well-spoken lady gave us our first example of' what kind of stylistic things a Mills & Boon aspirant should strive to achieve (and I quote):

"Nothing matters except this moment and our desire", he said urgently, "I need you, Amanda, you know that". "You say nothing matters", she insisted, "but how can we ignore the past?"

That's telling him, Amanda, I thought. Pasts didn't just disappear with the snap of a finger, did they?

"You must" the lady on the tape went on, "live with your heroine." This was a metaphor, not a lesbian reference. The writer also had to "sink yourself into her personality and experiences." And of course added our well-spoken lady, "You must fall in love with your hero. Nothing less than total commitment, all you M&B lovers!

"Don't make your heroine too perfect," my mentor went on, "She must be sweet all right, but not too good to be true." This was the age of realism. "Could you like someone who is perfect?" the lady enquired. Well, *could* you?? "On the other hand, don't make her too unattractive or she'll lose sympathy altogether!"

It was time for our second extract:

"Amanda glanced at the clock as she drove through the town at a furious pace. Nearly nine o'clock. She was going to be late for her hair appointment. Pressing her foot down firmly on the accelerator and ignoring the 30 miles per hour speed limit, she saw the needle of the speedometer jump over 70. What she didn't notice, until it was nearly too late, was the red light at the pedestrian crossing. "Too bad," she thought, and drove straight through it, catching the wheels of a push-chair as she did so. Screeching to a halt she jumped out and checked the car for damage. ''You stupid fool'' she shouted at the terrified mother, "You scratched my new sports car."

Amanda, I noted, was being a bit of a naughty girl here. On the other hand, sportscars didn't grow on trees, did they? And then there was the ferocious cost of panel-beating these days.

Neither would it have done to miss that hair appointment. We didn't want our heroines looking scraggly.

So how should I start my book? Here's extract number 4. Two extracts in fact: one the *do*, the other the *don't*. See if you can decipher which is better:

(1) "Amanda Taylor was 23 and had lived all her life in the small town of Milchester. She was very pretty, with blue eyes and blonde hair. She was the younger of two sisters and worked in a bank."

(2) "Amanda nodded, her blue eyes troubled as she thought how awful it would be to leave Milchester. 'But I've lived here all my life,' she protested."

Well – did you guess which was the *do*? If you chose extract No. 2, go straight to the top of the class. You have M&B written all over you, you lucky thing,

So what must your heroine look like? Well contrary to popular belief, the lady informs us, she need not be beautiful (surprise, surprise) nor of any specific age, though heroines aged from early to mid-twenties found favour with most age groups. (Let's hear it for the early to mid-twenties!).

What must she do for a living? In the old days of M&B (the company was established in 1908) she was often a stay-at-home type, but nowadays (yes, folks, we were now in the liberated nineties) she should be career-oriented, or at least enjoy her job. Such a job, if the writer wished, may be even "high-powered and unfeminine." Wow.

In recent years, M & B heroines have been everything from "commercial airline pilots to doctors in busy hospitals to garage mechanics." That's one in the eye for all those snotty feminists who look down on good ol' M & B as pulp fiction,

Neither is our M & B heroine waiting around for Mr. Right, On the contrary, maybe marriage is the *last* thing on her mind. Way to go, Amanda! From this point of view, her relationship to the hero presents an "exciting challenge to them both." Can't you feel your blood pressure rising?

And now it's time for another "This-one-is-right-and-this-one-is wrong" game. See if you can spot the turkey.

(1) "Oh yes, Luke," she breathed, "I'd be happy if you

ordered for me. I can't possibly decide. You do everything so much better than I do.''

(2) "For goodness sake, Luke, I'm not a child so don't treat me like one, mind. I'm perfectly capable of making up my own mind."

Tough decision, eh? Well I never said it would be easy. We can't have every Tom, Dick and Harriet writing M & B, can we? Okay, I'll spill the beans – it was Number 2. Did you guess? If so, congratters! You're almost there!

What sort of background must our heroine have? Again the local friendly tape-lady comes to the rescue in our time of need: "If your heroine is a girl-next-door type, the hero must be a man women dream about. That is why he has no shortage of girlfriends." He doesn't have to be classically handsome, or a millionaire (phew) or even a ''tempestuous Mediterranean type,'' but it's important that he's "overwhelmingly attractive." (As if we would have made him not so!)

Extract time:

> "Amanda noticed him immediately as he paused in the doorway of the room. Suddenly, every man she'd met faded into insignificance. He was gorgeous! Tall, with dark hair and a lean, hard-boned face that showed a wealth of experience."

So why should he be well-built? Need you ask? It's because "No one dreams of marrying a wimp." Too true. But he doesn't have to be aggressive or domineering. We must know why the heroine falls for him even if it's "against her better judgment." Could this be the garage mechanic, one wonders?

And now to plot. (We're getting warm). All plots are to an extent plagiaristic. Even *Jane Eyre*, for God's sake, was cadged from *Cinderella*. All the best stories have been told, so concentrate on how you tell yours. "Don't put in any petty worries, like overdue library books." Shame, shame! But neither, our mentor adds, should you put in overly serious ones either. "We're talking," she informs us rather sternly, "about escapism.'' Gotcha, girl. But escapism, she goes on, "must be based on reality. If the plot is too outrageous, the modern reader will have no patience with it." Well done, Modern Reader!

The central conflict between hero and heroine can either be internal or external. An example of an external plot would be "financial problems for the heroine's father, and the hero bales him out." Who said chivalry was dead?

But wait. "The heroine resents this because it reduces his self-respect." One up for our spunky heroine! I hope she makes more money than the hero in the finale!

An example of an internal conflict would be an ' emotional or moral issue, which puts hero and heroine at odds with one another, and with themselves.'' We're really getting down to the nitty gritties now. But fear not. "At the end, they must accept their differences, without altogether compromising their principles." Ah, the relief!

As regards the editing of your book, "You can't have your heroine getting dressed in the bedroom one minute and then appearing suddenly in the kitchen." (What a horrendous prospect). "If you want a scene-break, leave a 4-line space in your manuscript." I hope you're getting all this down.

And now to the crunch issue: "If there's a lengthy separation of hero and heroines, don't make it lengthy in terms of book-space." Twenty or thirty pages without our hero and/or heroine is not, repeat *not*, on. Heroes and heroines can't be expected to put up with being dumped in the narrative wilderness, one feels. Not by a long chalk.

We now come to the vexed subject of ...love scenes. How far should you "go"? The tape lady is open-ended on this:

"There are no hard-and-fast: rules. What's right for one story maybe wrong for another. Your heroine may or may not be a virgin but she's hardly likely to elicit sympathy if she's promiscuous." (Down with all those brazen hussies!) "Readers of romantic fiction like to be reminded of the connection between love and sex." Steady on there, my eyes are misting up.

The final section of the tape gives us an example of how your novel should start. Here's Amanda again:

"The rustle of palm trees in the breeze provided a pleasing accompaniment to the unceasing rhythm of the waves. Sunlight played with the water, highlighting the azure depth. Amanda stretched comfortably on the lounger, trying to decipher whether she had time for another dip before getting ready to go to the barbecue."

That was the end of the tape. After it whizzed to a close I spent a long time gazing out the window pondering its profundities.

Where would I go with my story now? I found myself immersed in the noumenal is-ness that was Amanda and her putative lover.

I put pen to paper. I tore it up. I tried again and tore that up too. Would I be good enough for M&B? How many times would I have to try until I got it right?

Character, plot, setting, dialogue – there were so many balls to throw in the air. How many would come down? How many would embarrass me? Could one of them my catharsis? Could one of them be Amanda's? An invisible power seemed to be pushing me onwards.

I let the spirit guide me. A force like levitation propelled me high into the air. I was terrified but excited too. It was like a divine presence inside me, pointing me to my destination. My head was muzzy, my legs like jelly.

But I still sat down at my rolltop. I took out my typewriter and set down the immortal words: "One day I will write for Mills & Boon..."

As I looked at what I had written it seemed now more than ever clear to me that all my life heretofore had been an approximation towards this one moment, this epiphany. As I folded the piece of paper away inside an envelope I felt the muse entering my soul. It said, "You will one day be rich and fulfilled ...rich and fulfilled... fulfilled and rich..."

I waited for more but nothing came. Was it the voice of God? Was it my publisher? I tore my hair out in a kind of abstract rage. I felt possessed.

Maybe this monster inside me was more than I could handle. Maybe one day it would gear me towards a destructive, a monstrous act. But I couldn't think about that now, I had to write, to write *anything*. I felt the rush of blood pounding inside my head as the words came to me like the fulfilment of a dream:

"She squeezed his hand tightly and knew this time it was for real. What matter that he had no prospects – no English even. Her adoration was enough for both of them, enough for anything. She would throw in her post in the bank and go with him to Peru."

"The more she thought about it, the more her parent's disapproval of him dissolved into thin air. She thought of all the years of artifice, of entertaining, all the years of exchanging platitudes with rajahs at exotic mansions. It was all like a bad dream now – replaced with her new fantasy – Cuthbert!"

"His cold blue eyes looked through her piercingly and she shivered. She felt as if she were in an ice-flow. But a moment later she was tremulous in his arms. She could feel the beads of sweat breaking out of every pore. 'Take me,' she whispered, biting his left nostril, "Take me now."

"He needed no second invitation. He slid his hand up under her dress and unclasped it. She felt herself becoming drowsy. She began to drown in his rosy hue. "I'm yours,' she said in a daze, 'yours alone.' From a far-away part of herself she felt his ecstasy squeeze into her, exploding inside her, becoming one with her."

She dug her nails hard into his back until it bled. He wailed gently. 'Let's stay like we are forever,' he murmured, 'Nothing matters except this.' He snuggled up beside her and she fell under his swoon again, like a little death. Her mind was gone from her now, her pleasure almost unbearable."

"No!" she shrieked as he tripped over his trousers and lay spreadeagled in pain, 'I can't. If you do it to me again I will die, surely.' 'Then let's die together,' he moaned. He took her up in his arms and carried her to the master bedroom where all his other virgins waited for their night of' bliss, all of them flying on gossamer wings to his pelvis."

That was it.

I'd finished my first chapter. Amanda lay in wait for me, and all the other Amandas. I was my hero. He was me. We moved one another. Our blood corpuscles melted into one another, making us one big me and one big Amanda.

My breath became heavy. I put the pages into an envelope and addressed them to London, to my editor. Sweat poured from me as I dropped it into the letterbox.

It was done. Complete – for now. Other chapters awaited. I was already composing one in my mind. This one, I decided, would have a sting in the tail to capture modern readers:

"Amanda woke up the next morning, her mouth oozing a fuzzy fluid, her mind a welter of conflicting lovelinesses. Pigeons cooed welcomingly on the balcony. She had a glass of iced tea. Her breasts surged with expectation.

Cuthbert was crying at the sink as he read a letter that had just been left by the bellboy.

'It's my mother,' he gasped, 'She has gallstones.'"

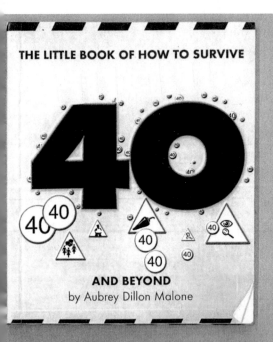

THE LITTLE BOOK OF HOW TO SURVIVE

40

AND BEYOND
by Aubrey Dillon Malone

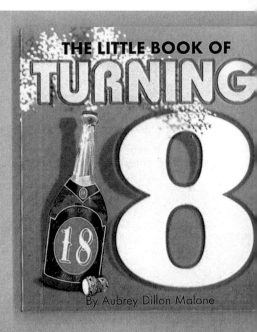

THE LITTLE BOOK OF

TURNING

18

By Aubrey Dillon Malone

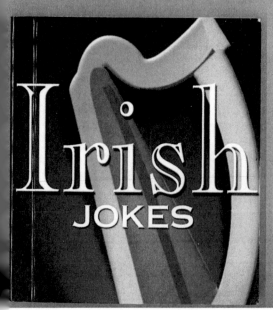

Irish JOKES

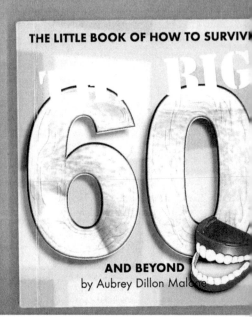

THE LITTLE BOOK OF HOW TO SURVIVE

BIG

60

AND BEYOND
by Aubrey Dillon Malone

Hemingway

One day in 1997 I was browsing in a second hand bookshop in Rathmines when I saw a little humour book published by a publisher I'd never heard of: Powerfresh. I was always interested in new publishers.

Every year I bought *The Writers and Artists Yearbook* mainly for that reason. Whenever I was trying to get a book placed I tended to ignore the big guns. It was too much like hard work trying to get them interested in anything. It was less difficult with smaller ones. Because I wasn't motivated by money, the size of the company I was dealing with didn't matter. I'd have preferred to make £100 each with ten companies than £1,000 with one. That meant ten books. There was always the chance of reprints too.

I rang Powerfresh. It was one of the most lucrative phone calls of my career. When you're not looking for money it often arrives. It's the inverse of Sod's Law.

They commissioned me to do a book, then another one, then another. They were all about birthdays and all about the size of a cigarette packet. I collected funny quotes about a milestone birthday – 18, 30, 40, 50, 60 – and they put the quotes together in the little book, just one quote per page.

They sold the books to greeting card shops all round the world. The idea was that a person would buy the card and then see the book, which was priced at under a fiver, and put it into the card as a gift. It was so simple. I did *Turning 18*, *The Big 3-0*, *The Big 4-0*, *The Big 5-0* and *The Big 6-0*. They also asked me to do a book of Irish jokes and later on some other books like *The Affluence of Incohol* and *Women's Wicked Wit*.

I now got another idea. Ernest Hemingway's centenary was coming up in 1999. I decided to write a biography of him to commemorate it. A very diligent book searcher called Sarah Fordham managed to locate a number of books written by his family and friends – and enemies – that I couldn't get through the bookshops. This was long before Amazon or any of the other social platforms. She put in the long searches and came up with the goods. Her fee was minimal. She just liked helping people.

HEMINGWAY

THE GRACE
& THE
PRESSURE

AUBREY DILLON-MALONE

My book didn't really say anything new about Hemingway. The thesis I wrote about him for my M.A. was about his style. I wanted to use it as a base for the biography but when I went out to UCD to ask for it they sent me into a room where there were about 1,000 theses in various stages of disarray on the floor, on filing cabinets, everywhere. Some of them were coming apart at the seams. I decided it would take me half a year to wade through them all to find my delightful 18,000 words so in the end I didn't bother.

When I was writing it I tried to contact Hemingway's third wife Martha Gellhorn for an interview but she didn't get back to me. Gellhorn committed suicide a few years later, at the ripe old age of 89. When I told Mary this she said, 'When she got that far, wouldn't you think she'd have stuck it out?' I could see her point but suicide was almost a religion for people associated with Hemingway.

His father killed himself. So did Hemingway himself, his sister Ursula, his brother Leicester and possibly his other sister Marcelline. The father of his first wife Hadley also committed suicide and, more recently, his grand-daughter Margaux. 'I'm curious to know how long a Hemingway can last in the natural way,' his son Jack speculated after the last tragedy.

As I was writing the book I learned that Hemingway's other son, Gregory, also died in strange circumstances. He was dressed as a woman on the night he passed away and arrested under the impression that he was one, dying in the woman's section of the prison in which he was placed after being arrested.

Gregory had been a doctor for most of his life. He was married to Valerie Danby-Smith, an *Irish Times* journalist who met Hemingway in Spain towards the end of his life and went on to become his secretary. There were rumours he had an affair with her when he was married to Mary, his last wife. Valerie met Gregory at Hemingway's funeral and the following year they married. They had five children.

I was intrigued to find out that Gregory was a cross-dresser, and also that Danby-Smith had a child by Brendan Behan. I got her phone number from a person I knew when I was writing the book and rang her up to ask her if she'd help me with my research. 'Who are you?' she asked me in the middle of one of my questions to her. When I told her my name she hung up.

After I finished the book I sent it off to all the usual places – academic publishers on both sides of the Atlantic and also commercial ones. I felt it could serve both markets. But over the next few months the rejection letters started arriving. It was my first experience of how difficult it was to get a book placed. I thought Hemingway's reputation and the forthcoming centenary would be selling points but obviously I got it wrong.

I never brooded over rejections. Anytime something came back I put it into another envelope and sent it somewhere else. If you sent something to 100 publishers and one accepted it, the other 99 didn't matter. I kept all the rejection letters to remind me of this. If I eventually got the book accepted, I wanted to keep them to show them to people who said things like "Writing is a handy number. You just sit on your arse all day. Try digging up the road."

I agreed with that and often said to people that I was privileged not to have to dig roads or go down mines or whatever. But it was important to let them know that writing wasn't as easy as they might have thought.

I enjoyed the research part and also the writing itself but getting the book onto a shelf was a struggle. It was like teaching. I enjoyed teaching itself but had a problem trying to keep control of the pupils. That was something they didn't teach you in training courses. In the whole year in Pat's I don't remember hearing the word "Discipline" once. And yet it was ultimately what drove me out of the job. I was determined that the difficulty of getting published wasn't going to drive me out of writing

In the end it came out with Robson Books. Jeremy Robson was a friend of the man who published my birthday books. When I told him I was finding it hard to get it taken on by anyone he said he'd have a word with Jeremy. In other words the acceptance came from a personal connection, word of mouth. What did that say about the industry?

It was like the way I got the *Image* job, from my father knowing Anne Reihill. Nepotism was rampant in Ireland and probably in other countries as well.

Ireland's former Taoiseach Jack Lynch once said his father told him the secret of success was written on every door. He thought he was referring to "Push" but he meant "Pull." Scoff if you like but I knew the Hemingway book deserved to be read. It may not have been the best Hemingway book out there but it was as good as most of them.

Jeremy Robson seemed to be distancing himself from the book as we approached the time of publication. I didn't know why. Every time I tried to contact him he was out. I got fed up ringing his secretary so I decided to leave it over to Vernon. He was great at sorting out things like that.

I don't think the book would have come out if it wasn't for Vernon but with all the to-ing and fro-ing they missed the centenary. There was huge coverage of Hemingway in all the papers on the day itself. A lot of biographies had come out on him and even a posthumous novel, *True at First Light*, which was edited by his son Patrick. I had imagined this day as my big chance for sales and now it was gone. A book I'd started two years earlier for this exact day was screamingly absent from the review pages.

I never saw it reviewed anywhere, nor did I ever see a copy of it in an Irish shop, nor any royalties for it. Neither did Robson send me any author copies.

In the later stages of the book I went into the relationship between Hemingway and Norman Mailer. Like myself, Hemingway admired *Advertisements for Myself* but didn't think much of Mailer's fiction, even *The Naked and the Dead*, the book that made him famous.

Of course Hemingway was always proprietorial about war books, imagining he'd written the best ones. It was probably the reason he trivialised works like *From Here to Eternity* and *The Young Lions*.

Shortly after my book was published I saw that Mailer was coming to Dublin to give a talk about literature. It was a subject he was always fascinating about. I made sure to be at it.

It was a buzz to be in the same room as him. He exuded such energy. Looking at him pumping the air from behind a rostrum was like watching someone punching out words like the pugilist he was.

He had an electric mind. Like any small men he had the look of a dictator about him. He engaged in a war of words with a feminist from the audience that night. It was no surprise to me. He was refreshingly behind the times when it came to being PC. After the lecture I went up to him with my Hemingway biography.

I found myself thinking of all the controversial events of his life – the time he headbutted Gore Vidal, the night he stabbed his wife, his campaign to get a man called Jack Henry Abbott (who'd been arrested for murder) released from prison only for Abbott to kill again after he got out.

I wanted to ask him about all these events. To tell him how big a part he'd played in my life. But there were too many people around. In the end I just handed him the book.

He thanked me for it. He seemed genuine but I felt I was probably one of hundreds of people who gave him books to read that he didn't get around to. I knew he'd sent Hemingway copies of his own books back in the day and that Hemingway hadn't replied to him. Who was I to put myself in such company?

I didn't expect he'd have time to read my book but it made me feel good to give it to him even if he threw it in a bin five minutes after getting it.

Celebrities

Mailer wasn't the only famous person I met during the years when I was busy both with books and journalism. One of the most memorable was the tennis player John McEnroe.

It was when he came to Dublin for a GOAL challenge. GOAL was a charitable organisation. I decided I wanted to meet him so I could do a profile of him for *In Dublin*. Hugo and Basil were big fans and so, to an extent, was Mary, even though she didn't play tennis. We'd all be in hysterics as "Superbrat" called out half-blind referees with insults like, "You moron. How did you ever get a job as a line judge – did you not see the chalk?"

I found out he was staying in the Berkeley Court Hotel so we trudged along there on the Dart. We managed to get past the doorman who was guarding the entrance. There was always extra security at places when celebrities were there. You never knew who might turn up – like the bozo who stabbed Monica Seles one time when she started beating Steffi Graf too much for his liking. I knew how he felt.

When we got to the lounge we saw him sitting with Mats Wilander. I'd had a few drinks so I was more excited than usual. I have a vague memory of throwing myself at his feet and going, "You're my idol" as he looked at me with a mixture of shock and pity. I'd done similar things to Jimmy White, which made people say things to me like, "Did you know 'fan' is short for 'fanatic'?' If it was, I was glad to be one. A fanatic, I mean. Even if McEnroe was looking at me with that "You cannot be serious" expression of his.

We eventually managed to extricate him from the company of Wilander. Hugo told him he had nine different kinds of service, a comment which seemed to intrigue him. Basil then took out his camera and asked him if he'd pose with us for a photograph.

He wasn't too pleased at having his evening interrupted by these zany folks but he said a grudging yes. After it was taken he didn't delay too long going back to Mats. I saw that look in his eyes that he gave to referees. It was the "That ball was *in*!" look. He was still the "angry young man" in those days rather than the cuddly Beeb commentator I now watch at Wimbledon every year.

Meeting John McEnroe

The next day we went to see him in an exhibition match he was playing with Pat Cash. I had no trouble getting in to it because I had my NUJ card but John O'Shea, the CEO of GOAL, made a big deal of letting Hugo and Basil in. "They're not journalists," he protested.

In the end we squeezed into the cheap seats. "Mac" wasn't the player he used to be but he still produced some magic touches. He reminded me of Alex Higgins with his rages and his genius. What a pity we don t have players like that anymore – and what a pity that the "mellow" McEnroe would go on to become a friend of Donald Trump. Who could have predicted it?

Another person I met during this time was Charlton Heston. He was in Dublin to promote his autobiography but he didn't like it when I pointed out a typo in it. I'd had the audacity to criticise Moses and he let me know it.

I felt he was going to break the two tablets of stone all over again. Suddenly I knew how Michael Moore must have felt when he confronted him about gun control in *Bowling for Columbine.*

I also ran into Billy Connolly one day. This wasn't in my capacity as a writer but when I was doing the courier work. He was on Stephens Green in the middle of a torrential shower and I was carrying about a dozen parcels and on my way to a drop in the Shelbourne Hotel. 'Let me shake your hand,' I said when I spotted him going into the hotel, 'I'm a journalist. I'd love to interview you.'

He looked at me as if I was from outer space. I had about six layers of clothing on me as well as leggings and a balaclava. I also had my expanding belt strapped around my waist with a load of parcels inside it, making me look like a suicide bomber. He exploded into laughter and then marched into the hotel. Obviously he thought I was a nutter. Maybe he was right.

Another person I met at this time was Leonard Cohen. I later put him into a book about the psychological problems of famous people called *On the Edge.* The·cliche about Cohen was that people put razor blades into the sleeves of his albums so they could slit their wrists after listening to them but in actual fact he turned out to be quite jolly. I was sorry Mary wasn't with me as she'd been with me from the very start of my obsession with him.

Cohen's friend Irving Layton had even met her in the Aran Islands once He was so captivated by her he wrote a poem for her.

When we were going out together first we used to play "Songs of Love and Hate" on an old-fashioned record player she had in the front room of her house. Hearing the sonorous syllables of this "bard of the bedsits" emanating from that little machine made me feel like a kindred soul to him. I wrote these words about that time:

> I was the soldier
> pining in the desert
> as he longed for Marianne
> somewhere on the other side
> of midnight
> on my lover's banjaxed stereo.
> I was the soldier
> sitting at the foot of chaos
> reminiscing on the decades
> of promise
> as his words wafted up
> through the floorboards.

On the Edge was positively reviewed by most of the critics but was heavily criticised by somebody in the Sunday Times who called herself Sue Denham. I didn't recognise the name and spent a number of days wondering who this snotty new journalist on the scene happened to be. A few weeks later I learned that she didn't exist. The name was a pun on the word 'Pseudonym·'. When criticism is anonymous it always makes you feel it's less trustworthy so that piece of news reassured me. As Sir Boyle Roche once said, "Anyone who has the audacity to write an anonymous letter should at least have the decency to put his name to it."

Seeing the article reminded me of "Sean Bocht" from the Western People all those years ago. That man gave me an early revulsion for people who denounced others anonymously. Now I had even more of a reason to hate them. I saw them as cowards just like snipers in war or hit-and-run drivers on the street. With social media in later years, people were given many more forums upon which to exercise their venom with impunity.

Pub Culture

Shortly after *On the Edge* was published, the Prion editor Andrew Goodfellow asked me if I'd like to write a guide to traditional Irish pubs. This didn't rate very highly on my list of priorities but I rarely said no to editors. As one of the older hookers on the publishing beat. I felt that work bred work. If you wrote the books you weren't madly excited about, the ones you did like had a better chance of following them.

My book *Historic Pubs of Dublin* was published by my London firm, Prion. It was later taken up by an Irish one, New Island. I don't think New Island would have been interested in it if I approached them with the idea even though the subject was Irish. They turned down most of the proposals I submitted to them over the years, as did most other Irish publishers. Its publication by Prion reminded me of what happened to *Fr. Ted*, a programme that was aired on Channel Four long before being "sold" to RTE. It was too "hot" for Ireland so Dermot Morgan went to "pagan" England with it. It's tame today but at the time it was written it wasn't.

Could you get anything more endemically Irish than *Fr. Ted*? Or *Historic Pubs of Dublin*? They say a man is never a prophet in his own country. I realise that's changed now. We celebrate our own. But it was the story of much of the last century for many of our writers, myself included.

I generally found it easier to get published in England or America than Ireland. That fact made me understand why people like Joyce or Beckett happier writing were abroad, or why John McGahern had to do so for a while when he lost his job here.

Begrudgery will always be alive and well in Ireland as long as familiarity breeds contempt. We see a book by someone and we say, "Sure I knew him when he had the arse out of his trousers – as if that means he couldn't write anything good. Meanwhile we genuflect before foreign scribes. Philip Larkin once said that the idea of a British writer having to emigrate would be ludicrous, but for many decades we took it for granted here.

For the next year or so I found myself in more pubs than I'd ever been in my life, with one big difference: I wasn't drinking now.

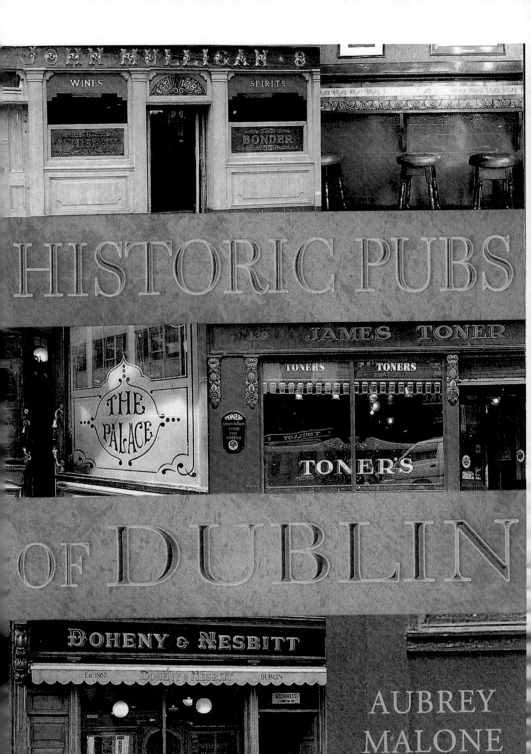

HISTORIC PUBS

OF DUBLIN

AUBREY
MALONE

This was a severe test of my self-discipline. I'm sure many barmen were surprised to see me with a pen in my hand instead of a pint. Some of them would have known me from the bad old days when I could be relied on to have "one too many."

I did an interview for it with a reporter called Philip Boucher-Hayes. He met me in a pub – it made sense – and took out his microphone. "What did you have for breakfast?" he said. I was used to doing interviews but mainly on the radio rather than face to face. I said, "Why would you want to know?" He said, "Relax. I'm only testing the microphone."

I didn't like the idea of going on TV in front of all the nation. That wasn't only because I was getting a bald patch and a beer belly but, slightly more importantly, I thought I was rubbish talking about my books. You could edit what you said in print and pre-recorded radio interviews but this was live TV. If you made a cock-up there was no hiding place. From that point of view it was even going to be worse than the Derek Jameson show I did for *Hollyweird*.

New Island arranged an interview for me on TV3 one Bank Holiday Monday to advertise it. I'd only been on TV once before, when a friend from the Elvis Club brought his camcorder into the radio centre of Beaumont hospital and filmed me talking to a deejay there. I thought it was a good idea to have my first TV appearance in a hospital. If I collapsed from stress there would be someone on hand to give me mouth-to-mouth resuscitation. Or, as might have been more likely, open heart surgery.

A small consolation was the fact that the interview was on a Bank Holiday Monday. Hopefully nobody I knew would be watching it.

The show was on at the crack of dawn so it was still dark when I got up. I set off for the studio with a new-found sympathy for TV-AM people. How could they have a social life when they had to be tucked up in bed shortly after tea?

My eyes were falling out of my head as Mark Cagney greeted me backstage. He was the man who was going to interview me. 'You don't have a thing to worry about,' he said to me, probably spotting the fact that my knees were shaking and my face chalk-white from fright.

I told him he reminded me of an anaesthetist. (I was still locked in the hospital idea). I felt if he asked me my name I'd have had trouble answering. Maybe that's not a good example seeing as I was going by two different names now anyway, being Peter in my social life and Aubrey in my writing one.

Part of my nerves came from the fact that I was worried about anyone I knew from the courier world watching. Mary tried to console me. 'It's a holiday weekend,' she said, 'They'll all be sleeping off their hangovers.' I forgave her for thinking all my friends were alcoholics – probably because they were.

The interview began. I found my mouth drying up. There was no water ready to hand.

Mark started firing questions at me. I went blank. Someone give me a drink, quick, I thought – even if it isn't from a historic pub. I tried to console myself by thinking I was only half-awake but deep down I knew the time wasn't the problem. I was.

After it was over I crawled back to the car feeling like I'd been dragged through a bush backwards. 'Never again,' I said to Mary. As we drove home I felt my eyes going. Most people were just on the way to work.

When we got home I fell into bed but I couldn't sleep. Every minute I felt the phone was going to ring and somebody I knew from the wrong side of the tracks was going to say, 'Jaysus Pether, what the fuck were you doin' on the telly?' (They always added a 'h' onto the Peter).

I suddenly thought of all the witty things I could have said to Mark about the book, things I'd been jotting down on pieces of paper over the past few weeks since I heard I was going to be on the telly. My father used to call this "l'esprit de l'escalier," a French term referring to the phrase you thought of on the staircase after leaving the room. Or, in my case, under the duvet after leaving the studio.

I feel someone should tell anyone who's about to interview a writer that we don't really like talking. That's why we become writers. If someone asks us a question, instead of answering it we'd prefer to direct them to a page of one of our books and say, "Here, read this." If it's a TV interview they could put a camera over, say, Page 17 and stay on it until viewers had the page read.

Then someone could turn the page and viewers could read Page 18. And so on until the end. If someone said to me, "Why have the interview at all if that's all they're going to do?" I would answer, "Precisely."

Because the pub book sold well, Andrew Goodfellow now asked me to do another one for him. I had suggested writing one about the eccentricities of famous people and he said he'd like that – with one proviso: I had to write it on a computer. All my books up to now had been done on my battered old Canon typewriter. He wanted me to be able to shift paragraphs around at the press of a button instead of working with cellotape and scissors, my preferred tools.

I said to him, This book is about eccentrics, Isn't it? Well I'm an eccentric so you have to let me do it the old-fashioned way.' He wasn't buying it. 'You're writing about them,' he said, 'but I don't want you to be one.' Obviously if Andrew was a film director he wouldn't have got on well with Method actors.

Prion was sold to another company at the end of the millennium but still traded under its own name for some titles and reprints. I was advised to sign a form saying I'd stay with them instead of demanding the reversion of my rights. I wanted to go with the new company but that offer wasn't on the table. I didn't know why. "This will be good for you," the MD said to me with the chirpiness of a dentist about to extract a recalcitrant molar. It was one of those, "Apart from that, Mrs Lincoln, I hope you enjoyed the play" moments.

I eventually burned the thermal head out of my Canon. Or maybe it committed suicide. I couldn't blame it after years of being battered senseless by the middle finger of my right hand and the middle finger of my left. That was the only way I knew to type – it was a style I learned from my father – but I got so fast over time I could nearly take down The News as it was being read.

Canon told me they couldn't replace the thermal head. The machine was still typing but every letter had a crack in the middle that made the typing look like bad photocopying.

I got a new one but a few months later the head went on that too. This time the problem was letters being chipped at the end rather than in the middle. So 'q' became 'o' and 'y' became 'v'. I now had two machines that were still typing but virtually useless.

Canon told me they were discontinuing the whole range. I was also informed that Canon ribbons were also being discontinued. The typewriters were useless to me without the ribbons so I bought about 1,000 of these. Considering I got 100 pages from a ribbon this was a hefty purchase. I started wondering which would run out first on my third and fourth typewriters, the ribbons or the thermal heads. Either way I'd be snookered.

Whenever I cried on Mary's shoulder about these kinds of things she told me I needed to be dragged kicking and screaming into the 21st century. Whereupon I reminded her of all the times she'd lost precious documents on her computer simply by hitting the wrong key. That could never happen on a manual machine.

When I finally bought a computer it was like my final compromise to the world of modernity. One or two editors still allowed me to send in hard copy but they were exceptions. Most of them told me I was like the Kerryman who tried to erase his computer errors by applying Tipp-ex to the screen. I had a soft spot for this gentleman.

Writing my books on a typewriter meant I had to use photocopying outlets a lot instead of simply pressing "Copy" on the computer, or "Save."

Many of these places had machines that seemed to have come out of the Stone Ages. They were set up in shops to accommodate people who needed to have something like their passport copied, not someone like me with 600 pages of their latest *opus* to save for posterity in case the copy I just submitted to a publisher (which was most likely winging its way back to me as yet another reject) went missing in the post. The one time you didn't copy it was the time it would indeed go missing, as that's the way with most things in life, isn't it?

The Stone Age machines spat out pages full of streaks. They also tended to break down a lot. And they tended to be placed immediately outside the counter of the places they were in, so you had to step aside roughly 137 times as the cashier came out to get something off a shelf. Sometimes I felt they were doing things like that just to annoy me. I spent so much time in these places they must have thought I was thinking of taking out shares in them.

Machines also ran out of paper, printed things sideways for no good reason – photocopying machines having minds of their own in matters like this – and snagged your pages up when it was coming up to closing time so you'd have to come back the next day for more fun.

When modern machines came in I was told they could do everything but make the dinner. That was fine but I didn't really want them to make my dinner. I wanted them to photocopy – and I found you'd need a degree of some sort to understand the controls.

The genius who built them seemed to have done so for the guy who wanted his passport copied (without streaks) not someone with the 600-page novel, because each page had to be done individually. I sometimes felt there were little men inside these machines sniggering manically as I tore the last remaining shreds of my hair out.

Writing novels, in time, became significantly easier than having to photocopy them.

Wings of Poesy

Mary's aunt Alice died in 2000. She was one of her mother's sisters. Alice minded her sister Angela for many years after Angela became ill. She never married. That was a shame as she'd have made a wonderful wife and mother.

As was the case with the D-Ms, she came from a family of nine, four boys and five girls. She suffered terribly from asthma over the years, which eventually necessitated the use of a nebuliser. I never heard her complaining about that or about anything else. She had a great ability to withstand pain but an equally great sensitivity towards the pain of others.

We often went down to visit her in Glenamaddy, the Galway village where Mary's mother had grown up. She also came up to visit us in Dublin every so often. Glenamaddy used to be a hubbub back in the day when it was a magnet for the youth of Galway with all its dance halls but few people went there by the time we started visiting it in the 1990s.

Alice spent many years in Dublin before going back to Glenamaddy to live. The death of her brother brought her back. Funerals often changed the courses of people's lives, what was meant to be a brief visit turning into a lifetime event.

Glenamaddy is a lovely village. Mary's cousins Claire and Dympna still live there. It was the subject of Big Tom's song "Four Country Roads." Big Tom was a legendary country & western singer in the showband era as most people know. His song referenced the square where Alice lived, the centre point of the village where the eponymous four roads converged in a kind of crooked quadrangle.

I have many fond memories of nights in Alice's house where we told stories into the small hours, buttressed by generous glasses of whiskey. During the course of such nights Mary told me stories of times she spent there as a child. She used to write letters to Alice asking to be invited there for the summer when she was in Galway, making sure she told Alice not to mention to her mother that it was she herself who'd suggested the visits.

I didn't get to know Alice until after Mary's mother died in 1992. She was minding Angela at that time. After Angela died she

had more time to visit us. She was a lady to her fingertips and great fun too. I never saw any bitterness in her about anything that went wrong in her life. No matter what happened she shrugged her shoulders and said, "Arrah sure that's the way." Maybe her whole generation reacted to suffering in that way - with a kind of Hemingwayesque dignity: grace under pressure.

After Alice died I went back to the world of poetry, publishing a book called *Pedagogue* with Lapwing, a Belfast company, in 2001.

Lapwing is run by Dennis Greig. He's been a voice to the voiceless for many years now. He hasn't had good health for a number of years which makes his commitment to what he does even more admirable.

Dennis arranged a launch of the book for me one night in the Writer's Centre on Parnell Square. He was launching two books that night, mine and one by another author of his. I brought Mary with me. The other guy brought three other people. I didn't expect to have to fight away the fans at the door but I thought there would be more than this at it. When the other guy read from his work, I tried to clap extra hard to make him feel good. He did the same for me. At least we had one another for some much-needed ego massages.

Afterwards I bought two copies of his book, one for me and one for Mary. He and his family (or friends) bought four of mine. In other words he was punished because of his numbers. There was nobody at the launch except our two sets of people. I imagined him putting my book on a shelf when he went home, never to be read. Such are the delights of poetry book launches - unless you're Harry Clifton.

Harry departed the world of poetry briefly in 2000 to publish a collection of stories. It was called *Berkeley's Telephone and Other Fictions*. One of the stories concerned his time doing night security. I reviewed the book in *Books Ireland*, writing, "When we were both struggling with finances (and our respective navels), Harry and I used to do night security work in Dublin's docklands. We often met up the morning after our shifts to exchange clocks. Then we'd go back to our beds to sleep for the day before another sojourn down to the docks to share our little shacks with mice, insects, stale cheese sandwiches and a copy of Immanuel Kant's *Critique of Pure Reason* and *Zen and the Art of Motorcycle Maintenance*.

I went on to write, "I eventually got sacked for going to the pictures one Paddy's Day after coming down with a dose of terminal boredom. I got a puncture on my bike on O'Connell Bridge and when I got back to the docks my boss was there with my P45. This surprised me somewhat considering he never seemed to have had a problem with me arriving in to work with a sleeping bag in one hand and an alarm clock in the other. Maybe his logic was that sleeping the sleep of the unjust was one thing, going AWOL quite another."

"As long as poets stick to poetry," Harry said "he's socially harmless, but the volatility of the poetic mind expressing itself in prose, with its dangerous social dimension, threatens everyone." I looked forward to seeing more of his fiction but he stopped there. Apart from a memoir he wrote about a year he spent in Italy with his wife Deirdre Madden (another great writer) he stuck to poetry.

I think I gave Dennis a bit of a seizure at the launch by reading one of my poems, "Overheard in Mulligan's" in a Dublin accent. It was meant to be an account of what a Dub in Mulligan's (the classic Dub pub) might say on a fairly typical night:

> *The theory of evolution, head,*
> *is an insult to the monkeys.*
> *All you have to do*
> *is look around you.*
> *The first man in the Bible*
> *killed his brother.*
> *Since then we've been going downhill.*
>
> *You can't go out of your house today*
> *without protection.*
> *A chap down the road*
> *got his arm broke*
> *for jumping the queue*
> *in a chipper.*
> *Another chap I know got headbutted*

in Fumbally Lane
in broad daylight.
Evolution how are ye.
The courts gave him a suspended sentence.
I know the suspended sentence
I'd give him:
From the neck.

This country is goin' down the toilet,
mark my words.
No one opens the door for you any more
or stands up in the bus.
I'm in my fifties now.
I remember manners, dacency,
people who'd buy you a pint
if you were on your uppers.

I'm on the dole too,
lost me job
to a bleedin' computer.
The gaffer who wrote '1984' had it right.

I got a golden handshake but
it was gone in a month,
pissed up against the wall of this kip.
Gave the best years of me life
to them tossers
and they threw me out on me ear.
Probably lose the gaff next.

When my ship comes in
it'll probably be the Titanic.
But what doesn't kill you makes you stronger,
 right?
The name of the game is survival.
Do it to him
before he does it to you.
The old lady is good to me though.

She's from the same generation as me.
We know what's important.
Christianity.
You don't have to be in a church to pray
you know, Jesus is everywhere,
even in my pint.

Pity about the priest scandals though.
Sure they're the same
as the rest of us.
Let him who is without fault
throw the first stone.
Who said that – Jesus?
If he didn't he should have.
Live and let live
and let the dead bury the dead.
That's my philosophy anyway.

Nippy tonight, isn't it?
What's your poison, head?
You wouldn't get me a half one, would ye?
I'd kill for one, that's the truth.
We're not here for a long time,
we're here for a good time, right?

I went home that night feeling a little deflated. I never expected much from launches but it was something of a comedown from the one for the Behan book. Not that I was surprised. Lapwing wasn't HarperCollins. And poetry wasn't prose. But eight people at a launch? Was it really worth Dennis' time coming down from Belfast?

I didn't feel my poems had resonance. They were things that could be tossed aside like disposable cameras. When I started out I wanted to write for posterity. Now, like a poet with the arrestingly appropriate name of Peter Reading, I felt I was only writing for, as he put it, "mutated arthropods." Would I end up like Leonard Cohen, crawling around a hotel room floor at 3 a.m. in my underwear, desperately looking for a word that rhymed with "orange"?

A writer once submitted a well-known poem to a pretentious journal with the words back to front and it was published. I wish I'd gotten that idea.

"Poetry," said Ted Hughes, "is a way of talking to your loved ones when it's too late." He would have known. Two of his lovers, Sylvia Plath and Assia Weevil, killed themselves over him. How must that have made him feel? To lose one lover, to paraphrase Oscar Wilde, was unfortunate. Losing two sounded like carelessness. I always felt a bit spooky reading his stuff after these events. If it was me I'd have put down my pen and gone into the Witness Protection Programme.

The Writer's Centre experience made me think it might be wise to spread myself around a little and get more attention for my poems. One night not long afterwards I was browsing through a poetry magazine when I noticed an ad from no less than the American Poetry Association which said that they were offering no less than $44.000 to writers the world over for contributions to their annual publication, *The American Poetry Anthology*. I decided to throw a few lyrics together and slap them in the post. If you don't throw you'll never know.

A couple of weeks later I received a letter from a Robert Nelson informing me that, yes, my work was deemed fit for the publication. And now here's the good bit. Mr Nelson said he was interested in five of the poems I submitted but due to the cost of typesetting, proof-reading and something called "paste up" he required that I purchase at least one copy of the anthology at my own expense. This would knock me back $40. If I wanted to have two poems published I was expected to buy two copies of the anthology. And so on.

It wouldn't have taken a genius to work out that the cost of my five poems – less than 100 lines *in toto* – was going to be $200.

There's more. If I wanted a photograph and biographical note included, this would cost me a further $50.

Towards the end of his letter, Mr Nelson very kindly informed me that if I purchased more than one anthology, the price would be reduced from $40 to $32.95. Gee. And – hold on to your hat – I could have a Presentation edition with leatherette binding and goldfoil printing for $55. This delightful addition, he added, would cost the average Joe in the street (i.e. somebody who wasn't, like me, a world class poet) a cracking 80 bucks. Aren't some people very generous all the same?

I was tempted to write to Mr Nelson and tell him that learning about his service was the most wonderful thing that had happened to me since the day I first put crayon to paper back in Junior Infants. But then I looked at the figures again and thought: Maybe I can't afford to be famous.

Dumbing Down

Humphrey Bogart once said that you weren't famous unless they could spell your name in Karachi. I wasn't even sure if they could spell mine in Kiltimagh.

My books were often put at the back of Easons where few people went. If they were at the front I'd usually find them so close to the floor you'd get sciatica reaching down to take them from the shelf. Some people I knew who sympathised with my plight offered to re-position them but I told them I wasn't that desperate. (Actually I was).

I needed a best seller. Robert James Waller came out of the wilderness and wrote *The Bridges of Madison County*. It was only a tiny book but it got everyone talking. What a masterpiece. Only a few of us knew it was too cute. They accused *Gatsby* of that too but we were still talking about F. Scott Fitzgerald all those years later. Would we be talking about Waller in the next millennium? I doubted it.

How would I get myself known? Mark Chapman shot John Lennon to become famous. I didn't want to do something like that to the remaining two Beatles, even though Ringo probably deserved it. There had to be a better way.

Should I employ an agent for my next book? Design a web page? Partner Pat Ingoldsby on College Green with a binbag full of copies of it? I ruled out the last idea pretty soon after hearing Pat had been "moved on" by the Gardaí. Was there no sympathy for struggling authors out there? Were we coming to a point where I'd have to cut off an ear like the beleaguered Vincent, or top myself like John Kennedy Toole after *Confederacy of Dunces* failed to find a home?

My problem, people told me, was that I didn't push myself. I needed to "get with the programme."

There was a time when a writer could be a retiring sort of chap who dressed in tweeds and lived in a country mansion like J.P. Donleavy, taking the dog for a walk in his grounds every so often before going back to his abode, leaving down his blackthorn stick and reading Mallarmé over cocktails. Today your average writer is a much duller figure who looks more like an accountant.

Still Rockin'

Tom Jones
A BIOGRAPHY

y Lolfa

Aubrey Malone

On social media, though, he probably has more "hits" than Tom Jones.

The industry was taking over the craft. I watched writers on television who knew how to play the game, people who would have been just as happy being real estate salesmen as authors. They were well turned out and well able to talk. The better they talked, I often noticed, the worse they wrote. Some of them gave such brilliant summations of their books you wondered if there was anything else to be gained upon reading them. Would the experience be anti-climactic?

These people had buckets of confidence. That was something I never had, even when I was talking to someone I knew who hadn't two brain cells to rub together. It was one of the reasons I ran away from publicity. That was never going to be any good in writing. Cue the definition of publishing in my *Cynic's Dictionary*: "A self-invasion of privacy."

Neither was I one of those writers who applied for grants or sinecures. I cried not to associate writing with any kind of financial gain. I'd haggle with someone at a fruit market for a few pence off a punnet of strawberries but if a publisher said to me, "I like your book but I have no money" I'd go, "Where do I sign?"

It wasn't as if I saw it writing as a noble occupation that shouldn't be sullied by the mention of filthy lucre. It was simply an acknowledgement of the fact that I felt lucky to be doing it. It beat working for a living. I was happy to accept editors' parsimonious terms. A lot of them probably wiped their hands in glee at my casualness.

Most of the writers I knew were my polar opposites. Two I was closely acquainted with actually "unsigned" contracts they'd put their names to after learning that the books in question weren't going to make them the kind of money they'd envisaged after submitting them to the publishers in question. I couldn't understand their attitude.

They were both minor talents. It wasn't as if people were queueing up to publish their books.

If someone expressed interest in what I wrote I practically embraced them. I understood those paupers from the old days who sat in the street waiting for someone to come along that they could write a poem for. I didn't ask publishers what kinds of royalties I was entitled to because in my eyes publication itself was reward enough. I'd nearly have paid them to publish my books – though I drew the line at vanity publishing. Not because I wasn't vain but because of the rip-off factor in such companies. They often took your money and pretended to run off copies of your book. There was no way of proving they didn't when, a year or so later, they came back to you with the sad news that it didn't quite hit the best seller lists. One reason for this might have been that nobody saw it. Another one - this was even more likely - was that it was shit.

One of the two writers who "unsigned" his contract said to me, "Don't tell anyone you know that you're under-pricing yourself or we'll all be out of a job." I said, "What job are you talking about?" The only thing I was aware of him having in print was a haiku or an obscure journal that about five people in the country read.

I think his "payment" for this was six copies of the journal, five of which he inflicted on his family, who stumped up two quid for the privilege of stuffing it in their pockets (and then, when he wasn't looking, probably the nearest wpb.) I hated that kind of preciousness, especially when it came from nobodies. I knew too many poets who stroked their chins ponderously in Dublin 4 dens as they wrote crap in free verse.

I sometimes rang distributors when my books were about to come out. They generally said things like, "Were not taking on any new clients at the moment." Translated into English that meant "You're a minor writer and we couldn't be bothered setting up an account for you." I can't recall any of them ever asking to see samples of the books so I could have just written the next *Ulysses* and they wouldn't know. If my book sold well I'd probably get a phone call from them

In Bed with the Enemy

An offbeat guide to relationships

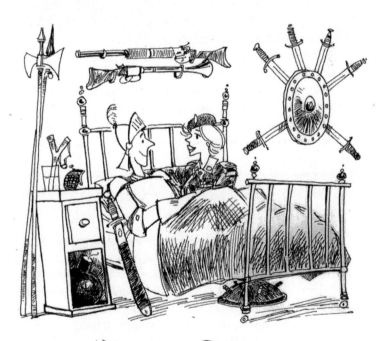

Aubrey Malone

asking if they could be a part of its distribution. People loved success stories, or rather the money accruing from them. But how could you get success without distribution? It was a vicious circle, like the old idea of people being drowned in the Middle Ages on the basis of them being deemed to be witches. If they rose to the surface they were indeed witches but if they didn't they weren't. So an innocent person had been drowned.

As the years went on I found myself becoming increasingly more supplanted by the "tecchie" brigade. My Canons kept breaking down and the ribbons kept getting more and more expensive. Often they were corroded when I bought them off eBay. It was a hard job trying to return them. I was paying fifty quid for a piece of unworkable cartridge.

Young writers told me I was mad. They had many more exciting ideas than me, and many more exciting ways to impart them. I cried on Keith's shoulder about feeling like an anachronism with my battered old typewriter trying to compete with their laptops. He was even more old-fashioned than me, writing his screenwriter book in longhand to be typed up by Clive in Zambia.

He spent over twenty years on his book and even at the end of that time it showed no signs of being finished. Was he afraid to finish it in case he'd have nothing to do? I knew the feeling. Every time I finished a book I started another one. Keith only thought of doing a second book (one about producers) years later.

During the twenty years, *Every Picture Tells a Story* (his title for the screenwriter book) was like *The Unfinished Symphony*. I commended him for his dedication to it. It was like his second wife, in contrast to me with my many literary mistresses that I alternated with one another in cavalier fashion. I imagined him sleeping beside it the way John Steinbeck did with *East of Eden*.

I tried to encourage him to approach publishers with it but he kept saying "It's not ready yet." I told him I rarely completed a book before sending it to publishers. I knew they didn't want you to do this. They liked to have an input into the direction it took. I couldn't imagine Keith derailing himself from his vision for the demands of these people. Neither could I see him asking for permission to use the photographs he planned to put in the book, none of which he'd got permission for, or all the quotes from books he'd amassed. He was in his own world, far from the strictures of the industry. A part of me envied him in his isolated mansion of ideas.

He had a stack of research material that must have been the size of a provincial library but his book was still no nearer to completion.

I can't get the illustrations I want for it,' he complained to me every time I saw him. He was still gathering data without seeking permission and still investigating the lives of people nobody had ever heard of who wrote scripts for films maybe a half dozen people in the country might have seen. I had a list of publishers as long as your arm that I wanted him to approach with his project but he always seemed bored when I brought that thorny subject up.

As time went on he seemed to care less and less about the book being published. He just wanted to finish it before he died. It was like Christopher Wren with St. Paul's: 'If you want to see my epitaph, look around you.' He told me I should understand obsessions because of the way I went on about Ballina. He was right but it was hard to see these things in yourself.

'You must have seen every film that was ever made by now,' I said to him one day. 'I have,' he replied, 'but sometimes I like to get better prints of them.' There was no way you could win a point with him.

I told him it was time to stop watching them and start writing about them instead. He disagreed. 'You have to write a book in your head before you put it on the page,' he claimed. He spent most of the time he wasn't watching films taking files out of cabinets and putting them into other ones, getting all his ducks in a row like the accountant he was.

His organisation was impeccable but I wondered if the whole enterprise wasn't some kind of guilt trip for taking premature retirement. He'd worked long and hard in Unidare but his puritan side wouldn't allow him to sit out the 'golden years' without some work ethic.

I wondered how many people would want to read a book about forties movies? I saw it all as therapy for him, a cathartic filling in of the days that allowed him to re-visit his past with a purpose.

'Maybe it isn't so much the movies you love as the past,' I suggested to him one day, 'You're trying to re-live the Ballina days from the Estoria.' He dismissed the accusation out of hand. I felt guilty afterwards for making it.

'What about copyright?' I'd ask him repeatedly. 'What about it?' he'd reply with cavalier disregard. He firmly believed that if he found a rare photograph of a screenwriter somewhere, that very discovery entitled him to use it in his book.

He had me searching for photos as well. Sometimes he asked me to get a book for him from England that I thought he wanted to read. As soon as I gave it to him he'd tear out a photograph and give it straight back to me. 'That's a screenwriter,' he'd say, 'The photo has him talking to a famous director. That means it's doubly precious to me. Readers of my book will look at the director and then get interested in the screenwriter.' But what if they weren't interested in either of them?

Clive worked on it from Zambia. Keith sent drafts of the book out to him to be typed on his computer. He even gave him instructions about typesetting. 'That should be the final step,' I said, 'You haven't even found a publisher and yet you're getting Clive to process the material as if it's ready for the bookshelves.'

I could never understand why he was fast-tracking the whole process when he hadn't even submitted a sample chapter to anyone. Was he afraid they'd say no? Sometimes I thought he'd be in a state if he managed to get some publisher interested in his book. He'd have been far too shy to do interviews or promotion.

In 2002 I wrote a book for a small publisher who allowed me to present it any way I wanted. It was a humorous guide to dating. I wanted to call it *Sleeping with the Enemy* but the editor thought Julia Roberts mightn't like this as she'd made a film of that name a few years before. For safety's sake we changed it to *In Bed with the Enemy*.

It was hastily cobbled together at the end but I could hardly complain: the editor had joined the British Army and was called out to sudden combat duty in Afghanistan just before it was due to be proofed. He even had to draw up a will before he left. Bad and all as writing was, I wouldn't have wanted to trade places with him. It also sounded like more fun thinking of sharing a bed with Julia Roberts than having your arse shot off by terrorists in the Middle East.

I worked hard trying to drum up publicity for the book, picking media contacts out of dog-eared little notebooks that went back years. It got a lot of reviews in Ireland but none at all 'across the pond'. The publisher asked me what I thought the reason was for this but I didn't know. Some months later I learned that the publicist hadn't even sent out review copies to the British media. Maybe she expected them to review it clairvoyantly.

I was getting a lot of publicity around this time from the *Evening Herald*. When I rang them and asked if they'd give it a plug they said they would. The next day a photographer arrived at the house. I was again faced with the worry of trying to avoid having my picture taken. I tried to stave him off by saying I'd cut myself shaving.

I gave myself a scratch on the cheek to bolster my case but he wasn't to be deterred and said he could shoot me in profile. I put a cap on my head to try and disguise myself and added my mother's glasses as he got his camera ready. I couldn't find my wig or my fake moustache but tried to hide my face behind a coffee mug before he said, 'Would you mind putting the cup down while I take the photograph, please?'

When it appeared, I went into my old panic mode and resolved never again to let any of the paparazzi within an ass's roar of the house. 'Maybe the time has come for you to lose your camera shyness,' Mary said, 'Most people around here are so far into their dotage they wouldn't give a monkey's if you were a serial killer, never mind a writer.'

She'd had her own photograph in a local paper a few times as a result of some voluntary work she'd done for the Vincent de Paul and enjoyed showing it to people.

'I realise you're the normal one,' I said, 'but you have to let me be myself. My books may be for sale but I'm not.'

'You and J. D. Salinger should get together,' she said, 'Maybe you could find a bunker for yourselves somewhere in Outer Mongolia.'

Bukowski

In 2003 I had a biography of Charles Bukowski, *The Hunchback of East Hollywood*, published by a company in Manchester that did off-the-wall stuff. I'd loved his writing from the first day I sampled it in a basement of Eason's Bookshop in Dublin where they sold remaindered copies of books. I started reading a poem, I don't know which one, and it went on for pages and pages. It read like prose but it was in poetic form. I couldn't put it down. I bought the book and never stopped buying them until I had everything he wrote.

I came late to Bukowski. His books weren't prescribed on any of my courses in Belfield, when I was there. He loved Hemingway but I didn't know that then. I don't think Hemingway would have thought much of him.

Universities didn't like Bukowski despite the fact that he often read his work in them. Or maybe because of that – he usually disgraced himself at the readings.

After I decided to do the book I wrote to John Martin, his publisher at Black Sparrow in Santa Rosa. Martin had 'discovered' Bukowski, paying him a stipend to write after he left his day job at the post office. I asked him if he'd be interested in me doing a collection of Bukowski's sayings. He said he thought this was a trivial idea and said no. 'There are too many books out about him at the moment,' he said. I found this amusing. Martin had published most of them.

As regards the sayings, he was probably right but I felt the world could have done with hearing his great pronouncements. ("Some people never go crazy. What truly horrible lives they must lead.') I hadn't thought of doing a biography of him at that stage. Howard Sounes had done what was seen as the definitive one. What could I add to it? There were a few short memoirs out there as well but they didn't seem to have much that Sounes didn't.

Bukowski changed my attitude not only to literature but to life. After reading him I knew I'd never be beholden to anyone again. I'd never be intimidated by anyone. I'd never be talked down to by anyone. Maybe I'd never even fully trust anyone. He turned everything I knew about life on its head. I'd never read

235

anyone who talked like him or wrote like him or acted like him. It was a miracle he'd survived what he put his body through. A lot of writers talked tough but he was the real deal. I also liked the fact that the Beats didn't embrace him into their fold.

Bukowski was in a different league. He'd have eaten these people without salt. The idea of me doing a book on a degenerate barfly whose main female company was alcoholic hookers would probably have had me run out of Ballina if I started the book there in my youth.

After the experience in Eason's I went in search of other books by him. They were hard to come by in those days. Apart from that one, Eason's didn't stock them. They didn't even have a way of ordering them from Black Sparrow. After a while I found a shop on the Quays called The Forbidden Planet. It sold graphic novels. They said they'd order them for me.

For the next few months I walked down the Quays with a huge sense of expectation when they phoned to say they had a new title in. They weren't cheap (some of them cost over £40) but I'd have paid ten times that amount for them. After I'd got through as many poetry books as I could find I went into the novels.

They were equally gripping. Then I got the letters and the articles. Did he ever stop writing? How did he do it with all that drink in him?

If his poems electrified me, reading about his life did it on the double. The nightmare upbringing, the *acne vulgaris*, the ten year drunk, nearly dying of a bleeding ulcer in the charity ward of a hospital in 1955, the miraculous comeback – you couldn't make it up.

I also found a lot to identify with in my own life. Like him I was partial to a drink (or three). I hated the politics around writing like he did and we both liked the sound of the typewriter. (He called it his machine gun.)

We had something else in common too. We both left jobs that were killing us to become writers. I was a teacher and he was a postal clerk – among other things.

I felt I had to do a book on him. Did I have anything to say that hadn't been said already? Maybe Sounes left some gaps that I could fill in.

After a few months I felt what I'd written would qualify as a sidebar to Sounes' book. It was never meant to be anything else. After finding a publisher for it I wrote to Martin to ask him for permission to quote from Bukowski's works.

He said no. Maybe he remembered me from the 'Sayings' idea. Even if he did, I was surprised. Was he not interested in the publicity my book would generate for his author?

Some publishers might have been but he wasn't. I suppose he didn't need me. Anything Bukowski wrote had gone viral by now. Martin had got so rich on him, any writings by people like me weren't going to buffet that by much.

I wasn't used to being blocked like that. I didn't have such problems with my Hemingway book. In fact when I rang the Library of Congress they provided me with all the visual material on Hemingway that I wanted. They also said I could use it without attribution or cost.

I didn't expect Martin to accord me such largesse when it came to the thorny subject of illustrations.

A man in Newcastle offered me the right to quote from an anthology of Bukowski's work that he'd edited. That was good news but my publisher wanted to bring the book out in a joint UK/US edition and the man from Newcastle only had permission for the quotations in the British Isles.

I ended up not being able to use them. The book suffered as a result of that as I'd already put the quotes into my text. Now I had to take them all out again. It meant many paragraphs lost their "meat."

The book only sold modestly. Bukowski audiences are a tough crowd. They don't take kindly to people like me jumping on his bandwagon. A lot of them thought I did it for the money.

Some of the reviewers pointed out that the production of the book was bad. In that they were right. The font was small. Reading it was like looking through a telescope backwards. Other reviews said my style of writing was over the top. They were right about that too. I was too immersed in the man to see my prose for what it was – purple.

Years later I re-wrote the book. A man in San Francisco

published it.

I toned down the style and added a lot of new stuff that I'd learned in the intervening years. It made it more solid. That isn't to say there weren't problems with it. I still couldn't quote from his works and I only had a few photographs of him.

They were given to me by one of his publishers, the editor of Sun Dog Press in Michigan. But somehow it came together. I was happy with it. The reassuring thing was that after I wrote it there were still books coming out by and about him for years afterwards – in fact right up to the present.

The beat goes on.

Diversification

I met my snooker hero Ronnie O'Sullivan in 2003. He'd replaced Jimmy White for me after Jimmy's game went west at the end of the millennium. Ronnie had won the world championship in 2001 and was the hottest property in the game. Mary heard him being interviewed on the radio one morning. He said he was going to be signing copies of his autobiography that day in Bewley's Hotel in Tallaght. Without thinking I said, "Let's see if we can see him." She was on for it. She'd heard me talking about him so much. We jumped into the car and went out there.

I thought I might interview him. I wondered if he'd talk about his father. He'd been imprisoned for murder. It was a sensitive subject.

No sooner were we in the door of the hotel than we were chatting like old friends. After all the years chasing Jimmy I couldn't quite take in how open he was, and how accessible. He was with his then coach Del Hill, a man who was six feet nine in height. He was so tall it was said he could spot the yellow ball from the other end of the table.

When I went up to the bar to get a drink, Ronnie started talking to Mary about Galway. He said he liked it as a city, that it was very friendly. She said, "There's some crime there now." She was sorry afterwards that she said that. It seemed to make Ronnie go quiet. She thought he might have been thinking about his father.

Ronnie and Del spent over an hour chatting to us. Afterwards we took some photos. As we were finishing, Ronnie looked at his watch and realised he was running out of time to get to the airport for his flight back to London. We ended up driving him there.

In the following weeks I started thinking about doing a biography of him. Until that happened, as was the case with Jimmy White, I contented myself writing articles about him. The best way to get them accepted, I learned, was to pitch a particular angle to an editor.

With Ronnie I focussed on the fact that he'd suffered from depression in the past. I'd been writing some articles for the magazine *Aware* at this point.

It was affiliated with an organisation of the same name that helped people with depression. The article chimed nicely with the tenor of the magazine. He was such an interesting guy both on and off the table he was easy to write about.

I did some more quotation anthologies now: one on Ireland called *Talk Nation* and another book for Powerfresh, *Pessimissimo*. The film and book list books I'd done with Prion came out in paperback.

I did one for a company called Clarion simply called *Quotable Quotes for Quoters*, and for a Welsh company, Ylolfa, called *Welsh Wit and Wisdom*.

Summersdale Press asked me to do one called *Golf Wit*. It was translated into foreign languages afterwards. A genial elderly man called Erwin Brecher published another quotation anthology of mine which I called *Life Through a Keyhole*.

I wrote a biography of a spine surgeon, Malachy Smyth, called *A Life in Medicine*.

Was I spreading myself too thin? I re-wrote *A Life in Medicine* as *Killing Pain* a few years later.

A few of my books started to come out in translations around now. I spotted them by accident. When I rang the publishers they said they didn't know anything about them. "Are these people making money from our work without us knowing?" I enquired. Nobody seemed too bothered. I made a few enquiries but I was never meant to be Woodward or Bernstein. Whoever they were, they got away with it.

I had a drink with the editor of a mainstream Irish company one night. I'd known him to speak to on the phone over the years. During those years I'd run a few ideas by him which didn't exactly make him jump up and down with excitement. That was a familiar pattern with me and mainstream companies. I often found myself wishing there were more offbeat ones out there. I'd worked with a few of these just as I'd worked with a few offbeat magazines but they tended to go to the wall. People said you got knocked down if you walked down the middle of the road. The analogy didn't really apply to publishing. The chances of fatalities there were much more if you were on the side – especially the left side.

He was wearing a two-toned shirt. He sat down to have a drink. I had Smithwicks and he had Bailey's. Already I felt things were going to go pear-shaped. It wasn't just the Bailey's. My father told me never to trust people with two-toned shirts. He said they usually had two-toned personalities as well.

"I'm interested in a book on cookery," he told me. There followed a long silence. I'd been thinking of offering him my brilliantly dark futuristic novel about a one-legged piano tuner from Killybegs who stabbed his mother-in-law to death and then cut the heads off his wife and children with a chainsaw. I now felt this would not go down too well with him. Could I somehow tie it in with cooking? Could he be a Jeffrey Dahmer or a Hannibal Lecter and like to eat corpses?

I understood his wish to produce a cookery book. I could hardly go in to Eason's without tripping over one.

As someone who cut his teeth on Hemingway, it was a bit sad to see coffee-tablers on every available shelf with foodstuffs I didn't know the name of sizzling in a pan on the cover instead of Ernesto with a dead lion beside him, like on my biog. of the great man.

After writing my biography of Elvis, it didn't do me any good either to hear that there was a new book coming out on him that focussed on his diet. It was going to be called *Are You Hungry Tonight?* Would we see something similar on Hemingway in time? There was already one out about his drinking habits (*To Have and Have Another*).

My own attitude to food was more basic. I couldn't understand those who agonised about it, who wrote food reviews using language more suited to Ph.D. theses. These writers condemned chefs who fell below their expectations with bile. I hated such writers but I hated the chefs too. People were dying of hunger all round the world.

In the previous few years I hadn't been able to turn on the television without seeing some idiot with a funny cap on his head regaling me with the delights of risotto or linguini or some other delicacy that floated his boat so I knew my publisher friend was on to something.

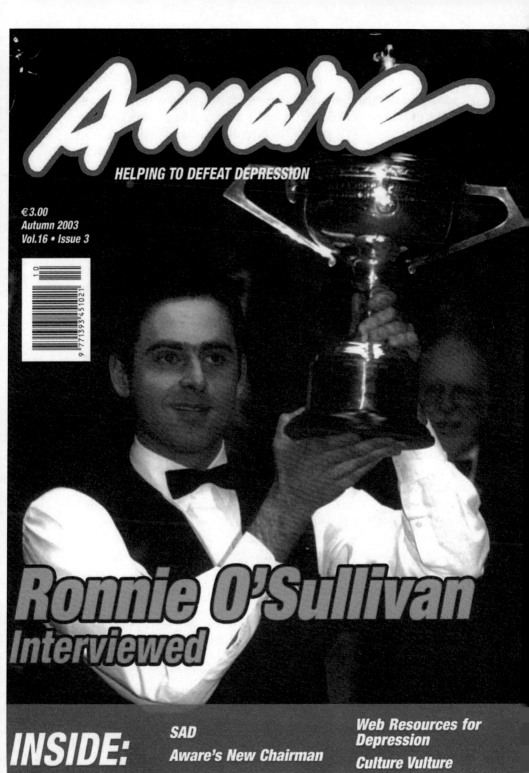

Aware

HELPING TO DEFEAT DEPRESSION

€3.00
Autumn 2003
Vol.16 • Issue 3

Ronnie O'Sullivan
Interviewed

INSIDE:
SAD
Aware's New Chairman

Web Resources for Depression
Culture Vulture

Should I "park"my dystopian novel and investigate the finer points of *coq au vin*? Wasn't it better to have a best-seller on your hands than starve in a garret clutching a manuscript that, even if it were published, would no doubt be banned?' I needed a few shekels and banned books didn't generally carry royalties, only hate mail from Mothers of Ten from Ballygobackwards. Or Killybegs.

Ideas for books? I thought of bringing one out about writers who travelled into outer space. The only problem was I couldn't think of any. What about writers who killed their wives? I couldn't think of anyone but William Burroughs and Louis Althusser. Three more were needed. The minimum number for a list in the last book was five. Where were all the disgruntled writer-husbands?

Another publisher wanted me to do a book about UFOs. He said sci-fi was the coming thing. I said, "I'm in my thirties. You should be talking to some pimply geek for that kind of stuff." He said, "Don't miss the boat. Over 3% of Americans believe they were raised by extra-terrestrials and brought to earth afterwards."

Where did people read shit like this – the *National Enquirer*? I said, "I live in Ireland." He said, "That's not the point. We sell in America. I know 3% isn't much but when you consider the size of America's population. We could make a kill if it took off. It could even be made into a movie."

I told him I'd think about it and I did. For about five seconds. Unfortunately, I was one of the 97% of people who, boringly, believed they were born on earth. I'm sure Steven Spielberg would have been disappointed with me. Maybe he could transport me to the U.S. in a flying saucer and I'd think differently. There seemed to be something in the air over there that made people come up with such beliefs.

I saw them on *Springer* every so often: "My orang-utan left me for another orang-utan." "My daughter is a boy and she's in love with me." "In a previous life my uncle was a goldfish bowl." I was living in the wrong country.

A third publisher suggested I do a book on science. Again I demurred. How old was the world? Who cared? Some say it's ten billion years, others say twenty billion. I'm not particularly concerned either way. I can hardly remember what I did yesterday. If someone says the dinosaurs are coming back I might be interested. Not in a book about them but one teaching me how I could run a bit faster if one of them was coming after me.

I was sitting in my car outside a school when the news of John McGahern's death came over the radio in 2006. The appropriateness of the location only registered with me later. I was shocked to hear he'd died as I didn't know he was ill. I'd interviewed him two years earlier for his 70th birthday.

He hadn't spoken about his battle with cancer on that occasion but it had been going on a long time by then. I later learned that he knew he probably wouldn't beat it. He was too much of a gentleman to mention it to me in case it would have upset me, which of course it would have.

I'd already interviewed him in 1990 about his book *Amongst Women*. He wasn't like your average writer. In fact he was more like a farmer to talk to. I was aware he farmed but didn't expect it to be his essence. He renewed my faith in the profession. One could be great and also natural – and have good manners. He sets a lot of store by this. A humble man, McGahern once said, "A writer should bow like a musician after a performance." It was lesser writers, I usually noticed, who were arrogant. His passing drew a large reaction. A figure of scandal in the early years of his writing career, by the end of it, with elegiac books like *That They May Face the Rising Sun* and *Memoir*, he'd become more like a national treasure.

Neil Jordan, a pupil of his when he taught in Clontarf before losing his job, gave an amusing tribute to him when he said, "When John taught me in Belgrave I just saw him as a teacher who wrote. By the time he died he'd become more like Padre Pio."

I wrote a guide to the Harry Potter books in 2007. There were about 17 million spotty teenagers out there who could have made a better fist of it than me. I picked their brains online. The book was the brainchild of a man called Jim Stanley, who was a friend of Des Duggan, one of the people I worked for in *Senior Times*. We decided to split anything we got from it three ways.

The *Harry Potter Guide* was the first book I wrote on the

computer. It was a necessary evil because most of my research came from there. I wrote the book like a robot so it suited it that it was composed in robot-like fashion sitting in front of a screen. I could never do anything creative that way.

We were getting the garage converted into a living room when I wrote it. The builders had to drill a hole about two feet thick. It was at the bottom of the stairs. All day long I listened to Kango hammers boring a hole in my skull as I studied the finer points of the Hogwarth whippersnapper's life.

I promised myself I'd never do another book on the computer. For future books I vowed to go back to my preferred way of writing: chaos.

I kept buying Canon ribbons off eBay even when they cost an arm and a leg – and more times than not didn't work. I liked writing little paragraphs and then cutting them out and pasting them together on sheets of A4.

I believe Jane Austen used to write on little pieces of paper too, hiding them under blotters if people came into the room. I was in good company.

If I made a mistake I re-typed the word and sellotaped it over the wrong one. I would then photocopy it. People in photocopying outlets who saw me arriving in with reams of pages told me I should topload them to save time. "Do you want to see your machine broken?" I'd reply.

I tried it once and the page got snagged inside it. A good day for me was when I came out of my little office with my fingers (and probably my jumper as well) full of Tipp-Ex and a piece of paper stuck to my shoe with cellotape hanging off it.

Rubbing Tipp-Ex marks off trousers and jumpers with thick cloths often tore them so much I had to throw them out but it was worth it. Sometimes I stitched – or superglued – them together.

I liked the noise the typewriter made. In that I was like Bukowski. He compared the sound of his machine made to the rat-tat-tat of a rifle.

The woman next door complained that I was keeping her awake half the night by typing into the small hours. At least she didn't bang on the walls with a broom handle like the people in Bukowski's rooming houses did.

Aubrey MALONE

Harry Potter
de A à Z

TOUT CE QUE VOUS AVEZ TOUJOURS VOULU SAVOIR
SUR LA SAGA DU PETIT SORCIER ET SA CRÉATRICE

L'univers Harry Potter expliqué de A à Z

Le guide non officiel de toute la SAGA

City

RICHARD BURTON • DYLAN THOMAS • RACHEL ROBERTS • ANTHONY HOPKINS

Welsh Drinkers

AUBREY MALONE

It was at the bottom of the stairs. All day long I listened to Kango hammers boring a hole in my skull as I studied the finer points of the Hogwarth whippersnapper's life.

I promised myself I'd never do another book on the computer. For future books I vowed to go back to my preferred way of writing: chaos.

I kept buying Canon ribbons off eBay even when they cost an arm and a leg – and more times than not didn't work. I liked writing little paragraphs and then cutting them out and pasting them together on sheets of A4.

I believe Jane Austen used to write on little pieces of paper too, hiding them under blotters if people came into the room. I was in good company.

If I made a mistake I re-typed the word and sellotaped it over the wrong one. I would then photocopy it. People in photocopying outlets who saw me arriving in with reams of pages told me I should topload them to save time. "Do you want to see your machine broken?" I'd reply.

I tried it once and the page got snagged inside it. A good day for me was when I came out of my little office with my fingers (and probably my jumper as well) full of Tipp-Ex and a piece of paper stuck to my shoe with cellotape hanging off it.

Rubbing Tipp-Ex marks off trousers and jumpers with thick cloths often tore them so much I had to throw them out but it was worth it. Sometimes I stitched – or superglued – them together.

I liked the noise the typewriter made. In that I was like Bukowski. He compared the sound of his machine made to the rat-tat-tat of a rifle.

The woman next door complained that I was keeping her awake half the night by typing into the small hours. At least she didn't bang on the walls with a broom handle like the people in Bukowski's rooming houses did.

Other books followed: More quotation anthologies for Summersdale and Powerfresh (which had now become Little Black Dog).

I did another poetry collection for Dennis Greig (*Idle Time*), a biography of Jimmy White, *Whirlwind*, a book about Hollywood and spirituality (no, they weren't mutually exclusive) which I called *Sacred Profanity*, and two more books for Ylolfa, *Famous Welsh Drinkers* and *Still Rockin'*, the latter a biography of Tom Jones.

In 2011 I wrote a study of censorship for the American company, McFarland.

It was the first of five books I'd do for them in time. I was also writing a lot of stories during these years but I didn't see them as being commercial. Most of them I stuffed in shoeboxes in the attic alongside my more purple poetry.

Mordecai Richler once said, "Everyone writes a book too many." I'd written many books too many. I would have been the first to admit I did some of them for that very reason – to write a book.

It was like an athlete running races to get more trophies, a compulsion to keep the process going. I often wrote when I had nothing to say and then I kept on saying it. It was verbal diarrhoea – coupled with intellectual constipation.

Maybe I was trying to over-compensate for my quietness when I was young. The shy man's revenge. If so, God help the reader. He had to suffer my self-help expostulations.

There was no pattern to my books. I alternated fiction with non-fiction and poetry with prose. Serious biographies of film stars and writers were followed by trivial anthologies of quotations.

As the quote books piled up, publishers began to seek me out for more. I did about ten of them for Powerfresh and its successors and another dozen for Summersdale.

These companies knew I could do them quickly. I kept buying other books of quotations to draw from and I was also reading biographies and autobiographies as well as comic books.

For a while I built my days around collecting quotes. I remember saying to one editor that in Stone Age times people went out hunting animals, returning with so many scalps for the dinner. I went out hunting for quotes, coming home from libraries with ten or twenty every day that I slotted into my various manuscripts.

"I don't know what a quote is," Hugo said to me one day, "Isn't everything we say a quote of some sort?" He was right. I didn't know where one drew the line between something that could be construed as a quote and something that wasn't.

Readers' appetites for quote books eventually died off. It was probably due to the internet. Why should people fork out money for anthologies when all they had to do was turn on their computers and google any subject they were interested in?

Just as singers were suffering from people downloading their tunes, often illegally, and stand-up comedians not getting the same turn-outs for their shows because it was so easy to watch people on YouTube or wherever, so I felt the pinch with my little offerings.

The problem was that, when the fad passed, I already had another ten or so of these books ready to go, like food off the deli counter.

Where would I send them now? My speed came against me sometimes, resulting in a lot of work being done that went nowhere. Sometimes I went up to the attic and looked at bags and bags of pages getting more dog-eared by the minute in their perch beside the water tank. I was often tempted to drop them into it.

Modern Woman closed down that year. I was sorry to see it go. Margot's husband Jack had sold his shares in *The Meath Chronicle* by now and she didn't feel she had the same authority in editing "*The Woman*."

I met her less and less in the following years. That was mainly my fault. Navan was a long way away. Because of a claustrophobia problem I wasn't good travelling on buses. She wasn't in Dublin much now on junkets because she wasn't covering anything anymore.

There were also things going wrong in her personal life. Her daughter died, which broke her heart. Then she developed health problems – a detached retina in one of her eyes which subsequently affected the other one as well, eventually leaving her what they called "legally blind."

She was too proud to get a seeing eye dog. That meant she went out less. The things the rest of us take for granted were suddenly major chores for her, like putting on a cup of tea. I think she burned herself a few times. As far as I know she only had 5% vision.

We talked on the phone every so often. If she was having a glass of wine she'd grow melancholic and cry.

Her husband Jack was a great standby to her at this time. So were her. sisters. But I felt she lost a lot of her spirit after *Modern Woman* went out of her life.

In many ways she turned into a recluse now. Her work with a mental health organisation she worked with also trailed off. She'd done so much for it over the years, raising huge amounts of money for it. I felt it was now time for her to sit back and let Navan do something for her.

What could that be? I didn't know. "Eaten bread is soon forgot" she said to me,

Margot asked me to write a little playlet once for the back cover of *Modem Woman*. That experience got me thinking of doing something more extensive in that line. I wasn't especially good at dialogue – Mary was – but I went through a phase of writing plays now.

One of them – not my best, I hasten to add – was aired on the radio. It was about my courier days. I called it *Unlucky for Some*. I was courier Number 13, driving from pillar to post as my boss barked instructions at me.

It wasn't exactly Shakespeare but it was nice to be able to tell people to listen in to something I wrote that was going out to the whole country.

Unlike books, which people read at different times, when you have something like this it makes you understand the buzz actors or singers get at live performances.

You also have actors delivering your lines. If they're good they embellish them.

The buzz I got from it made me write another one. It was set on New Year's Eve and featured a soldier coming home from the Lebanon to a couple he's friendly with.

The surprise is that he turns out to be the father of one of their sons.

There were a lot of flashbacks in it featuring this son and a girl he's going out with. He's confused about what he wants from life. The mother has a drink problem. Her marriage is falling apart. It was all a bit chaotic.

I sent it to Hugh Leonard, a well-known playwright. He was the man who said, '*Hamlet* is a good play but there are too many quotations in it.'

He sent it back saying, "I think there's something here but I'm not sure what. God help you, it looks like you may be a playwright but you're not there yet. Send it to the Abbey with a note saying I said they should refuse it but to watch out for your next one." I didn't know what to make of that.

Who'd send something somewhere on the proviso that they knew it wasn't going to be accepted. As for the "next one," I might never get around to doing that.

I sent it to a theatre that had just opened up near me. It was an intimate little venue situated above a pub, specialising in plays by new and unknown writers.

I'd been at a few of them. It was a nice idea for a night out. You bought a drink in the pub and brought it upstairs. People sat at benches around the stage. It was small and intimate like the Focus Theatre.

The Focus was my favourite theatre in Dublin but unfortunately it closed down some years ago. It was run by Deirdre O'Connell, the wife of the Dubliners' Luke Kelly, with a distinctly Stanislavski emphasis.

I saw some brilliant plays there over the years by people like Strindberg and other European writers. It was so small you had to cross the stage to get to the loo.

This was a tiny little cubicle off the equally tiny drinking area where you clustered together with anyone else who liked sipping wine in a firetrap between the acts.

I didn't have any great hopes they'd take my play, or even read it, so I was surprised when I got a letter from the director one day saying "We got your play. It might be suitable for us. The problem is that there are ten people in it. The most we could accommodate in our limited space is eight, and even that would be tearing it."

I wrote out two of them and sent it back to him again. This time his comments were more detailed. Some of the speeches were too long. The time scale of the play was confusing. He wasn't sure if the flashback sequences would work.

I felt like saying, "Why didn't you say that in your last letter? It would have saved me the trouble of re-writing the thing." But I re-wrote it a third time to please him, taking all his points on board, and then sent it to him again.

This time it came back with a bald, "We're cutting back on submissions at the moment as we have a backlog."

I've found time-wasters like this annoyingly prevalent in all walks of the writing game. They say one thing when they mean another. It's better to lance the wound early on instead of giving people mixed signals which confuse them.

As I've gotten older I think I can read the signs better. I don't think I'd fall for the idea of re-writing something today unless I'd sat down for a coffee with the director in question and talked turkey with him to find out if he was genuinely interested.

My play may not have been very good but I don't think that was the point. I think it was better than some of the ones I've seen in this theatre.

Why wasn't it accepted? I don't know. Some directors do "favours" for writers for any number of reasons.

They're friends of theirs, or relations, or they owe them a favour, or they have a large social circle and can guarantee people to turn up for the performances, or they pay them money to have it staged etc. etc. They might even have been patrons of the bar downstairs so an element of nudge-wink could be going on there.

The point is that acceptance or rejection of work has often very little to do with its quality. More important is politics, which is a huge aspect of all branches of writing as it is of every other activity in life.

I went back to writing books, or rather trying to find publishers for them. I sent a round robin email to various universities about a project I was working on that dealt with conflict between stars.

I felt I had a better chance with university presses than commercial ones.

They didn't offer much money but I didn't care about that. The problem with them was that my style of writing was sometimes too conversational for them.

Once again I went to my "Bible," *The Writers and Artists*

Yearbook, for the addresses of publishers, sending my missive everywhere from Alaska to Mexico.

You'd never know, I thought, some eskimo in an igloo might be at a loose end at the North Pole, or a gaucho sitting in a sombrero in Mexico. A few days later I got a reply from a man called Patrick McGilligan. I vaguely recognised the name. He'd written a few books of interviews with screenwriters that Keith had. "Are you the man who writes the screenwriters books?" I asked. He said, "That's me." I told him Keith had read all his books.

You can't beat the personal touch. He may have been flattered that I knew about him, or that Keith did. He wasn't interested in my Hollywood conflict idea but shortly afterwards he wrote to me asking me if I'd like to do a biography of Maureen O'Hara.

I wasn't over the moon about the idea. She'd never been one of my favourite actresses. Out of 100 subjects I might have wished for, she'd have been about 99. I'd read her autobiography, *'Tis Herself*, and enjoyed it moderately but no more. But it was work. I rarely refused that.

Sometimes I took on books I didn't like at first and grew into them as time went on. Besides, it might lead to other projects down the line. I said to Pat, "Are you aware she's written her autobiography?" In retrospect I think I was probably trying to talk myself out of the job by asking him this. He said he did but by the way he said it I wasn't sure. Was there not a danger people would feel they knew everything about her already? Could I add anything new? It wasn't as if there were any skeletons in her cupboard. The ones that were already there had been bought out to dance in her own book. Nonetheless I told him I'd do it.

He said I'd have to submit a proposal. This turned out to be something of a nightmare. My first effort was dismissed as being "too sketchy" for the blind peers who spent their time surveying these kinds of things. Ditto for the second one. And the third. I found myself wondering who these blind peers were. I imagined them as having long beards and crumpled tweed suits and sitting

ADVANCE READING COPY · NOT FOR SALE

MAUREEN O'HARA

THE BIOGRAPHY

AUBREY MALONE

in dusty rooms surrounded with heaps of mildewed books in various stages of disarray on their shelves. Would I ever see them? Or even get to talk to them? The "blind" part seemed to fly in the face of that.

After a few months of submitting proposal after proposal I said to Pat, "This is draining me. Can I not just get on to the book? The way things are going, I'm not going to have any energy left for it when I get down to it."

"That's the problem," he said, "You may not be able to get down to it." I didn't know what he meant.

"Are you saying you don't want me to do the book?" I said.

He said, "If it was left to me I'd want you to do it but there's one peer who doesn't want you to." I wondered who it was.

"Can I speak to him?" I said.

He said I couldn't. It would go against the whole nature of the process. I just had to do a better proposal. "And by the way," he added, "It's not a him, it's a her." Ouch. I thought of an expression my father liked to use: "Cherchez la femme." Sometimes, he said, women were "deadlier than the male."

By now I'd bought various books on Maureen and on people who'd worked with her. I'd also ordered most of her films from Amazon and even contacted her film studio in America for material about her, and various institutes of film studies that Keith got press books from over the years.

"We'll have to cancel the contract if you can't do a better proposal," Pat said to me. I later learned that the person blocking me was a woman who lectured in TCD, my father's old alma mater. There was me thinking my enemy was 5,000 miles away when she was just down the road. She was, of course, American. I knew she had to be.

I suspended all my research and wrote a proposal that finally pleased her. I was over the moon at her acceptance. I'd got the green light. Now all that remained was the tiny task of writing the book.

I felt I'd have to talk to Maureen to give myself any chance of competing with *'Tis Herself* but any overture I made to her in the coming months was met with a deafening silence. Maybe she'd heard through the grapevine that I was doing the book.

Actresses don't generally like biographers unless they can dictate how the biography is going to go, in other words that it's going to portray them as the Mother Teresas they believe themselves to be. Mine was an unauthorised one so she wasn't going to be able to do that. In a way I was relieved. I'd read about fifty interviews she did and most of them were the same: She stood up to directors. She was proud of her Irish passport. She had a troubled relationship with John Ford. She loved John Wayne. Did I really want to listen to her going through all this guff again? In the end I did it without her participation.

Clive James once said that autobiographies should really be called "alibiographies" because people rarely washed their dirty linen in public. I was interested to know if Maureen had told us the full story about her life in her book. Was her first husband, for instance, really as bad as she made out? Or indeed her second one?

We'd only heard one side of the story. I don't think she'd have been too pleased if I asked her these questions. I'd probably have had to run to John Wayne for protection. (Oops, he was long dead by now).

Sadly, the freedom of expression I gained by not talking to her didn't count for much because the publishers wanted a book that eulogised her. Anytime I passed even the tiniest criticism of her as a person (or indeed an actress) it was cut out. I don't know why. Maybe they didn't want to antagonise the 44 million Irish-Americans that would be displaying the book on their coffee tables with the Waterford crystal and the medals won by Sinead and Seamus at the Feis in Coney Island.

Maureen died after it came out. She was a great age so that wasn't too much of a surprise. A few years later the paperback of it was published. I was asked to add a final chapter documenting everything that happened in the interim. That was an enjoyable task. There was no "blind peer" making my life misery anymore.

It also came out as an audio book. I bought this to send down to Margot Davis in Navan. I used to enjoy sending her my books before she got her eye problems. She couldn't read at all now. We often talked on the phone.

She'd ask me how I was getting on with my writing but I felt that was trivial now in comparison to everything she'd been going through in the last number of years. She had a big computer screen that magnified words but she didn't like it.

She thanked me for the book. It began with a line that I felt would draw her in: "They have a statue of her in Kells." (Margot grew up in that town). But audio books could never compensate for "the real thing." She told me music was her best therapy now.

My writing changed after I stopped doing articles for Margot. She brought out the humour in me. I wrote a lot of articles for her on the funny sides of relationships, even the funny side of break-ups. I wrote about disgruntled wives writing notes to deadbeat hubbies saying things like "Your dinner is in someone else's oven." She loved things like that. Other editors wanted more hardboiled material.

One of the most satirical books I wrote was *The Mammoth Book of Irish Humour*. There was a time that comedy was tame. These days it's more like character assassination. I milked as much venom for that book as I could find. It was my way of taking society's temperature.

Sometimes I wrote things that were insensitive to people I knew. I never intended to but it happened. Maybe every writer does at some point. I think of Truman Capote with Marlon Brando (the Kyoto interview) or Ernest Hemingway with Scott Fitzgerald ("Poor Scott...")

Keith said to me one day, "You're a different person when you take up a pen. He meant it as a compliment I think – but it worked the other way too. When I got on a roll sometimes I said too much. The "different person" took over. Most people had the common sense to tear up things they wrote that crossed a line. I didn't seem to have that gift. I remembered the letters my father wrote that my mother asked me not to post when we were in Ballina. Maybe I inherited the streak from him.

Mary was like my mother. If I showed her something I wrote that involved a person we knew she'd say, "Tear it up. You got the benefit from writing it. Now it's finished." That was hard for me to do. It was like a perverse form of showing off. If I worked hard at an article I wanted to have something to show for it. I should have been aware of people's sensitivities because I was sensitive myself. How would I feel if someone wrote something about me? Nobody in my family ever did. I was a protected species in that regard. If someone reviewed a book of mine negatively (like the infamous Sue Denham) it upset me.

I developed a thick skin as the years went on – you had to with social media being so eviscerating – but for my first few books I was vulnerable. Praise is like oxygen to a writer but as Hemingway said, "If you believe the good stuff you have to believe the bad." At the start of my writing life I became defensive if I was attacked, not realising that this was what literary critics did for a living – they criticised.

The film director Luchino Visconti said to Dirk Bogarde one day, "We create, they destroy." It was the same with literary critics. I had to learn to ignore them. They were filling a column because they were paid to do so. Damning something sounded more important than praising it. When you praised, you looked up. When you damned you looked down. That gave the person more esteem.

It took me years to realise that it was all a game. You had the eunuchs and you had the harem. The people who couldn't do things had a go at the people who could. Their words didn't matter. All that mattered was whether your books sold or not. It's hard to see that sometimes, particularly when the long knives came out or their comments were gratuitous. You might have worked for a year on something and see it denounced in a sentence. I couldn't complain. I'd done it myself when I was working for Hibernia all those years ago. Nobody is as cruel as the young.

Sean Haughey once said of his father Charlie – the disgraced politician – "Everyone hated him except the people." It was an interesting comment. Haughey is almost universally reviled today but some people still see the charisma that enabled him to get away with his machinations. "Lovable rogue" is the cliche for people like this. Poor Sean – a decent man but one lacking his father's ability to "work" a crowd – had his career cut short because of being his son. The Haughey "curse," if we may call it that, came down to his generation.

After I finished the Maureen book I looked around at all the books I'd used to research it. They were literally spilling out of my shelves. I did what I always did when I finished a book, i.e. I took them all out and shoved them into the attic. Likewise all the drafts of the book, all the sheets of paper I'd got from film archives, and all the DVDs of her films that I'd searched high and low for. I watched a lot of films not only for this book but every one I did on the cinema.

Keith gave me many from his vast library as well, many of them coming from a dealer he did business with in Maine called Roberta Mitchell. As he got older he developed scruples about ordering them from Roberta, saying they were bootlegs and that she didn't have a license to download them from TV, which was how she'd been able to sell them cheaply to him.

I tried to explain to him that if she wasn't allowed to do this she wouldn't have been able to stay in business for as long as she did but he wouldn't listen. The irony was that he'd alerted me to the fact that Roberta existed. She sold films for as little as $5 a go. That was about a quarter of what you'd pay from Amazon. Strictly speaking they were bootlegs but she wasn't selling them "under the counter."

Keith's conscience wouldn't let him watch Roberta's films eventually so they just lay there on a shelf in his house. He gave a lot of them to me but refused to watch the ones I'd bought from her even if I'd bought some specifically for him. Then Roberta retired. When she was travelling to her retirement place in a truck one day, there was ice on the road and it skidded. All her films fell out and went down an incline. It was tragic.

Afterwards I found another man who ran a similar type of business. This was John Andrushkoff from Quebec. He goes by the name of JR. We became friends over the years. I now deal with him all the time. JR gave me films starring Tony Curtis for my book on Curtis and on Maureen O'Hara for my biography of her.

When I wrote *Hollywood's Second Sex*, my book on the women of Hollywood, he sold me films on any number of actresses. All I had to do was mention someone and he came up with the goods. There's no end to his library. I wouldn't like to think how many DVDs he has in it. He's been collecting them

261

since he was hardly out of the cradle. He's in his eighties now but still active. No matter what you want he'll find it for you like that other Canadian resource, the Mounted Police, he "always gets his man."

Mary and myself had somewhat different attitudes to JR's films. I'd be watching them with an eye for a future book. For Mary they were ends in themselves.

My preferred decade, like Keith's was the forties. We'd be watching a film directed by someone like Preston Sturges. I'd say something like, "This is Sturges' third film but the first to show him developing his style. Watch the camera angles here. Some of them made him unpopular with the moguls. They thought he was trying to be *avant garde*. He uses a filter that gives the film a kind of orange hue. Listen to the music as well. It ushers in Phase 2 of his career. He was before his time but of it too. His films saved the studio."

Pleased with myself, I would then go out to the kitchen to make a cup of tea. When I came back Mary would say something like, "You missed a good scene. Joel McCrea is pretending to be in love with Jean Arthur but I don't think he is. He doesn't really listen when she talks. I don't think the relationship will last. Jean's parents originally came from Russia but they're living in Australia now. They raised a family of seven but only four survived. There was some kind of plague. Jean loves her mother but doesn't get on with her father. I think she'll go to Sydney with her mother. Joel will panic when he thinks he's going to lose her and beg her to marry him. She'll tell him it won't work because she wants to have a career and she knows he's not the type of man who would be happy with that. He's really old-fashioned but covers it up. He wants to bring her to a log cabin and cut wood for a living. Jean would be bored to tears with that. I bet her mother will talk sense into Joel and they'll get back together at the end."

I would then say, "I've only been gone from the room for ninety seconds. Where did you get all that?" And she'd say, "It was obvious. Now what's that you were saying about the camera angles? And where's my cup of tea?"

Somebody once said, "Men, women. Women, men. It will never work." He knew what he was talking about.

Sunset Boulevard

Keith died in 2015. He'd fought a brave battle against Parkinson's disease, becoming more and more benign if that was possible) the more it got a grip on him. But he slowed down with the years. He even stopped writing his book at one point, which was anathema.

He did some unusual things in his last years, like playing the mouth organ and putting bets on football matches. He even started watching snooker on the television.

Sometimes when I visited him I saw the life going out of him. As he sat there shaking with his terrible disease he'd look at me with a kind of pleading. It was an expression that said, "What have I done to deserve this?" He'd have a smile on his face but it was a sad one. It was a smile that said, "I know I can't beat the disease but I won't let it kill my spirit." As the saying went, he had Parkinson's but Parkinson's didn't have him.

He knew he would soon be going to his "reward." He was even surer than Cagney at the end of *Angels with Dirty Faces* when he stopped being the Hard Man to do a favour for his padre friend Spencer Tracy, feigning "yellowness" for the Dead End Kids. The priests in Muredach's – both the college and the cathedral – had done a good job on him.

His death came out of the blue. He hadn't been attending doctors but then he never had. In the end it was his heart that got him rather than the Parkinson's. He left life – as he'd done everything else during it – His Way.

I wrote this poem for him after seeing him in the funeral parlour in Ballymun, silent for once as everyone chattered around him:

> *How can you have left us, Keith,*
> *With all those millions of facts*
> *Stored up in your encyclopaedic brain,*
> *The names of stars nobody ever heard of*
> *And producers and directors*
> *And second unit cameramen*
> *And set designers*
> *And grips*

And crew hands
And roadies
And stunt men
And of course writers
Because you spent the last 25 years
Writing a book about these people
Before abandoning it
As suddenly as you took it up.

How can you have left us
Without even a goodbye,
Or showing us one of those films
You insisted on showing after midnight,
The ones with the bad dialogue
And the shotgun delivery of the stars,
And the corny plots you loved
And the predictable plot twists
And the happy-ever-after endings.

You died at home
Which was a tribute
To all the people
Who kept you out of nursing homes.
We were relieved about that
Because we feared the day
You'd have to go to hospital
Even more than you did.
We knew you hated doctors,
remembering how
You used to quote Brady, our relation,
When he said,
'The best part of a hospital
Is the ootside'
in his Scottish voice.

Earlier today
I stood over your coffin,
I remembered you sitting

In the front room
Of your house
In Ardmore Drive
In the grey chair with the board across it
That you used for your tea
With your glasses half way down your nose
And the remote in your hand
Like Alan Ladd with a gun in a film noir.
You got excited
When you put on one of his old movies for us
The ones with the grainy texture
And the muffled sound.
You used to turn the volume up loud
As the credits came down
And the MGM lion roared.
You'd turn it up higher
If we dared to talk
At any point
Because that was the one unforgiveable sin
At your showings.
Turning up the volume
Was your way of telling us
To shut up
Because you were too nice
To say it in words.

I was born in 1953
The year 'Shane' came to town,
That made me feel special
Because 'Shane' was the greatest film ever made.
We knew that because you told us it was,
If you said something it was true
Because you knew everything about films,
You were Moses leading us to the Promised Land.

Your eyes lit up with joy
As Shane rescued Joe Starrett
Or Errol Flynn rode into the valley of death

Or James Cagney cheated the electric chair.
As I looked at you
Looking at the screen
From your grey chair
With your knuckles tight
And your eyes on fire
I'd realise you were back
In Ballina all those years ago with Clive,
Skipping off school to go to the Estoria,
Our home from home,
For the double feature that was
'Retained' –
That magic word.
You hoped none of the priests from Muredach's would be
there
To ask you why you weren't at home
Doing the lessons
That seemed so drab
In contrast to the buckskin of Shane
Or the golden curls of Jeanette Mcdonald
Or trenchcoat of Bogie from 'Casablanca'
Or the wagon train heading east
Away from the injuns.

I never knew you growing up
Because you were the eldest
And I was the youngest
And there was a whole world between us
But years later
I became a part of your world,
The world of Bogart and Cagney
And all the other stars
Nobody ever heard of
Whose faces I knew from the books
You left lying around the house
To entrance us.

Today you lie still
for the first time in years
the Parkinson's
not annoying you for once.

I hope you're whooping it up
with all the stars
you made into family
in that big studio in the sky.·

Piranha Fish

After the Maureen experience I decided I needed a bit more order in my writing. Someone to protect me from bad treatment by publishers. In other words, an agent. Could he (or she) be relied on to do that?

Somebody once said they were people who created trouble between writers and publishers. Maybe they did, but maybe I needed someone to do that to stop them rolling me over. An agent, I felt, would have stepped in and sorted out the nonsense with the "blind peers" on the Maureen book. He, or she, could have stopped them having all that silent power over me as they "peered" at my work from behind their secret screens.

Up to now I'd always seen them as the piranha fish of publishing, gobbling up everything they could and giving little back. Chelsey Fox was a good one but there was no way she would have been able to cope with the number of titles I was working with.

Vernon Futerman (pictured on previous page) was a gentleman but perhaps too "old world" for the aggressive turn the book industry was taking at the time he wound down. Ray Santilli had stung me with the Elvis book. I knew I'd have to be more careful from now on.

A writer at the Frankfurt Book Fair, Joseph O'Connor said once, is basically an inconvenience. I've never been at this but I'll take his word for it as I know it's a marketplace and writers aren't generally renowned for being good at marketing, or at least they weren't when Joseph made that remark.

We might say in the same vein that film directors are inconveniences at film festivals. They want to discuss their film, unlike their agent, who'd be busy talking percentages with some rich fuddy-duddy who knew SFA about films but was good at writing cheques.

I decided to look for an agent in that vein, someone who'd be tough enough to "save" me from the publishers who were, I felt, taking advantage of me.

Unfortunately, the one I picked drove me further and further into the inferno.

He was American. Let's call him Philip. That's not his real name. (Considering there are some delicate matters that have arisen in my various connections with agents and publishers over the years, it's best not to identify people like this). He appeared very friendly to me for the first few months I dealt with him and I felt we could strike up a really strong author-agent relationship. "You really need an agent," he said.

He set me up with the Public Lending Rights system, which was good. It meant I got a stipend every time one of my books was borrowed from a library. Then he dug up some unpaid royalties I was due for the Harry Potter book. These were the two best things he did but they didn't make me much money. The PLR allowance was small and the Harry Potter money was divided between myself Des and Jim so I only got a third of it.

Money, in any case, wasn't my priority. Getting books published was, and as time went on, I didn't notice him being particularly pro-active about sending my ideas to publishers. He was more interested in collecting royalties on the ones I already had out.

I got five contracts in the year I worked with this man, including my "Hollywood conflict" book "*Star Wars*" (not to be confused with the George Lucas movie) which was due to be brought out by an Indian publisher based in London at the time I employed Philip. There was also the Maureen book, an anthology of quotations about travel called *It's Great to be Back on Terra Cotta*, and a book I was contracted to do by Constable Publishing called *The Mammoth Book of Irish Humour*.

Philip wanted to be brought in on all these contracts even though it was me who got them. I put his name on *Harry Potter*, *Star Wars* and *It's Good to be Back on Terra Cotta* but held back on the other two. I wanted to see if he'd get me any contracts of his own rather than piggybacking on my ones.

Why should I give him 15% of everything I'd be getting from these publishers if all he did was send out requests for royalties? In that guise he wouldn't have been more than a debt collector.

I always knew I was lucky that I didn't have to write to eat. I like money as much as the next man but I tend to think it will arrive when it arrives. If you hassle publishers on matters like this, it creates a bad atmosphere. Philip was good at reminding publishers of overdue payments but he didn't show much interest in submitting my proposals to them.

One day I said to him, "Are you ever going to be able to get me a contract?" He replied, "I don't think so." I was impressed by his honesty but it made me wonder what I was doing with him. I decided not to keep him on after the year of our collaboration expired.

Star Wars was due to come out as we neared the date of the expiration of our contract. So was my Maureen O'Hara biography and *The Mammoth Book of Irish Humour*. Philip wanted to be in on both of these as he knew they were both potential moneyspinners. I'd been offered a huge advance for the Constable book (£7,500) so his interest in this was especially keen on that one

He was shocked when I told him I wasn't going to put his name on either the Maureen O'Hara contract or the Constable one. 'You have to,' he said, 'They're both within our contractual year.' I said, 'I haven't signed either contract yet.' (I'm going back a bit in time here).

Philip got his revenge on me by going to the Indian publisher and telling him not to publish *Star Wars*. This must be the only time in history that an agent has actually advised a publisher *not* to publish one of his client's books. The reason I know he did so is because after that publisher told me he wasn't going to publish the book.

I took him to court and won an award from him. It was an open and shut case as I had the contract. In his depositions to the judge, however, which I was privy to, he included an email from Philip to him in which he said, 'Don't publish Aubrey's book' Charming message!

Why had he so much influence on this man? I don't know. It was probably due to the fact that Philip put a lot of his other authors in touch with him after hearing about him from me. They became very involved with one another.

That was another thing that annoyed me about Philip. He used my contacts to make contacts of his own. He even got a book out with one of his other authors through Constable after my one.

It had to be only a matter of time, I thought, when he approached Kentucky UP, the publishers of the Maureen O'Hara book, or Summersdale. He actually did that, and also placed books for his other clients with Michael O'Mara, who did *Hollyweird*, and HarperCollins, who did *Harry Potter*. Coincidence? I didn't think so.

He put all five of the books I got contracts for in that year on his website under the title, 'Books I Helped Place.' I said, 'You didn't help place any of these titles. Please take them off your site.' He did that. I noticed that a lot of the other books he 'helped place' were from vanity presses. That didn't take much savoir faire.

I was awarded a token sum from this publisher in the Small Claims court. It hardly paid my expenses but I felt I'd made my point. I tried to chase Philip as well but got nowhere.

Philip was supposed to be my literary midwife. Instead he turned into an abortionist. Neither was *Star Wars* the first contract I had that was cancelled.

I'd had other ones scotched over the years. A book of music quotes was commissioned by a man who gave me a £600 advance for it. He then changed his mind. A company called The Friday Project contracted me to write a book of clothes quotes and then welshed on the deal. There were others as well.

I wondered if it happened in other walks of life. Could you imagine getting a contract for a deal in an insurance firm, for instance, and having it cancelled? It seemed to me that publishing offered more 'outs' for people changing their mind about deals than any other walk of life.

I never felt I could challenge these people. There was always some small print clause that would get them out of it. In many ways the contracts weren't worth the paper they were written on. I wondered if this kind of thing happened in other walks of life. If you were fired from a clerical post, surely you could go to the Labour Court.

I chased the Indian publisher through the Small Claim Court, a good resource for writers who've been badly treated, but very laborious. The problem with these kinds of things was that living in Ireland came against me.

If a contract was signed in England and I wanted to pursue someone legally, I'd have to go over there or employ a British solicitor to represent me. That's what I had to do for the *Star Wars* case. Once again, as with the Elvis one, it wasn't about money for me. It was about making people accountable if they dumped on you.

Very few of the agents I worked with over the years showed much interest in my books. All they wanted to know was where I wanted to send them. They didn't seem in any way concerned about whether they were any good or not.

I never had a problem with that. Everyone has their function. I can discuss the merits of my books, or their lack of merit, with fellow writers. The problem with fellow writers is that even if they tell you you've written the book of the century, and they probably will (after you tell them they have as well) they most likely won't have any suggestions about the pesky little problem of getting it on a shelf.

I sometimes phoned agents when I had a book just finished. Flushed with excitement I'd ask them if they wanted to see it but they never did. With the exception of people like Peggy Ramsey, who represented Joe Orton, agents just want to make deals. If they can make one with a bad book easier than a good one they're just as happy. For agents, as someone said, the deal is the sex, the book the cigarette afterwards.

And how do you get the deal?

It's all about who you know. The Hollywood agent Swifty Lazar made many of his ones on the golf course or at his legendary parties.

A literary agent is more interested in massaging a publisher's ego when he's three sheets to the wind on Christmas Eve than trying to convince him his client has just written something as moving as Robert Emmet's "Speech from the Dock."

As long as he can get him to sign along the dotted line it doesn't matter if he's selling him *Hamlet* or 'Three Little Piggies went to the market.'

THE MAMMOTH BOOK OF

IRISH HUMOUR

NO SELF-
RESPECTING
PERSON WANTS
TO STAY IN
IRELAND

Edited by
Aubrey Malone

Resetting the Dial

The Philip experience chastened me. It made me realise I needed to be more careful in any further negotiations with anyone. 'You don't need me,' he said to me one day, 'You're doing all right on your own.'

A lot of agents said things like that to me over the years. It wasn't hard to see why. I had a lot of titles out there. But many of them were from 'used car salesmen.' There had to be some middle ground.

I looked around at what other people were doing. How was it that people less seasoned than me seemed to be able to get lucrative deals without even trying? Could I unearth some of my short stories and make them marketable?

John Connolly got a £1 million advance for his novel *Every Dead Thing* in 1999. Not to be sneezed at. I didn't read it but I saw that it featured some gory scenes in America's Deep South.

My stories concerned drab love affairs in the bogs of Ireland. Clearly I was out of date. Maybe I needed Johnny Murphy and Bridget O'Connor to jump on a plane to the U.S. of A and engage in some alligator-wrestling in Louisiana, after which Johnny would go to a clambake and dance with the decapitated Bridget over sarsaparillas. The world had moved on since Liam Flaherty.

The next time I was in Eason's I started flipping through the latest Patricia Cornwell outpouring. She also had a taste for the macabre. After reading a few blood-curdling scenes I remembered why I hadn't gone on for Medicine in UCD: the sight of even a drop of blood made me pass out. Not exactly the best credentials for a career in gory novel-writing.'

By now all my own titles had disappeared from the shelves in Eason's. Now and again I might see some of my academic books in the more upmarket shops but you'd probably need a magnifying glass to find them.

Salescon titles like this were probably about one a year. To this day I never saw a copy of my Maureen O'Hara book on a shelf in Ireland.

Despite numerous calls to my publisher to try and remedy this state of affairs, the first, and to date only, biography of

Ireland's most famous celluloid export remains curiously absent from our shops. As for *The Mammoth Book of Irish Humour*, the sales on this haven't even recouped half my advance in the decade since it's been published.

Going into bookshops since I became a writer has been a decidedly different experience for me than when I used to go in as a reader.

In the old days, when I walked into one of these shops I got a big beaming smile and somebody rushed over to me and said. 'Can I help you, sir?' I thought this was very urbane altogether – riffling through tomes by Henrik Ibsen and Solzhenitsyn and being oh-so-refined about it.

In latter times. however. I've been going into these shops to sell my own books. and the reaction I get is somewhat different – to say the least. Now it's case of, "Oh, bad time, sir, to sell books." Or. "No, I don't think that would be for us."

All this makes me re-evaluate the past. When these people were being nice to me before, I imagined it was because we were fellow intellectuals mutually savouring the rarefied delights of the written word. I'm afraid I miscalculated badly. What we really were was seller and buyer. Now that I've become the seller, the smiles are gone.

Bookshops aren't about culture; they're about making a buck. That's what you learn when you jump over the counter.

To try and blot out the mechanics of what I was doing I went back to my poetry, bringing out another book with Dennis Grieg now.. I called it *Mature Student* after a poem it contained about my father. (The 'mature' was used advisedly).

We put him on the cover as well. I felt it would be less of a problem than it had been when he was on the cover of *The Things That Were.* The title poem went like this:

> *His father was a self-made man*
> *and he lived in his shadow.*
> *His mother spoiled him rotten.*
> *I know nothing of his childhood.*
> *His story began for me in TCD*
> *where he studied for one bar*

and ended in another one.

He graduated by default at 33.
Marriage by elopement followed
and then a brace of children
that arrived almost by rote
until work
that fearsome word,
was sandwiched
between nights in Tony Crane's
with friends he thought
he'd left behind
when he substituted books
for the clearer knowledge
of intuition.

Insecurity warred with bravado
as his thirties slipped by,
the haze of cigar smoke and whiskey
replaced by the genial enquiries
of judges,
guardians of the peace,
and his conscience.
Through the thin veil of laughter
he negotiated a trajectory
of industriousness,
knuckling down to support
his novena of children
as the buzzards gathered
to dent that fragile sensibility.

In 2018 I wrote a book about alcoholic writers. I wanted to call it *The Bottle and the Pen*. The publishers, McFarland, preferred the more sober (no pun intended) *Writing Under the Influence*.

That's the title we eventually used. Maybe it sounded more literary than my one. Andrew Goodfellow had a similar attitude when he replaced my title for my funny definitions anthology,

Writing Under the Influence

Alcohol and the Works of 13 American Authors

Aubrey Malone

Daffynitions, with the more sniffy *The Cynic's Dictionary*. I agreed with him on that occasion because it meant the book became a kind of updated version of Ambrose Bierce's *The Devil's Dictionary*.

I always found the hardest part of a book to write was the first sentence. That wasn't a problem with *Writing Under the Influence* as I'd already published biographies of two alcoholic novelists, Hemingway and Bukowski. I knew I could write these two chapters in my sleep.

The biography of Hemingway also involved studying the life of F. Scott Fitzgerald, another lush, so I was nearly three chapters into the book in my mind. I didn't think it would take too much work to write the other ones. I sourced the life of people like John Berryman, John Cheever, Eugene O'Neill, Raymond Carver and others and soon had the book done and dusted – or so I thought.

"What about women alcoholics?' my editor asked. He was right. Why should men have all the fun, guzzling as they wrote? I dived into the lives of Dorothy Parker, Anne Sexton and Edna St. Vincent Millay and had three more chapters done relatively quickly. Then my editor said, "What about African-American writers?"

By now I felt we were getting a bit tokenistic. I contemplated doing a chapter on James Baldwin but couldn't find much that was interesting about him. I felt the idea of putting in a black man (am I still allowed to say "black"?) just for the sake of it wouldn't make much sense if it turned out to be a dull chapter so we scrapped that idea.

I also wrote a book about the Oscar ceremonies. Most of the books I'd read on this theme focussed on the winners. I thought a more interesting slant would be the losers. The book was called, *And the Loser Is*

Sometimes I learned as I read into the subject, the winners even turned out to be losers in the sense that they became victims of what was called "The Oscar Curse." This had its most graphic manifestation in the case of Gig Young.

He won a Best Supporting Actor Oscar for *They Shoot Horses Don't They?* in 1969 and went on to shoot his wife and himself some years later. Could I make a connection between the two events? You're darn right I could.

I over-egged the omelette in the book, making out that the Academy got it wrong every year. That wouldn't have been possible. I felt if I let them off the hook I'd lose my theme but I lost it more by over-arguing it.

A reader pointed out some errors that were in it on a review he posted on Amazon, causing my editor to withdraw it from the shelves until they were corrected.

"This guy seems to know a lot about the Oscars," I said to him, "Why don't you employ him for the re-write?" He did that, which resulted in us working together. Better to have him inside the tent peeing out, as I think Lyndon Johnson once said of Edgar Hoover, than outside peeing in.

I didn't mind him correcting the typos but then he got cocky and started picking holes in my views on films. This was a step too far for me so I suggested he'd done his bit. It was now time for us to part.

He was a valuable asset for the reprint but as time went on I felt the old adage about putting a beggar on horseback applied. "Let him write his own book if he knows that much," was my attitude.

The publishers of the book told me they needed some endorsements from academics on the dust jacket to help make the book sell. These had to be high-ranking yokels from universities. I looked up my little black book where I had the details of a few people I'd used for a previous book. The usual suspects. An internet search threw up a few more.

I approached one man, a kind of writer for hire, and asked him if he'd say some nice things about my book.

"How much would it be worth to me?" he asked. Uh-oh. We were going down that road.

"Would $100 be okay?" I said.

He agreed grudgingly. His puff was okay but hardly over-the-top. I needed him to say I was God's gift to the writing cosmos whereas he only said I was adequate. Maybe I'd have to up the payment for the grand slam puff.

I then went to another person I knew, a university professor from one of America's more prestigious colleges. It turned out he was just after bringing out a book as well.

"I'll endorse your one if you endorse mine," he said. I was beginning to see how the process worked. Prostitution in only slightly more cultured form. You show me yours and I'll show you mine.

It got even worse. "I have an idea," he said, "that will make this easier for both of us. You write your endorsement and I'll write mine. Then we'll swap."

I was beginning to feel like Farley Granger in Alfred Hitchcock's *Strangers on a Train* where Robert Walker, a nutcase, offers to bump off an inconvenient woman in Granger's life if Granger does the honours for him with someone he himself wants to "rub out."

"Okay," I said. So I wrote that my book was the greatest one on the Oscar ceremonies that had ever been written (take a bow, Aubrey) and he did likewise for some Anglo-Irish thingie he was working on. I never read it.

My *piece de resistance* was to follow. I now went to a bigshot writer who'd done a biography of Steve McQueen. I felt a few words from him on how wonderful I was would really bump up sales.

"Have you quoted from my book in your book?' he asked.

"Er, no."

"Have you quoted from any biography of Steve?"

I said I had. He wanted to hear the quote. When I gave it, he said, "That quote is in my book too. If you give me as the source I'll give you your puff."

Oh brave new world that has such people in it.

Penniless Press

I started working for a British company called Penniless Press in 2019. It's run by the no-nonsense Ken Clay, one of the few people in publishing today who doesn't let the mechanics of the business get in the way of what he wants to do. Not for him the piranha fish, the real estate salesmen or the horse traders. Like Dennis Greig he sidesteps the middlemen paralysing the book trade. Instead he publishes people who probably wouldn't get their books on shelves otherwise – like me – and does so without any fuss at all. If you send him a manuscript he decides to publish he'll have it set in three minutes, or three minutes and twenty seconds on a slow day. The cover could take an extra five. Then he gets you an ISBN. number and puts it on Amazon (another 57 seconds).

He can. also create books from other books, a la Frankenstein. And he brings out a magazine every few months, *The Crazy Oik*, and also writes himself. So why isn't he the CEO of Sinclair-Stevenson or Weidenfeld & Nicolson? Probably for the same reason Ralph Nader never became president of America. He's simply not interested. When writing becomes a business, he feels, the fun goes out of it.

The Crazy Oik is probably the last magazine left in England where one can be politically incorrect without having to apologise for it. There was a time we mightn't have even noticed such rambunctiousness. Now it's almost obsolete due to our "woke" enlightenment. We should enjoy it while it lasts.

Ken has put up with all my fussiness over the years in the structure and pagination of my books. His tweaks on my covers often run into double figures. This is done without complaint as he realises I have a large dose of OCD to go with my ADHD.

Penniless Press gave me the motivation to go back to my childhood. When I left Ballina it became the last place on my mind. I was focussed on my future rather than my past. But then one day you wake up and realise what you lost, what you ignored. Why didn't I make more of my opportunities when I was growing up? Why didn't I listen to my father more? All those stories he told me when I was busy rushing out to meet someone. That someone meant nothing now, and my father was gone.

I tried to log into my memory banks and dredge up incidents, even trivial ones, to blacken pages. Stories became poems and poems became stories. It was all part of the one matrix.

I published a trilogy of short stories and poems with Penniless Press: *Ballina Stories and Poems*, *More Ballina Stories and Poems* and *Ballina and Beyond*. I also did three novels with them: *After This Our Exile*, *A Nursing Life* and *Sins of the Father*. *A Nursing Life* was narrated from the viewpoint of a woman.

I tried to get into her head in the same way as I'd tried to get into Elvis Presley's head for *The Elvis Diaries*. *Sins of the Father* was a re-write of *The Things That Were*. I tried to iron out all the mistakes I'd made in that book in the same way as I tried to fix the problems with *The Hunchback of East Hollywood* when I re-wrote it as *Bukowski*.

Ken Clay freed my hand up in a way no editor had done since Margot Davis. Ken is an editor who likes to give writers their head. He doesn't interfere with the way they write in the way another editor might, even – or especially – when they're being eccentric. It means you're being allowed to write without looking over your shoulder. That's often where the best stuff comes from.

I "Ballina-ised" the stories in the Penniless Press trilogy. There was no way I could have written fifty stories about my home town in the sixteen years I was there. Maybe I wrote some of them in my head in those years but I'd put precious little on paper before I came to Dublin. The themes were general but for the sake of, ahem, 'artistic unity' the word 'Ballina' appeared in all three titles in the trilogy. That gave them a shape.

It also gave them a target readership. When I asked the editor of the *Western People* if he'd be interested in me writing for him one time he said, "Only if you cover local themes." 'We're not much bothered about what happens east of the Shannon." John Healy once said, 'All news is local." This is what Paddy Kavanagh captures so graphically in his poems, the idea that Shancoduff is the centre of the universe as far as its residents are concerned. It's probably the same for every village in Ireland, if not the world.

A Nursing Life resembled many of my stories in what you

might call its 'Dick Whittington' theme, i.e. the heroine going from a country area to the "big smoke." I had that experience in life so it wasn't surprising that it would come out in my books. I mentioned the point about first novels being autobiographical. They write us rather than us writing them. I tried to diversify my style in the stories but over the longer length it proved to be impossible. I tried to create an anti-self by writing as a woman in *A Nursing Life* but an anti-self is still a kind of self.

Maybe it's like people who say they're anti-Catholic. The point is, anti-Catholic is still a kind of Catholic. You can be anti-Catholic, non-Catholic, a lapsed Catholic or any other kind of one but no Catholic, in my view, can be unCatholic. Because it's in our DNA. A Jesuit is supposed to have said once, "Give me a boy of seven and I'll have him for life." It's probably true.

Look at Joyce. He once said he had religion injected backwards into him but a backwards injection, similarly, is still an injection. That's why we see religion filling his books even if he took a reaction against it. The same is true of the presence of Ireland, which he also deserted, in his books. It's often been said that if Dublin was destroyed, it could be re-built using the pages of *Ulysses*. But Joyce couldn't live there.

It was the same with John McGahern. In the sixties he had to leave Ireland to write. He was different from Joyce in that he came back but they shared a disenchantment with Catholicism. Joyce was once asked if he'd become a Protestant. He replied, "I may have lost my faith but I haven't lost my reason." It was one of the kinder things he said about religion during his life.

Graham Greene is another writer whose books scream religion even when he's denouncing it. I learned that from an early age due to Padraic Loftus exposing us to *The Heart of the Matter* in Muredachs. It's infused with Catholic guilt. "Greeneland" is also infused with characters like the "whiskey priest" of *The Power and the Glory*. Greene, like Joyce and McGahern, used religion for his inspiration even when he was going through the dark night of the soul. One is reminded of Beckett's "The bastard – he doesn't exist!" reference to God in *Endgame*.

I killed off my Tortured Adolescent persona with *A Nursing*

Life. This had been a monkey on my back for as long as I could remember. (Even back to Junior Infants when I made those crayon scrawls?) I came down from my Olympian heights to where everyone else lived, and even have a bit of a laugh too, something that I used to regard as "infra dig" for writers. That didn't mean I had to be Bobo the Clown. It was all about balance.

Ken allows me run off some copies of my Penniless Press books with a printer I know in Dublin, Gerry Kelly. Gerry is keenly priced. That's probably why he works with many of the biggest publishing companies in the country. He also does a great job. I distribute the books to family and friends and also give some to the libraries and charity shops. It means they're at least being read and not costing me an arm and a leg to have them printed.

Even though most of the charity shops were grateful for the books I gave them, sometimes I felt I overdid it. No shop likes to have one author dominating their shelves. For years I did that with the Vincent de Paul. Then one day I saw they weren't stocking my books. The shelves became taken over with chicklit. There's nothing wrong with chicklit but every shop should have variety.

I used to bring big loads of books to the charity shops, mixing different titles and picking a range of shops scattered across the city. The gratitude of the people in these places was touching but the experience of carrying heavy loads had a price. I ended up with nerve pain from carrying them. It started with a shooting pain down my left arm on Christmas Eve a few years ago. What a time to think you're having heart problems. Mary suggested going to A&E but I didn't fancy having my Christmas dinner on a trolley. Instead we ferreted out this clinic that saw people 24/7.

They couldn't detect heart problems but suggested I see my GP in the new year. When I did that he diagnosed something call cervical neuritis. It was a neck problem that radiated down to my fingers. Eventually the pain in my arm went away but the feeling never came back to my fingers. It meant that I had to avoid my index finger anytime I was typing from then on.

Basil had a similar problem. He put his hand through a

BALLINA
STORIES & POEMS

AUBREY MALONE

window back in the sixties when he was in our cousin's house in Sandymount. It was the day John F. Kennedy was passing through town. Basil saw him in College Green, waving to him with a bandaged hand. He ended up having to type with his fourth finger. We were both like Kenneth Tynan, sticking our fourth fingers up in the air at the keyboard. I always liked the way Tynan held a cigarette between his fourth finger and his middle one.

Spending time in charity shops means you see a lot of remaindered books. Don't believe they're remaindered because they're bad any more than you should believe books are best sellers because they're good. Often it's the opposite.

I don't have a problem with anything I write being remaindered. A few years ago I got an email from History Press to say they were remaindering my book *To Hell with the Diet*. They said they had 111 copies left and were about to pulp them. If I wanted them, they said they could offer them to me at £1 each.

I wrote a cheque to them for that amount. When they arrived, I circulated them through the libraries and charity shops and even something called Legal Deposit. Every book printed is supposed to be lodged in this system. You bring the books in to TCD and they send them to various libraries in the UK A lot of writers don't bother doing this. I feel they're missing out. Books that are sent to libraries are there for perpetuity. What more could a writer want?

I didn't think *To Hell with the Diet* was anything special. It was just quotes about the joys of food. I didn't even make up the quotes. I didn't like it when my editor re-jigged them from the original A-Z format I'd used. It worked so well for me with *The Cynic's Dictionary*. She must have had her reasons. Why didn't the book sell better? I didn't mind that either. My policy was to just keep churning them out. If you threw enough dirt at a wall, some of it might stick. If it didn't, so what? "On to the next one" was always my policy.

To Hell with the Diet was inspired, for want of a better word, by a book I once saw called *How to Start Smoking*. I was struck by it as I'd seen dozens of books with titles like *How to Stop Smoking*. My original title for it was *How to Gain Weight*. I thought that might be a good corollary to all the ones with titles like *How to Lose Weight*. The publishers preferred the title we ended up with. That was okay, even if I'd have preferred the other one. Maybe it was my revenge on the publisher who wanted me to write the cookery book. (A recent book on the diet theme from Jimmy Carr had the best title of all in my view: "*Put it Down, Fattie.*")

Maybe all these attitudes of mine suggest I'm not a "real" writer. I was once reading a book when a letter fell out of it. It was a wacky one written by a man to a woman he'd been seeing years ago. He was now married to someone else but not happy with them.

The letter was written from a hotel in England with the letterhead of the hotel on the top of it. Presumably the man's wife was with him in the hotel room as he wrote it. He still carried a torch for his old girlfriend. You could practically see his tears on the page. I felt so sorry for him. I found his letter much more interesting than the book I was reading. Not very literary of me.

That was a second hand book I bought off Amazon. I much prefer second hand books to new ones. I even prefer the smell of them. It makes them more personal. If they've got notes down the margins, better again. But please spare me people who put their names on the inside covers of books as if to say, "Don't even think about stealing this." That's okay if you're under twelve.

I don't prefer second hand books to new ones because I'm a cheapskate. The point is, I like reading something with someone else's fingerprints on it. It gives it a live-in feel. And then there are all those messages scattered here there and everywhere by people who couldn't find a Basildon Bond close to hand and went for the first piece of paper they could lay their hands on.

Sometimes these missives – to friends, lovers, relations, even enemies – are almost as long as the books on which they're inscribed.

I saw this one on a coffee-tabler on Flower Arranging once: "I've dropped Scooter down to the vet. He howled all the way and near bit my foot off. Zip insists on accompanying me to the homoeopath – worse luck. Tell Dolly I got these cough mints and the serge top she's been pining for. I'll get onto you later about Gerry's gall bladder. What's the story on the budgie ? Or Norma's neck brace? I've decided to give Joe the bullet by the way. Myself and Dezzie are going on the trip to Tipp. 'Spect us when you see us. Ciao, Jackie." All human life is there.

Or how about this one I found in the Forward to a Kama Sutra paperback: "A few new positions for you, Da. Just remember the population explosion." Da sounds like quite a character, doesn't he? Not to mention son – or was it daughter?

In my years stravaging through second hand bookshops (and assiduously checking out the dust jackets) I've come across everything from rough drafts to divorce layers, *billets doux* to stormtossed lovers, heady threats to unreasonable bosses… and lonelyhearted replies to obscure dating agencies. People seem to have no shyness whatsoever about spreading their hearts across pages that will soon be discarded – eventually ending up in the hip pocket of some recession-hit bibliophile like myself in months or years to come.

Do people never think to rip these pages out after they're finished with them or is it all the result of some perverse need to confide the details of their personal lives to some (im)perfect stranger? And could the likes of Jeffrey Archer or Maeve Binchy or Deirdre Purcell or Rosalind Pilcher ever have foreseen the kind of things that would end up on any blank pages they've left at the beginnings or ends of their novels? Some of the latter are more interesting than what's in the books proper.

I'll never forget the one that said simply: "Hi, Dorothy. I'm just scribbling this on the way out to work. Make your own breakfast. There's sambos in the fridge. Don't on your life mention anything about what happened last night to Diana."

Another one I saw – in the Intro to the de luxe edition of *Oedipus Rex* – went: "To Mom: who will understand". Was this the real Oedipus, one wonders?

My favourite, which I recently found on the end of page 34 of a fifth-hand copy of Elmore Leonard's *52 Pick Up*, says: "When I got to the Opera House last night the bird had flown. What's up? I met Iggy at the docks and sorted him out. Is there   a problem at the Rotterdam end? You know the stuff is Grade A. Sammy's going to run with it if he can get clearance. I have to be out of

Dublin in three hours or it's curtains. If I don't hear from you before then the deal is off and Iggy takes a dive. It's up to you." It was signed "Fingers."

My conscience told me I should probably have turned this scrawl over to the Drugs Squad so the calligraphic experts, or even the forensic ones, could check it out. My problem was that I hated to leave a Leanard book unfinished and, at page 34, the action was just going to get heavy with the (anti)hero or whether he'd get enough "bottle" to take them on.

I went on a trip to Arklow after my first Penniless Press books came out. There were a few charity shops in the town so I decided to bring them in to them.

When the lady in the first one saw *After This Our Exile* she said, "That's from a prayer, isn't it?" I told her it was. She started giggling with delight. "I'm not as stupid as I look, you know," she said, causing another woman standing beside her to go, "And that's saying something." They continued to make smart comments which made me want to get out of the shop ASAP. Most people in charity shops were fine but sometimes you got ones that seemed to enjoy making fun of you or your book.

Some writers were sniffy about their books being in charity shops. My brother-in-law said to me one day, "I saw your book in a charity shop." It was almost as if he was embarrassed for me. I said, "I put it there!"

It didn't matter to me if someone with blue blood from Balmoral or Buckingham Palace was reading it or a hobo who couldn't afford the original list price and threw a quid across the counter of Oxfam. What was the difference? A reader was a reader. Charles Bukowski prided himself on the fact that he was the most read writer in prisons, and also the one who had most books stolen from libraries. I imagine he'd have gone down a bomb in the charity shops if they existed in his time. No doubt he'd have been a patron of them himself before he became famous if they did.

My father used to say of Hilaire Belloc, "His sins were scarlet but his books were read." If books weren't being read, what was the point of writing them? If they were gathering dust on book shelves, you might as well have them stacked in a corner in your garage. Many writers got remaindered copies from publishers or author copies from subsidy companies and don't know what to do with them.

Now and again someone knocks on the door of my house with a book in his hand and a rather pathetic look on his face. "Would you like to buy my book?" he says, adding something like "I lost my job."

I find it difficult to say no even if I know I'm not going to read it. It's not easy to throw yourself at the mercy of readers in this way. I wouldn't have the courage to do it anymore than I'd have the courage to operate a stall in College Green like Pat Ingoldsby does, or wherever else he hangs his hat these days. But it beats selling encyclopaedias that are written by someone else – something else out-of-work people have done over the years.

Revisiting my poems for Ken led me back to Dennis Greig. I hadn't published anything with him for some years. In fact I thought my last collection with him was going to be my last, period. But then Penniless Press happened. It revived an urge in me that gave rise to the book *Ballina Remembered*. This was my first experience of linking all the poems in a book with a theme.

None of them had been published, or even sent, anywhere else before they ended up in that book. I tried various poetry journals with my poems over the years without much success. I had the occasional one published but most of the others were sent back. Some were kept by editors until their "reading season" started. I was never the most patient of people so didn't relish the idea of someone spending six months sitting on a poem that may not have been longer than a page. Life is too short for that. I also found that poetry editors tended to go for "name names" in their publications. Already published ones got more exposure while unpublished ones were left to wither on the vine.

Dennis became ill just before *Ballina Remembered* was about to come out. He had a rare blood disorder that I couldn't even pronounce. It meant the book was going to be delayed. When he wasn't getting better I asked him if I could help with the editing.

He said I could. I then asked him if I could put some photos in it. Poetry books with photos were rare. Some would say they trivialised the book. I didn't care. Since they were autobiographical, the book lent itself to them being in it.

Dennis was also agreeable to the idea of Gerry Kelly running off some copies for my personal use. In that he was again like Ken Clay. In a sense I felt *Ballina Remembered* was like a Penniless Press book. At this time Ken was also looking at a snooker memoir I wrote, and some more quotation anthologies I wanted to put out. I didn't like swamping him with manuscripts (or depleting an already depleted stock of ISBNs) but he was as obliging as ever.

Denis did me a favour by getting sick as the delay in publication gave me time to write some more poems for the book. I was sorry for him of course but I put the time to good use. I often felt I submitted books to publishers too soon. When I was proofing them I saw so many things that needed to be changed I often infuriated them. They'd say, "Why didn't you fix that when you were writing the book?"

I never had an answer to that question. All I could say was, "Every time a writer sees a page in a different format, something new strikes him." It was always a relief to me when I parted with the text because I knew I'd be doing something with it forever if it was left in my hands. There was never a book of mine that came out to my satisfaction. No sooner was I presented with a copy than I'd gasp at something I hated. Maybe every writer feels the same. The day we get it right is the day we should give it all up.

I don't know where my poems come from. Kris Kristofferson has a nice term for how he writes his songs. He says they "occur" to him. Philip Larkin said he had no idea how he wrote his ones. It wasn't like "making a window frame or seducing women." I wouldn't have thought he'd have been particularly adept at either of these activities, though he seemed to have no difficulty getting so women.

What were they attracted to? His mind? His poetic genius? I've often thought these things were over-rated when it came to attraction. Women who said a man's mind was more important to them than how he looked usually ended up with men like George Clooney. The exception was Sophia Loren. Her husband Carlo Ponti was no oil painting but she stayed with him despite half the hot-blooded males on the planet lusting after her. Maybe that was it. She knew it was lust.

Someone once defined poetry as the process of dropping a rose petal into the Grand Canyon and expecting to hear an echo. I'll go along with that definition. I've written a few I like but don't expect to be asked onto *The South Bank Show* to talk about them. One reason for this is that *The South Bank Show* no longer exists. Another is that probably only about ten people in Britain know I do.

The success of poetry, like any other form of writing, depends on how you work at it. My UCD colleague Harry Clifton, like Philip Larkin, was capable of spending a year on a poem, or even a verse. I usually write mine in a few minutes. (You're welcome to say, "It shows.")

Harry used to submit his poetry to various journals before collecting them in book form. You can see the names of such journals in the frontispieces of his books. Most of, them I've never heard of. They were like the building bricks to his final construct. That's dedication.

The last Penniless Press book I did was *My Life in Snooker*, an account of my relationships with my three heroes of the baize: Alex Higgins, Jimmy White and Ronnie O'Sullivan. After I finished it I sent a copy to *Snooker Scene*, the game's flagship magazine. They'd given me some illustrations for it. The editor said he'd run a feature on it but I'd have to write it.

That was no problem. I asked him if I could put an email address in the piece that readers could contact to buy copies. He said that wouldn't be a problem either. I was relieved to hear this as the book trod on some corns. I mentioned, for instance, that Steve Davis had been unfaithful to his wife, and also that he'd been a hate figure of mine throughout his playing career. Considering the fact that he was "Mr Snooker" as far as the magazine was concerned, I didn't think this was going to go down too well.

I also passed criticisms of my three heroes, saying Alex was nuts, Jimmy had a mental block about winning the world championship and Ronnie often came out with comments that suggested he'd taken leave of his senses. It probably helped that I added that all three men were geniuses. And most geniuses were mad, right?

I've just finished Ken Clay's book *The Malletts*, a paean to his mother's family. They lived in and around Grappenhall in Warrington, an area that combines elements of Mancunian and Liverpudlian culture, the latter moreso. Co-written with his cousin Colin, it's a spellbinding read, calling up a world that's more or less gone now, a jolly old pre-Thatcherite Britain where everyone is a character of some sort.

Most of them indulge in the kind of slagging that I see as more Irish than British, or maybe that's just because Ken highlights that aspect of it, being an *aficion* of slagging himself. If people are on their high horses he pulls them down. Sometimes he pulls them down even if they aren't.

There are lots of hilarious anecdotes in the book, most notably one in which Ken flirts with the idea that he's not his nominal father's son. This is unlikely as he looks too much like him but it makes for a good story. (If facts conflict with the legend, as John Ford said, print the legend).

The book is so bedecked with illustrations it doubles as a kind of family album, replete with Ken's familiarly eccentric captions.

The most memorable character in it is his uncle Bill. He has an almost permanent glint in his eye. The others have lived-in faces which Ken, a keen photographer (as they say) captures well. He shows them in their Sunday best, on the road, spending a day at the beach or at 208 Manchester Road, the place where most of the book's "action" takes place.

The young men resemble those who would have been plucked from their jobs in the forties to go off and fight "jerry," the women like their curly-haired, long-frocked sweethearts whose 8x10 glossies they'd have sellotaped to their lockers at the front.

It's into this environment that Ken is born, a war baby looking bewildered by the turbulent world in front of him, as well he might. A few years later he's holding his mother's hand on the way to "the pictures." Cinemas were the "great escape" for all of us in all eras, war or no.

The book has a wingspan of 1920 to 1960 so we get to know

his cast of characters in all their weathers. Even after they've settled down with wives and families they still like to knock out a good time at "208."

There are wild parties, singing (without karaoke) and fun-loving folk generally conducting themselves likes anglicised versions of the Royal Tenenbaums.

Ken inks in the biographical details of these people with forensic efficiency. He's like someone from *www.ancestry.com*, telling us where they came from, what they did, how they lived and, often tragically, died. He mixes jokes with heartache as they negotiate their kiss-me-at-the-end-of-the-pier, paid-on-Friday-broke-on-Monday *zeitgeists*. They drift in and out of jobs by day and by night trip the light fantastic.

Most of the people in *The Malletts* are gone now. Ken in many ways is the last of the Mohicans. This makes him the ideal candidate to chronicle the multiple figaries of his lost Eden.

It should only be a matter of time before he. submits this manuscript to someone like his namesake Ken Loach – or Mike Leigh – to make a movie of it in a more hardscrabble way than those feelgood flicks Richard Curtis mainlines.

I'm seeing people like Celia Imrie and Emma Thompson as the main leads, or maybe Imelda Staunton and Maggie Smith, with Keira Knightley and Felicity Jones as their younger selves. For the men, maybe we could have Bill Nighy and Jim Broadbent. Dame Judi Dench is the granny telling them to keep the noise down.

And warning Bill to keep the ash off the bloody turkey.

Bill Mallett presents the Xmas turkey 1956 with his characteristic garnish of fag ash

Brando

I embarked on a biography of Marlon Brando in 2016. He'd been my favourite actor from the first time I saw him on screen. I can't remember when that was, or even what film he was in. I just knew that even when he was appearing in junk, and like most actors he was in a lot of junk, he made it compulsive viewing.

Hugo was the first person who talked about him in the family. Keith wasn't really into him. He preferred the traditional stars. That was probably understandable as he'd grown up watching them. Brando changed acting forever. I'm not sure Keith wanted that. It was as if it spelt the end of the Dream Factory. Maybe it goes back to why people go to films – to escape their problems or to see them amplified on a screen. Hugo and myself probably went for the latter.

Even if I can't remember the first film I saw Brando in, I remember the first film of his I remember coming to Ballina. It was *Southwest to Sonora*, which was showing for two nights in the Estoria. Hugo went to it both nights. When he came home on the first night I was in bed. I remember him coming up to my room and acting out some of the scenes. That was something Keith liked to do too in earlier years

Hugo was good at imitating Brando. He did the drawl and the slouch and the pause between sentences as he looked away from you - something Robert De Niro would go on to do as well. This isn't surprising as he's the closest thing to a successor to Brando as we got after Brando stopped caring about his films.

Hugo was particularly taken with the scene at the beginning of the film where Brando's horse is stolen by John Saxon's gang. He's drunk at the time and Saxon makes fun of him. When he sobers up he decides to go after Saxon to get the horse back. "That horse meant a lot of things to me," he says to the person he's staying with at the time. I still remember the way Hugo drawled that line.

Southwest to Sonora was made during Brando's fallow period in the sixties, a time when he was largely just doing dross. Many would say this was dross too, but it was Brando.

BRANDO – THE FUN SIDE

Aubrey Malone

He made a minor western into something special. A few years earlier Hugo saw another great film Brando made during his so-called fallow period, *Reflections in a Golden Eye*.

Brando's renaissance came a few years later. We all know about that. *The Godfather* made him bankable again and *Last Tango in Paris*, the film he made after that, continued his revival, as did *Apocalypse Now*. There wasn't much of note after that. When his son Christian shot the fiancé of his daughter he seemed to sink into a gloom that was only partially relieved by the cameos that characterised his later career.

In my book I decided to focus on his humour. All his other biographers emphasised "Moody Marlon" – a person we knew all too well. I felt there was another side to him from various anecdotes I'd heard over the years. He also showed his funny side in interviews. and in a few comedy films he'd made – though he would have been the first to admit he wasn't a particularly good comedy actor.

The more I researched my subject, the more I realised the humour wasn't just an aspect of his life, it was the over-riding factor in it. Almost from the cradle he was creating havoc with his pranks, and they went on for the next seven decades. I had my book.

For the next few months I searched high and low for more anecdotes. It was easy to go to the index of the bigger biographies and find, "Brando, Marlon, comic side." There was just a few pages in each. But one book led to another, and then another.

Before I knew where I was I had books by his secretary, his co-stars, his directors, he ex-wives, his friends, his architect, his lawyer, even the daughter of one of his dentists, who became someone he could goof off with in his later years. There were lots of people who knew him only marginally but who could testify to this side of him.

I often gave out about Amazon but I found these books at the flick of a button. Research that would have taken me months, even years, in the old days was done in a matter of weeks as my book grew into the size of a biography.

After finishing it I sent it to the usual round of publishers. One from Virginia seemed the most enthusiastic so I offered it to them. All went well for the first year. The editor, Sarah (not her real name) was all powered up about it and showered me with praise. She put me onto her proof reader, Suzie, and even the girl who handled orders, Deborah. Again these aren't the real names of the people. I've changed them because this is not a pretty story and if they happen to read the book I don't want to embarrass them.

I proofed the book with Suzie and gave her the names of a number of editors on both sides of the Atlantic that Deborah, hopefully, could send copies out to for review when the time came.

I left the book in their hands fully expecting it to come out with them. They seemed like a friendly company with lots of happy authors. They hadn't produced any film books to date – their main area was fiction – but they seemed delighted to be expanding their operation with my book, which they thought was both funny and original.

It was round about 2017 that things started to go pear-shaped. I emailed Sarah a few times to know if they were getting ready to publish the book but she didn't reply. I then rang her but just got her answering machine. I waited a few weeks and then emailed and rang again. By now I was starting to worry if there was a problem. Eventually she came back saying she was having a few staffing problems and also a few financial ones. I said that was fine. There was no rush on it.

I left her for another few months thinking everything was still fine. I was working on a few other books by now- I usually had a few on the go - and didn't think much about the Brando one. But as 2017 went into 2018 and there was still no word from Sarah, I started to become a bit concerned.

My calls to her now became more frequent but I kept getting the answering machine. Neither were my emails answered. I also had the email addresses of Suzie and Deborah but they weren't replying either. After a few months I got one from Deborah saying not to worry. "Sarah is very busy with other projects at the moment," she said. I said I'd appreciate it if she told me that herself. She said she'd ask her to.

I didn't know whether she did or not because the silence

continued right through 2018. Eventually I realised I had to do something so I contacted my union. I asked them to write her a letter. They did so but she didn't reply to it. I now started to think they'd given up on the book so I sent it to another publisher, a Spanish-American one that I'd had a previous film book out with.

This company said it was interested. I was sent a contract but didn't sign it. I told Virginia I'd sent the book to this other company. I wanted to make sure they weren't taking it as otherwise I would be in a situation I described as the literary equivalent of bigamy.

I started to think I needed to delve deeper into this company. When I did, I found there were many more disgruntled authors than me. A few of them hadn't been paid royalties, being continually fobbed off with excuses.

Some of the authors I got in touch with felt their books hadn't been presented properly. Others had books that were cancelled without any apparent reason, or delayed interminably like mine was. I was beginning to realise I wasn't the only one who'd been shafted.

One of the authors I contacted had employed a lawyer to deal with her case. I contacted her and asked her if she'd put me on to this lawyer.

She said, "Can you not get one of your own?" I said it was difficult because it would have to be an American one and I didn't know any of these. Another author I managed to contact was actually a religious minister. He said he was withdrawing his book from the company and going elsewhere with it.

I also contacted a woman running a society called Authors Beware. She said if we could all get together, maybe we could organise some kind of a heave against it. I didn't want to go that far. Despite all my frustrations, I just wanted to get my book out.

As we got into 2019 I started to think I'd sign with the Spanish people. Then out of the blue I got an email from Sarah again. She seemed to have this knack of knowing when I was thinking of moving from her. Did she want my book or not? Was she enjoying toying with me like a cat with a ball of wool?

She was as friendly as ever on the email, acting as if there was nothing at all unusual in all the delays. She explained that she'd had problems with staffing, money, health, you name it. "So what's happening about the book?" I said. "Don't worry," she said, "It will definitely come out. Sorry about all the problems."

Afterwards she went into another silence. By now I was expecting this. My emails and phone calls went unanswered, leading to me conducting all sorts of searches on websites to find out where she might be. There was no physical address for her company and none of her other colleagues, all extravagantly described on her website, had email addresses. At one stage I even found myself trying to track down the lawyer who co-signed the contract. By now the company was starting to remind me of Kayser Sosa in the film *The Usual Suspects,* a character who fools people into thinking he exists.

My brother Basil pre-ordered a copy. Both of us wondered if we'd ever see it. Sarah was keeping her hands so close to her chest it was a bit like the Third Secret of Fatima.

I got on to some of her other authors now. One of them told me not to worry. She'd had lunch with Sarah recently and in the course of it she told her she really enjoyed my book. She also put it as one of her "likes" on Goodreads, a book website.

My fears were allayed – for the moment. But then she went into a shell again. 2019 turned into all the other years: a promise, a silence, another promise, another silence. A book I'd started with such enthusiasm was turning into a drudge. What would Brando have done? Probably make her an offer she couldn't refuse, I thought.

Covid hit us in 2020. It derailed everything. Life stopped all over the world because of that damn Wuhan bat. Priorities changed. Formerly negligible things became suddenly important. We did ourselves up to put out the bins.

It became the highlight of the week. The publishing business became as beleaguered as every other one so once again I realised Brando was going to be put on the back burner. I put him out of my mind and tried to concentrate on my other books and the journalism I was doing.

In 2021, to my surprise, I heard from Sarah again. By now I was starting to think she'd fallen off the planet. It happened one night when I happened to ring Deborah's number on a whim.

Instead of Deborah answering, Sarah did. It was my first time hearing her voice "live." All the other times had been on her answerphone.

"I suppose you're wondering about your book," she said. "You could say that," I said. By now I had almost a casual attitude to it. Too much had happened. "Well don't worry," she said, "It's definitely coming out soon. Things are just chaotic at the moment." I felt like saying, "They seem to have been chaotic since 2016."

I then said, "When I rang the number I thought I would be talking to Deborah." "Deborah is off work," she said, "She's taking care of her partner." I asked her what was wrong with him.

She said he'd had a terrible accident. He was a lumberjack and he'd fallen from a branch he was cutting onto the roof of a house. Then the branch fell on top of him, doubling his injuries. I was shocked to hear all this.

"Don't worry," she said, "He's in good hands. I've brought my daughter up with the right values." "Deborah is your daughter?" I said.

She said, "Didn't you know?" I said, "How could I have? She always refers to you as Sarah." I now began to wonder why she hadn't called her 'Mom' in all the emails we'd exchanged over the years.

Sarah then told me there was a 'Go Fund Me' page for Deborah's partner. She directed me to it. The details on the page made the man's injuries sound horrific.

I felt I should contribute to the cost of his recovery so I said I'd send $100 to it as a goodwill gesture. It was only a paltry amount but she sounded very grateful for it. I then started to think Deborah's partner would need much more money than this.

I said, "What if I gave you $1,000 in exchange for some of the Brando books?"

She seemed very interested in this idea. "How many would you send me?" I asked.

She went quiet for a while. Then she said, "You would have to order the through the sales portal Deborah gave you. Your author code will ensure you qualify for a reduction."

She was referring to an ordering procedure I'd found difficult to negotiate. I'd pre-ordered my copy of the book through this, as had Basil and a few friends I'd directed to it, hoping the orders would get Sarah motivated to finally bring it out.

I didn't want to mix my offer for the injured lumberjack's recovery to be lumped in with this, especially when I knew I was going to have problems ordering more than one copy per time, and not knowing how the distribution worked in cases like this. Would the books all arrive one by one? Or would they not arrive at all? Imagine if I parted with $1,000 and had nothing to show for it?

I said, "I'd prefer if you just put a bunch of books in the post and sent them to me." "I can't do that," she said, "We have to do it through the portal." All of a sudden my $1,000 idea didn't sound like a good one to me. My momentary burst of goodwill had all the life sucked out of it by this administrative mechanism. I said, "Let's put all that aside for the moment. I could give you a percentage of my royalties for the fund instead. That might work better." I could see she wasn't pleased. "As you wish," she said. Then she went offline.

I didn't hear from her again until 2022. She said Suzie was working on the final proofs. All that remained was to put in the photos. My heart leaped.

It looked like the book was finally going to come out. I contacted Jerry Ohlingers, a company that had provided me with images for all my McFarland books in the past, and asked them if they had any of Brando.

They said they had as many as I wanted. I ordered twenty from them. They were only $15 each.

Ohlingers didn't carry permissions but neither McFarland nor Sarah's company seemed to have a problem with that. Small companies or scholarly ones didn't usually get pursued by the big guns on matters like this.

Suzie had also got some images from the New York Public library that were in the public domain, and I'd got permission to use an oil painting of a Brando image from *One Eyed Jacks* as well.

Everything was going swimmingly at last. Suzie had also managed to locate some images of the young Brando taken by a man called Carl Van Duchten which didn't require a permissions fee so the photo section was now complete.

The final text, with the photos in place, was sent to me online. "Just give it a last look through," Sarah said, "and we're away."

I don't like reading texts on a computer so I emailed a printer I knew to print out the text. An hour or so later he emailed me to say he had it done so I collected it from him.

It looked beautiful. I liked Sarah's lay-out and design. She also had all the photos spread strategically through the text at suitable intervals. And she'd done an Index. All I had to do was read it to see was there anything glaringly wrong.

I flipped through it looking for typos and saw a few. There were also some sentences that I thought were phrased poorly by me. A few others had been changed by Suzie. I wondered why. Some of the photos also bled into the text. I knew I needed to point out all those things and that this would take a while so I put it aside for moment, emailing Sarah to say I'd got it and that it looked great apart from a few editorial blips.

A visit to my sister's house in Cork beckoned in late 2022. She was having a number of the family down there for a get-together.

Clive came from Africa and my niece Joy from London. My cousin Colin, who lived in America as well, was also going to be there with his wife and children, as was Ruth's daughter Fiona. Basil was coming from America too but he'd got Covid and was delayed. June travelled with Joy from Dublin,

I went down with Mary, booking into an airbnb in Garryvoe, a beach town about twenty miles from my sister's house. When we got settled in we drove to it. Everyone was in great form. No sooner was I sitting down than they started asking me about the Brando book.

"It's finally corning out," I said. They were all overjoyed. For the first time in years I felt I could enjoy a holiday without the worry of its non-appearance hovering over me.

After I got back to Dublin I started reading the text and jotting down notes on it. There were a lot of things I thought

Issue 114 November - December 2021 **NOW** €3.50/£3.00

Senior *Times*

The magazine for people who don't act their age

The Brando legacy

50 years after The Godfather

ISSN 1649-2056

9 771649 205095   12>

Spry
FINANCE

needed to be done to make it right. I put all my observations on a Word document and sent it to Suzie, emphasising that they were all suggestions rather than demands. The document ran to forty pages. I was aware it was very detailed but I felt I wanted the book to be perfect after having waited so long for it to come out.

Another silence now began. Uh-oh, I thought, did they not like my comments?

I checked the website for the book. It had been on it for many years now. There was a nice description of it and a cover that had been re-designed since an original one from 2017. The posting said "Out soon!" and gave a description of its contents, basically saying that this was a book every Brando lover must read. The publication date was given as April 3, 2023. It would have been his 99th birthday.

December arrived. In the course of the month I made some more calls to Sarah. Again there were no answers from her. The new year began the same way. Yet still her website said of the book, "Out soon!" in big red letters. What was going on?

To try and calm my nerves I kept myself busy. That often helped in situations like this. I decided to look for some photos of Brando that might look well in the book as the photo section wasn't completed yet. I googled "Marlon Brando Photographs" and found a dozen that we could potentially use. I sent a few to Suzanne in separate emails as I didn't know how to put them in a file. There was no answer from her. Then I sent a few more. Still no reply. After I sent a third set she emailed me saying, "Stop sending me photographs. You're clogging up my 'In' tray. I've had to delete all of them. Don't send any more."

I said, "Have you looked at them?" She said, "They're not proper prints. You've pulled them down from the net." I said, "They're only examples. If you like them I can get higher res ones from Jerry Ohlinger. I'll pay for them." She repeated, "Don't send any more."

Her aggressive tone reminded me of something I'd forgotten from 2015 when I'd first submitted the manuscript. As I chronicled some of Brando's childhood misdemeanours, a sticky note appended to one of the margins said, "This writer is condoning juvenile delinquency."

almost fell off my seat laughing when I read it. It was Marlon Brando we were talking about, not someone on the Jeremy Kyle show. I wrote back, "These are just stories I'm recounting. That's what a biographer does. I'm not condoning or condemning anything." My message wasn't responded to and in time I forgot about it. Until now. Was it Suzie who'd put in the sticky note? Anything was possible.

We got to April. I remembered what Brando said about his marriage to Anna Kashfi: "I was born on April 3 but after I married Anna I felt it should have been April 1." She's pretended to be Indian to attract him – he liked Eurasian women – but she was actually born in Cardiff as Joanne O'Callaghan. Kashfi was Welsh? There must have been a bit of Ireland in there too. "She's as Irish as Paddy's pig," Brando gasped.

Now it was me who felt like the April Fool. The days crawled by... April 1, April 2 ...then suddenly we were at D Day. Or should I say B Day.

There was no sign of the book. I emailed Sarah to ask her what was happening. No reply. At least she was consistent. She'd been blanking me for seven years now with few exceptions. Why should she be any different now?

I finally had enough and told her I was taking the book from her. I demanded the reversion of rights. Again no reply. I went to the union. They sent her a letter confirming my position. An email I'd asked my union to send her five years before had failed to flush her out. Would this one? I wrote her a stern letter outlining my frustrations with her over the years, telling her she'd aged me with her endless vacillations and false promises. I told her I was now on my last nerve.

She went into one of her familiar silences over the next few weeks.

I couldn't understand why they would want to back out of the book at the eleventh hour. We'd all been through so much. Were they going to junk all their editing and proofing? How many hours of wasted time would that amount to? The fact that Suzie had done an index was even weirder. I knew how long indexes took. People were paid up to a grand to do them Some of the ones I'd done for McFarland almost took me a month.

Then I got another one of her oblique emails. She said her health was bad and that she was "out of pocket." I didn't know what to make of that. I knew she hadn't been well for years. She'd often talked about her various maladies even on her web postings. This sounded more serious.

I asked her if she was looking for money. I think she was but she didn't want to say so. "Out of pocket means out of sorts in this country," she said. That wasn't true. I looked it up.

I couldn't understand why she was saying this. Was she taunting me? Sometimes I felt she was more interested in playing games with me than she was in the book.

I said, "I'll have to go to him if you definitely wash your hands of it but you've put so much work into it, as I have, I think it's a pity to waste all that."

"You sound like you're dawdling now," she said, "What do you mean?" She was still toying with me.

I felt sorry for her, sorry for her and for myself. We were like two boxers tired of punching one another. I asked her if she was going to revert the rights of the book to me. She said, "Do you want me to?" I said, "No, but you've been dawdling so long I have to do something. You need to shit or get off the pot."

My vulgarity seemed to bring out an anger in her.

She said, "You seem to be bluffing. Why haven't you gone to this other publisher if they'll take it."

I said it was like a woman who's living with a man who doesn't love her. She wants him to stay with her but she knows the relationship is no good. I was starting to sound like a rejected lover from a bad soap opera.

She said, "I know you're a good guy but you've made some big mistakes with the book."

"Like what?" I asked.

"You criticised Suzie's proofing," she said.

I was wondering why she was so protective of her. Then a penny dropped. "Is Suzie another family member?" I asked.

"Suzie is my little sister," she told me.

All the pieces were starting to fall into place for me. I was dealing with a mini-Mafia. First Deborah and now Suzie. Seven years of emails to Suzie and she hadn't told me she was related to

310

Sarah any more than Deborah had.

I said I didn't mean to criticise Suzie. I was just fussy about editing. I always had been.

"Suzie has been proofing books for thirty years," she said, "and you come in and give out about the way she laid out the photographs." I said, "They were bleeding into the text." She said, "Do you not think we knew that?" I said I couldn't read people's minds. I just called things as I saw them.

"And then there was your fit of pique on April 3," she said.

"That was long overdue," I said, "Seven years to be exact."

"Your document was over forty pages," she said. I said I was sorry for the length but I wanted to get everything in. I repeated what I'd said already: "They were suggestions, not demands."

I asked her again if she was going to revert the rights to me. I was beginning to sound like Krapp's Last Tape by now. I didn't expect her to answer me but she did.

She said, "I'll send you the reversion of rights letter but you won't be allowed to use our settings or the photos we got from the New York Library." God forbid that she'd allow me a photo. I said I wasn't intending to.

"You'll send me the letter?" I said. I couldn't believe it. After so many months – years – of delays it was huge for me. I was really getting nothing after all those years but it felt like everything. Deprivation did that to you.

"Yes."

I breathed a sigh of relief. We were ending on a whimper rather than a bang. By now I'd almost forgotten about the book, forgotten about why I wrote it. My relationship with this woman had superseded everything.

I sent the book to the Spanish-American company that said they were interested in it four years previously. It was the year Sarah went missing, the first year I realised something was seriously wrong. They were my default publisher. A man called Lucien sent me a contract for it. I'd asked him if I would be getting an advance. He said they didn't do advances. "What about $100 as a goodwill gesture?" I said. He said okay. He wanted to send me the cheque but I said not to bother, that I had his word for it.

They came back to me fairly quickly.

Lucien had gone from the company now, they said, but they still wanted the book. There would, however, be some stipulations. The new editor wanted the names and email addresses of four experts in the film field who could review it favourably. I said "Lucien didn't mention anything about that." They said it was a new system now.

Suddenly I was sorry I hadn't asked Lucien to send me on the measly 100 bucks. It would have been some kind of guarantee. I still hadn't signed the contract. Now I was back in Maureen O'Hara territory, having to suss out some sycophants who'd tell me I was wonderful for a fee. Did I have the stomach to go through all that again? For a minute I thought I might have been better off helping Sarah not be "out of pocket." Maybe her message was a cry for help that I'd ruined with my "fit of pique."

They reviewed the manuscript and said, "We're confused. This is a funny book but we're a serious publisher." I said, "The name of it is *Brando – The Fun Side*." How could it not be funny? If it was serious it wouldn't be true to its title.''

They said they couldn't take it. I said I had a contract for it. They said that was irrelevant now.

Back to the drawing board. Brando had been a hero of mine all my life but now he'd turned into a nightmare. Was there ever going to be any end to it all? Should I not just take a match to the book and make a bonfire of it? It might have been the best thing for all of us.

To get my mind off him I started working on another book, one about the breakdown of the studio system. I got the idea one day when I was up in the attic and saw about a hundred books on the floor, all of them about Hollywood. Was there any connecting thread between them? I couldn't see one.

Then I thought: Why not be a Keith and write a book about Hollywood itself, about the way it changed from a mogul-based industry to an actor-centred one? I knew this was a theme close to his heart. Maybe his spirit could guide me from above.

I started writing and it began to take shape. After I had a few chapters done I sent it to McFarland. They wrote back saying they'd look at it and let me know. The tone sounded bored.

Thanks for nothing.

As I waited for them to come back to me I pitched the Brando idea to a few of my usual suspects in London, citing his forthcoming centenary as a selling point. They didn't reply. That wasn't surprising. Most publishers only replied to agented proposals. One or two said the centenary was too soon, that they needed two years minimum between receiving a proposal and getting a book on a shelf.

I didn't bother asking McFarland. They'd more or less poured cold water on the idea when I first mooted it to them years before.

Instead I sent it to a company called Bear Manor Media. Within 24 hours the editor came back to me with one word: "Deal!" I couldn't believe what I was seeing on my computer screen. Seven years of agony and now a one word acceptance after a day. To coin a phrase, it was an offer I couldn't refuse.

A few weeks after signing with Bear Manor I got an email from McFarland about my studio book. They said, "This looks like too big a project. We imagine it could run to many hundreds of pages. That would be too unmanageable for us." I said I was going to fast-forward through all the decades. They said that mightn't do justice to the theme. At the end of the email, the editor said in a P.S.: "What's happening with your Brando book, by the way? We might be more interested in looking at that." I said, 'You told me you weren't interested in it seven years ago." They said, "The temperature has changed now." I said, "It's too late. I've just signed with another company."

It was Murphy's Law. A feast or a famine. From no publisher to two within a month – after a seven year drought. Why hadn't I mentioned it to them after finally wresting it from Sarah? Probably because I didn't want to be a pest. Now I knew I wouldn't have been one. Things changed in publishing like they did in every aspect of life. It was important to keep your options open. If I'd asked them about it I could have kept Bear Manor for my studio book. Then I'd have had everything placed.

By now I was beginning to feel like Mrs Bennett from Jane Austen, trying to get all my daughters married off. People often said my books were like children to me. Not having "real" children, I suspected they were right. "The only difference," I used to reply, "is that you don't have to get up in the middle of the night to tend to them." (Well not often anyway). In such a scenario, publishers became like orphanages. But to pursue the analogy, so many of my babies had been aborted over the years. Was the studio book going to be another one?

I couldn't think straight anymore. Too many books and too many headaches. I put the typewriter away and tried to get my mind off everything. After a few days, for the lack of anything better to do, I looked up the website of the Virginia company to see if they'd taken Brando off their list. They had, but beside where it used to be I saw a notice saying, "We're not looking at submissions at the moment. The editor is unwell."

We were all suffering. That posting made me lose my anger at Sarah. What did books matter when one's health was at stake? I started to think of Anthony Burgess of all people. I'd stood beside Burgess years before at a function. He was talking about Salman Rushdie. "Rushdie knew what he was doing with *The Satanic Verses*," he said to the people he was talking to, "I have no sympathy for him at all about the fatwa."

Burgess, I learned later, was a workaholic. His widow Liana told Erica Jong that writing killed him. She advised Jong's husband Ken to stop Jong going the same way. Ken said, "I couldn't stop her from writing even if I wanted to." Mary felt the same about me. Liana said to Ken, "Life is more important than writing."

I certainly found myself agreeing with that after the Brando experience. But it was good to have another book out with Bear Manor.

I'd had two others published with this company before Brando, one on *Shane*, the film we all loved in Ballina, and another on *The Misfits*. Most of my film books were on actors but I'd done two little ones on Michael Collins and *Ryan's Daughter* back in the nineties. The Bear Manor books were much more detailed.

Ben Ohmart is the editor. He reminds me of Ken Clay in some ways. Both of them are in publishing for the love of it and both produce many titles. Hardly a week goes by but Ben sends me an email of a new crop of books. He's like a bottomless well.

I'd been putting ideas to him for about ten years before he took *Shane* on. My approach was always too academic for him before that.

He's more interested in the inside track of films than a discursive study of them. I didn't have access to family histories of stars and that ruled me out to a large extent with him. *Shane* was different because I got information about the making of it from a CD-ROM made by a man called Walt Farmer. Walt had died in 2002 but I managed to track down his widow, Kay, who sent it to me. It had all sorts of information about what went on in 1951 in Jackson, Wyoming when it was being made there. (It wasn't released until two years later).

The CD also had loads of photos, credited to a woman who was also called Kay. I got in touch with her after getting her details from the Jackson police station. They were slow to give me her details at first because of data protection but a police officer there had previously worked in the library and she was sympathetic to my query. She put me in touch with Kay, who lived in California.

I expected her to be a much older woman if she'd been on the set of a 1951 film. Instead I heard a young voice when I rang her. "You must have been in nappies when you took the photos," I said. She said she hadn't been on the set. Rather that she'd bought the photos from Walt. When I asked her if I could buy them from her she said, "I'm afraid I don't own them anymore. I sold them." Suddenly things were beginning to look like the Brando book all over again. But Kay told me she was good friends with the person she sold them to and she didn't think there'd be a problem with me using them.

That turned out to be the case. The other woman, who lived close to her in California, loved Ireland and liked the idea behind my book. She was a writer herself and had actually written a novel set in Ireland. Her husband, a retired accountant, had also written a book, a tourist guide to Ireland and Scotland emphasising the Celtic connection between the two countries. Suddenly everything was beginning to come together. The other woman gave me permission to use the photos and didn't even charge me for them.

315

The Misfits

The Film
That Ended a
Marriage

Shane was different because I got information about the making of it from a CD-ROM made by a man called Walt Farmer. Walt had died in 2002 but I managed to track down his widow, Kay, who sent it to me. It had all sorts of information about what went on in 1951 in Jackson, Wyoming when it was being made there. (It wasn't released until two years later).

The CD also had loads of photos, credited to a woman who was also called Kay. I got in touch with her after getting her details from the Jackson police station. They were slow to give me her details at first because of data protection but a police officer there had previously worked in the library and she was sympathetic to my query. She put me in touch with Kay, who lived in California.

I expected her to be a much older woman if she'd been on the set of a 1951 film. Instead I heard a young voice when I rang her. "You must have been in nappies when you took the photos," I said. She said she hadn't been on the set. Rather that she'd bought the photos from Walt. When I asked her if I could buy them from her she said, "I'm afraid I don't own them anymore. I sold them." Suddenly things were beginning to look like the Brando book all over again. But Kay told me she was good friends with the person she sold them to and she didn't think there'd be a problem with me using them.

That turned out to be the case. The other woman, who lived close to her in California, loved Ireland and liked the idea behind my book. She was a writer herself and had actually written a novel set in Ireland. Her husband, a retired accountant, had also written a book, a tourist guide to Ireland and Scotland emphasising the Celtic connection between the two countries. Suddenly everything was beginning to come together. The other woman gave me permission to use the photos and didn't even charge me for them.

The book I wrote for Bear Manor on *The Misfits* was equally interesting for me. I set it against the backdrop of the crumbling marriage between Marilyn Monroe, who of course had the lead role in it, and Arthur Miller, who wrote the script. Marilyn had been fed up of playing 'dumb blonde' roles at this point and asked Miller to write a serious role for her.

He did that, but in the process leaked many details of her marriage to the public, which annoyed her more than if he'd written a 'bubblehead' role for her. The film was the last straw in an already fraught relationship.

In the course of my research for the book I bought a book on the making of the film. Imagine my surprise when, on getting to page 181 I read these words: "Mary Malone, the Hollywood correspondent of the *London Daily Mirror*, offered a member of the crew a case of champagne if he called her if anything happened on the set, not specifying what that might be. The crew member asked her if that was all that was on offer. Malone replied, 'Well I might be able to promise you something else if it's really good."

This was my cousin talking – Paddy Dillon-Malone's sister and Uncle Louis' daughter. It was a small world, to be sure.

But I still wouldn't like to have to paint it.

Burn Out

I eventually burned myself out at writing just like I did at teaching. One day I even thought that I couldn't breathe, that the walls were coming in on top of me. My head was a jumble of facts. I felt like someone coming off stage in a rock concert, their head buzzing with the cheers of the audience.

How was I going to wind down? People said, "You have to take breaks" but even on breaks I was thinking of what I was going to do when they finished. I couldn't even relax on holidays. Often I brought my typewriter with me. I was nearly capable of bringing it to the beach. Mary told me her boss in O'Connors never took holidays, that he was a workaholic. Madonna once said, "Holidays are only for people who don't like their jobs." I liked my job but it didn't like me. You could have too much of a good thing.

Things eventually got to a stage where I felt my health was suffering. If I was in the middle of a chapter of something I was doing and felt a bug coming on, I wasn't capable of stopping until I felt better. I kept myself going on black coffee and high calorie chocolate. They gave me temporary bursts of energy but afterwards I'd be drained. I worked hard for short periods but then had to do nothing when my batteries ran out. I'd write notes to myself that piled up, waiting for the time I'd be able to transfer them onto the typewriter.

When I reached rock bottom I got to hate going in to the office. I knew it was going to tempt me back into doing things. I asked Mary to hide the keys of it from me once. I got to hate the books, the typewriter, the reams of paper looking up at me pleadingly as they waited to be filled.

I knew I needed to get away from the weirdness of so many of the people I was reading about and back to straightforward ones like *Michael Collins*. Writing a book meant you had to get involved in these lives but if you got too involved you became like a Method actor who couldn't go back to his real identity once the cameras stopped rolling. Why did I have to throw myself so much into what I was doing? It was the way I'd been at the courier work too. When I was doing that I tried to convince myself that the secret of eternal life lay in side every packet I was asked to deliver. It was a way of trying to give significance to a soul-destroying job, of pretending it was important when I knew it wasn't, or that I was the only person who could do it.

The point was that, with or without me, the packages would be delivered, With or without me the children I used to teach would have been educated. And with or without me, books would also be written, written probably much better by other people than by me.

It took me years to realise that. When I was doing my Tony Curtis book I told myself that this was going to be the definitive biography of him.

Likewise with Hemingway and Bukowski. Otherwise why do them? A girl I used to act with in Delta-K, the drama group I joined in the late seventies, said to me one day, "You're the most intense person I ever met." That might have been okay if we were doing Strindberg or Anouilh but we weren't. We were doing Lennox Robinson.

I bought books I didn't read. It was a kind of compulsion in me. Mary said she often bought clothes she didn't want. She called it "retail therapy." The main buzz she got was walking in the door of the shop knowing she was going to come out with something nice. Strength of character was taking the item of clothing from the rack and then putting it back. I couldn't do that with the books.

I bought them with the best intentions of reading them but they always looked better on the shelves of the shops rather than in my library. Once I possessed them I lost interest in them. The thrill was in the chase.

Clutter in the attic built up. The shelves in my library were stacked so tight, every time I bought a book I felt I'd have to throw another one out to make room for it. I felt I was in some kind of exchange programme.

I walked up and down among the shelves saying to myself, "Which book have I not looked at recently?" I was like that with clothes too, keeping things I hadn't worn in decades. Mary told me to throw out anything I hadn't worn in the last year.

MICHAEL COLLINS

A Neil Jordan Film

Ireland's
buccaneering hero
hits the screen

By Aubrey Dillon-Malone

For some reason I wasn't able to do that. Maybe it went back to a childhood sense of thrift, to my mother telling me to finish everything that was on my plate at meal-times. She felt constrained to do that with nine mouths to feed and only a limited amount of money coming in from my father

Cluttermania ran right through my family. Ruth had it with clothes too. Keith piled up film books. His library kept growing as he researched his screenwriter book. I'd run into him sometimes in dusty arcades as he sought out obscure biographies of people I'd never heard of. In another section of the same arcade I might find an 18th century novel from some French dilettante and add it to my collection.

Eventually the shelves "burned out" too. I had to shift some of the books up to the attic. I didn't have shelves up there so they were just stuffed into boxes.

That too became full over the years. I found myself tripping over the boxes every time I went up there. What was next, I wondered. Would I have to put them under the floorboards? Or on the roof? It seemed like the last frontier.

I wrote a biography of the director Sidney Lumet, the first to be done. It was my first Hollywood book that wasn't about a star or a theme. Unfortunately, in the same week, another writer, Maura Spiegel, came out with another biography of Lumet. What were the chances of that happening? I felt I was poxed. So much of writing was about timing.

The Lumet book was done for McFarland. Would I have better luck with an Irish publisher? In the *Writer's Yearbook* I noticed the name of a new company, Maverick House. I rang them to ask if they were interested in film books. Jason O'Toole, the editor, said to me, "Crime is where it's at now, Aubrey. You should try that."

After I put down the phone I looked up the Maverick catalogue. I found it frightening to see the number of books they had on the subject. Crime had become a genre all to itself in our island of Saints and Scholars. In the bookshops you found it in the Real Life section, not the Fiction one.

People like Paul Williams of the *Sunday World* were as busy as the chicklit writers who seemed to define the previous era. In bookshops there was blood and guts on one side and sex and Sangria on the other.

When a drug baron was shot in the head down the road from where I lived, the man in the local hardware shop said to me, "It's getting closer." His words chilled me.

One of the biggest hits in RTÉ's recent history was a series about Dublin's drug 'culture' (a term I despise) called *Love/Hate*. Mary said to me, "Why wouldn't you try writing something like that?" Not only would I not have wanted to write it, I couldn't even watch it.

"That sort of thing is going on outside our door," I said, "They should be making documentaries about it, not something that purports to be fiction." Newspapers gave drug barons cuddly names which seemed to normalise what they were doing. In years to come we'd witness bodies being chopped up, which reminded me of some of the gorier films I'd seen about Mafia crime in the U.S.

The biggest growth area in book sales at this time was "True Crime." It meant people were gobbling up stories about people wiping one another out a few hundred yards up the road from us. I found it boring.

There was a certain kind of romance in reading about Jesse James or Bonnie and Clyde but the thuggery of the drug world had no romance in it, just brutality. I knew people had to write about it as it was news just as much as any other kind of crime was but some of the reporters – not all of them men – seemed to me to be actually getting off on it.

Veronica Guerin had died in the attempt to "out" these people. Some other reporters after her time also got death threats but it seemed to me that most of them were more intent on reporting crime than trying to erase it. I didn't see that as a justifiable "career."

Books about "The Missings" – people who'd been presumed to be murdered but who were never found - was another huge area in the True Crime genre. It was something else I could never get into.

I understood the need for grieving relatives to have closure on the disappearance of their loved ones but 99% of searches for these people tended to turn up blank Why did they persist in carrying them out on half-baked confessions from killers? In time "The Missings" became household names – Annie McCarrick, Jo Jo Dullard and many others.

They weren't just in Ireland. Hardly a week went by but I saw some article on the kidnapped toddler Madeline McCann. Many of these subsequently turned into books. Editors knew her image sold papers. There was a feeding frenzy around her that ran the risk of turning into voyeurism.

It can't have done any good to her parents any more than the stream of articles of people like Ian Huntley and Maxine Carr did for the parents of Jessica Chapman and Holly Wells, the two young girls who were murdered in such a grisly manner in Soham in 2002. There were murders committed in every country every day of the week but only some became iconic. In the same week as "Maddie" was kidnapped, so were other children not far from where she was taken in Portugal. Did they not deserve mention too? At times it seemed to be only children of the well-to-do were mourned.

Something similar happened with Peter Sutcliffe, the Yorkshire Ripper. I recently read a book about Sutcliffe. It emphasised one thing: It was only when he started murdering "innocent" girls (i.e. non-prostitutes) that the hunt for him was stepped up.

Another book I read at this time was one co-written by Tony McCullagh and Neil Featherstonehaugh called *They Never Came Home*. It was about the fire in the Stardust ballroom in Artane in 1982. It took Ireland 42 years to get justice for the 48 people who died that night. Why? Most likely because they were working class. I saw the smoke coming from the building on the night. It continues to haunt me.

I now live in Artane myself. The people around here are down-to-earth and genuine. Few enough of them are affluent. Was this the "crime" of the 48 victims of the Stardust fire?

McCullagh made this point on a recent documentary about the tragedy that came in the wake of a landmark decision to finally record the deaths as being "unlawful killings" rather than the result of arson.

This was a new book that will set the record straight on such matters rather than another one telling me about scumbags cutting up body parts and becoming near-celebrities as a result.

In 2020 I wrote a book about homosexuality in films called *Queer Cinema*. It was a difficult book to write, not because of the subject but rather the arch tone I was asked to adopt. Films can be serious and so can sexuality but both can also be funny. I wanted to explore that aspect of the subject but from early on in the editing process I was led away from this. To give a small example, I wanted to put a joke in the book, a comment Conan O'Brien made about the relationship between Anne Heche and Ellen De Generes: "They're talking about having a baby. I hope it comes out quicker than Anne." (Heche had been in the closet for years before embarking on the relationship with De Generes.)

There was no way my editor would agree to what she called an "offensive" joke like this in such a "profound" book. I sympathised with her about the terrible treatment gay people had undergone throughout the ages. Indeed, a lot of the book was about that very subject. But at a certain point I feel it's important to take your foot off the didactic pedal and just tell stories. I'd done this in my book *Censoring Hollywood* for McFarland.

As our relationship went on, the difference between our attitudes grew bigger and bigger. It even got to the stage where she accused me of homophobia. This was after I told her another joke: "Forty years ago homosexuality was condemned. Thirty years ago it was discouraged. Twenty years ago it was tolerated. Ten years ago it was encouraged. I'm getting out before it becomes compulsory." Some gay people I knew laughed at this. She didn't. I knew we'd have problems working together as the book went on so I was mightily relieved when she was later replaced with another editor.

Strict controls were also placed upon the language I was required to use. I wanted to refer to "people of colour" as blacks but was told I had to use the term "African-American." This despite the fact that I knew many people "of colour" who preferred to be called black.

CENSORING HOLLYWOOD

Sex and Violence in
Film and on the
Cutting Room
Floor

AUBREY
MALONE

I wanted to explore that aspect of the subject but from early on in the editing process I was led away from this. To give a small example, I wanted to put a joke in the book, a comment Conan O'Brien made about the relationship between Anne Heche and Ellen De Generes: "They're talking about having a baby. I hope it comes out quicker than Anne." (Heche had been in the closet for years before embarking on the relationship with De Generes.)

There was no way my editor would agree to what she called an "offensive" joke like this in such a "profound" book. I sympathised with her about the terrible treatment gay people had undergone throughout the ages. Indeed, a lot of the book was about that very subject. But at a certain point I feel it's important to take your foot off the didactic pedal and just tell stories. I'd done this in my book *Censoring Hollywood* for McFarland.

As our relationship went on, the difference between our attitudes grew bigger and bigger. It even got to the stage where she accused me of homophobia. This was after I told her another joke: "Forty years ago homosexuality was condemned. Thirty years ago it was discouraged. Twenty years ago it was tolerated. Ten years ago it was encouraged. I'm getting out before it becomes compulsory." Some gay people I knew laughed at this. She didn't. I knew we'd have problems working together as the book went on so I was mightily relieved when she was later replaced with another editor.

Strict controls were also placed upon the language I was required to use. I wanted to refer to "people of colour" as blacks but was told I had to use the term "African-American." This despite the fact that I knew many people "of colour" who preferred to be called black.

I remembered an experience I'd had in the Mater hospital in the 1980s when I happened to say to a surgeon "The black doctor saw me yesterday." He put on a look of horror and said, "You can't use terms like that. You have to say negro." He was a brilliant surgeon but behind the times in terms of linguistics. I knew that "negro" had been jettisoned in favour of "black" hut he hadn't.

Using the "right" terminology was apparent even in the title. When I mentioned to my editor that "Queer" was a pejorative term for gay people when I was young, she snapped at me, "Well it isn't now." That was before she was replaced. The famous Irish gay man Mícheál Mac Liammóir said in the 1960s that he preferred to be called queer than homosexual. He was in the minority at that time.

By 2020, however, all that had changed. Would we ever go back to our "old" vocabulary? That was in the lap of the gods. I didn't care greatly either way. Words were just words. I was more concerned about actions. We could be politically correct, or "woke" (the new term for that) in words until they came out our ears but this didn't seem to impact on people's actions. "Queer-bashing" was still going on, as was the murder of blacks - sorry, African-Americans.

Nobody seemed to be too perturbed about this as long as we called them by their right names. I was reminded of Rex Harrison saying in *My Fair Lady*, "The French don't care what they do as long as they pronounce it properly."

There were no photographs in *Queer Cinema*. I thought that was a bad mistake. A film book without photos for me was the ultimate no-no. Philistine that I am, it's always the first thing I look for in such a book when I'm browsing in a bookshop. When I asked the editor why she wasn't putting them in – she'd promised she would when I signed the contract – she said, "Most people know what the people you're writing about look like anyway." I thought that was classic. If one pursued her logic, no film book since the turn of the century needed photos.

How had publishers been so silly up until this? Everyone knew what Charlie Chaplin looked like, and Al Jolson and Lillian Gish and Mary Pickford and Greta Garbo and Mabel Normand. Why should we patronise readers by reminding them?

After I finished *Queer Cinema* I had another drink with the publisher who'd asked me to do the cookery book. Was he still interested in one, I asked, not because I wanted to do one but to see what he'd say.

Things had changed now, he told me as he supped his Guinness. (Thankfully he'd gotten off the Bailey's). He told me his publishing "arm" was focussing on YA now. "What's that?" I said. "Young Adult," he chirped.

He said he was "theoretically" interested in dark apocalyptic stuff like *The Hunger Games*. On the "soft" side, would I be interested in trying a "neo Mills & Boon" book? "Come again?" I said. He said, "Schmaltz with a bit of how's-your-father."

There was also an opening for biographies of musical celebs who were getting on in years. "Legendary figures," he said, by which I deduced he meant over-the-hill crooners with a foot in the grave.

In the following weeks I sussed out a few he mentioned to me. Sadly, I discovered nothing even vaguely interesting had happened in their lives. A lot of them weren't just over the hill; they were never on it in the first place, having voices that just barely cut it on the chicken-and-chips circuit during the showband boom, and then only because most of the people listening to them were ossified.

Would I consider that? I imagined myself approaching some fossil as a "writer for hire" and having them look at me with an expression that said, "This guy is so desperate for work he's even willing to break bread with me to try and put flesh on the bones of my dismal life."

"Maybe you'd have a go at it," he urged. If I could find that his subject had been sexually abused in his youth, that would be a bonus. "Most books have those kinds of chapters now," he beamed. It could be a draw. Or maybe the guy thought he was gay at one stage of his life. Or flirted with cocaine after his first marriage collapsed. Or declared bankruptcy after the manager who'd been godfather to his kids hared off to Andalusia with nine-tenths of his earnings over the years.

There was always some "story behind the story" with these people, he suggested. If there wasn't, maybe I could make one up. I said, "Is this meant to be fiction or a biography?" He said, "You're the writer. You decide."

In an attempt to find something slightly more attractive than such an admittedly fascinating enterprise I came up with the idea of doing a biography of John McGahern. I'd interviewed him in 1989.

His letters had just come out. These gave me the infrastructure for the book. I also found cuttings about him that

I'd taken from newspapers over the years. I found these totally by accident one day. I must have conceived the idea of a biography years before and then forgot about it.

I had my 1990 interview with him on a cassette tape but it got snagged up in the machine when I tried to play it. How could I have expected anything different from a tape that was over thirty years old?

A company on Burgh Quay managed to stick it together and convert it to a CD for me. The noise behind us in the pub made it almost impossible for me to hear what McGahern was saying unless I turned it up to a near deafening level but it was still like gold dust for me to give my book something other biographies wouldn't have.

I called it *Leitrim Observed*. It was cheeky of me to do it as I'm not in any way a part of the McGahern "industry." Neither was I particularly well acquainted with him. I only met him twice and though we kept in touch by phone and post, there were many more people who, I felt, were more qualified to write his biography.

A man called Denis Sampson made two stabs at it but one was overly academic and the other only covered his early years. If nothing else I felt I was filling a gap.

I wanted to do the book because so far there was no full length biography published on him to date. I liked being first at something. I wrote the first Jimmy White biography, the first Maureen O'Hara one, and the first Sidney Lumet one too. But I didn't feel comfortable writing it.

The people who do biographies of writers either know their subject well or have lectured about them or have an "in" with a publisher. All I had was the fact that I liked his books and had a passing acquaintance with him over the years. That meant it was going to be a hard sell - - especially when I heard Faber were planning an official biography of him soon.

Clearly this was going to blow me out of the water when it was published. I was left with a relatively short window of opportunity to make sales.

My main chance, I thought, was in Leitrim, where he lived for most of his life, but I met with resistance here from the loyal cohort of his friends and fans who seemed to be waiting for the "real" biography to come out. It was going to be written by Frank Shovlin, the man who edited his letters, and have the collaboration of McGahern's widow Madeline.

Just my luck. It was like what happened with my Lumet biography some years before. There always seemed to be a faster gun over the ridge whenever I tackled a "big" subject – with infinitely more resources at their disposal.

The *Leitrim Observer* blanked any overture I made to them regarding a feature about my book or a review of it. Likewise the John McGahern Museum.

Even the people who'd helped me with illustrations seemed to cool towards me when the book came out. Had someone got to them? Surely Ireland had advanced beyond the days when it was a valley of squinting windows. Were there not enough slices in the cake for both of us?

The editor wanted me to do a launch for the book and also a signing and a podcast. I was expected to organise all these. I'd have had a problem doing them even if he organised them.

When he asked me to do them I said, "Do you have any more jokes?"

I put a lot of effort into getting the book reviewed. I also emailed practically every library and bookshop in the country asking them if they'd stock it. The uptake on "cold calls" like this is generally small and so it proved here. They work better if they come from the editor. Otherwise it looks like a self-published book.

The last book I wrote was a revamp of my 1999 biography of Hemingway. I wanted to do this as I felt I'd learned a lot about writing since that year. And also a lot about Hemingway.

Ken Clay created a Word document from that book so I could edit it. It was written long before I had Word so I'd have had to start from scratch if it wasn't for Ken's mastery. He tore out each page individually from the book and then scanned it. I'd have eaten it first.

I was glad to have the opportunity to correct the flaws from the original book. I'd done something similar in turning *The Hunchback of East Hollywood* into *Bukowski*. Not everyone gets the chance to write a book twice. I hoped I'd gotten it right the second time. There was also a lot of over-writing in the original book that I tried to remedy by adopting a low key Hemingway tone.

In the 24 year interim between the two books, a lot of information had come out on him. A writer called Bernice Kert had been one of the few women to write major books on him before 1999.

I used her book as research for my original book. For the new one I drew on other women who'd written books on him. The fact that women writers had joined the biographical fold was good news for all of us. For too long Hemingway had been seen solely as a "man's writer." That was a pity.

There was more to him than big game hunting and corridas.

Time's Winged Chariot

Cher said recently that she felt "older than dirt." Sometimes I do too. Is it time to retire? To pack the typewriter away and go back to "real life" -whatever that is? Hemingway said, "A writer never retires" but look what happened to him. Maybe he should have. Writer's block killed him just as much as all the accidents he had, or all the shock treatments.

It's hard to write "The End" on the last page of a book even if it's not for the last time.

People say to me, "You're lucky to have found something you're passionate about." I wish I could agree. Most days I have to nearly bribe myself to turn on the typewriter even to write a sentence.

Every book both fulfils and destroys something in you. Oscar Wilde said, "Each man kills the thing he loves." I couldn't watch Jimmy White playing snooker after writing my biography of him. The same thing applied to looking at Tony Curtis films after my book on him came out. I didn't find it so much with Hemingway or Elvis, maybe because these people were so, complicated. Material about them is like a bottomless well.

The thing about washing my hands of someone didn't apply to Ronnie O'Sullivan either after I wrote *My Life in Snooker*. That's probably because he was only a part of it. Why did it apply to Jimmy and Tony? I don't know. Maybe when you've put every thought you ever had about a person down on paper it's almost like you've commodified them. Watching them do what they do afterwards somehow seems like *Groundhog Day*. Will the same thing happen with Brando? I hope not. If it does, it might be time to give it all up. My heroes are dwindling with each passing tome.

Why did, I destroy so many of them by putting them into the boxes books necessitate? Why couldn't I be more like John McGahern or Philip Larkin or Harry, bringing out just one a year, or even less than that. It might get me more respect from people – or from myself.

Someone said that poems were never finished, merely abandoned. I feel like that about many of my books. I ended them not when I should have but when I got an idea for other ones.

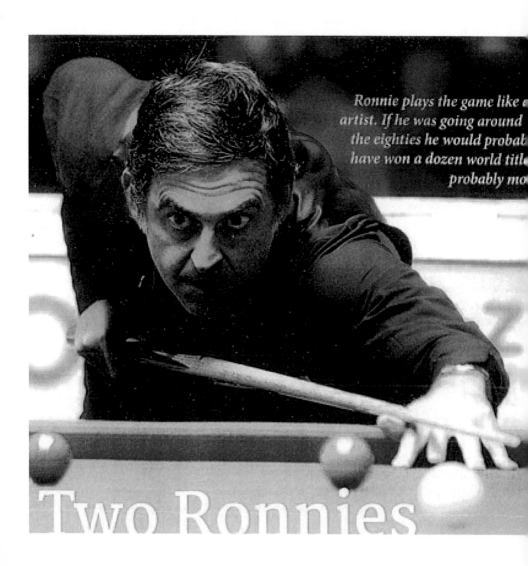

Ronnie plays the game like *an* artist. If he was going around *in* the eighties he would *probably* have won a dozen world *titles,* probably mo*re*

Two Ronnies

The reason for that was that I needed to keep the process going. I finished my book on Ronnie O'Sullivan almost in mid-air simply to get on to my next project.

It was a kind of panic induced by the fear that one day I might wake up and there would be nothing on the horizon, no job to get out of bed for. If I was happy at teaching I'd have stayed in it till I dropped. I like activity. It wasn't the work I disliked in teaching, it was the job.

My books don't get many reviews now. There was a time I would have worried about that. Now I'm not so sure. Do reviews sell books or is it word of mouth? Or good networking?

These days I feel reviews are a bit like your family or friends praising what you write. It would be unusual that they wouldn't but can you believe them? The expression "a face only a mother could love" springs to mind.

When you're famous, people give you cars but you don't need them then. Nothing succeeds like success and nothing fails like failure.

There's more injustice in writing than there is in most other walks of life. Bad runners don't generally win races. Bad footballers don't generally score goals. But a lot of bad writers become rich on potboilers. Some of them also win prizes.

I rang an editor once that I'd been submitting various articles to without reply. He said, "You didn't put your phone number on any of your submissions. We don't work through letterboxes." His comments made me feel very inefficient. The next time I sent something to him I added my phone number but he didn't reply to it. I realise now that this was just an excuse on his part to avoid having to deal with me.

I should have known. We spend the first half of our lives beating ourselves up for mistakes we think we've made and the second half realising we didn't really make any, that it was the outside world that was to blame. Unfortunately, by the time we get to the second half it's too late to make our mark. Instead we just spend it giving out about the bastards who failed to publish us.

When people ask me if there's money in writing I say, "Maybe, but not for me." I got some good advances in the old days but they were rare. I also worked for some magazines that paid very well but they tended to close down over time. The moderate payers tend to last longer, maybe for that reason.

I am now 71 years of age. Yesterday I was 58, the day before that 37. The years slip away and we forget growing old. I remember being 70 but I don't remember being 60 or 50. Once you get past 30 (the real crisis) you find yourself accepting the fact that youth is gone. Everything afterwards is just a detail. It's only when your body starts betraying you that the full fore of ageing hits you. Your mind stays at the age it always was – in my case about 12...

Mary once knew a woman whose nickname was Baby Higgins. The name stuck even when she got into her seventies as her family still saw her that way. Maybe, I thought, I could be another Baby Higgins.

Each time I go to my local hospital now the doctors seem to get younger. The last one who attended me looked about 12. It's rare to see an Irish one now. I have nothing against foreign doctors – they're probably all geniuses – but it knocks you back a bit when they can't pronounce your name or address. I'm living in fear that I'll wind up in surgery some day being booked in for a hysterectomy.

One day my GP told me I could do with losing my beer belly. "Don't criticise it," I said to him, "That took a lot of money to grow." He wasn't amused.

I went to a gym for a while. Most of the other people there didn't seem to need one. They were only there, it seemed, to show off their six pack stomachs and their biceps. "Gotta get rid of that flab," they'd say to me, "I was thinner last week." It was a bit like Raquel Welch telling you she couldn't get a date in high school. I got out of there fast.

I kept my exercise equipment in the house years after I stopped using it, eventually convincing myself that I could lose weight simply by looking at it in a kind of osmosis. The cross trainer became a clothes horse, the treadmill belt a storage area for boxes of books.

My father was 71 when he died. I have many similarities to him Some people tell me I look like him. In other ways we're different. In a poem called 'Between Two Stools' I wrote about the contrast between us, going back to the year I left Ballina:

> *I am now the age my father was*
> *when he died.*
> *It doesn't feel like it.*
> *I'm still that 16 year old boy*
> *thrown on life's surge*
> *as Ballina became*
> *a glorious thing of the past*
> *and Dublin*
> *a dull thing of the future.*
> *'Think of it as an adventure,'*
> *he said, but I couldn't do that.*
> *For me the adventure*
> *would have been staying*
> *where I was.*
> *He was boyish like me*
> *but in a different way.*
> *No matter how childish he acted*
> *he was always my father,*
> *a man who commanded a room*
> *just by entering it.*
> *I never had that.*
> *I was small as a boy.*
> *In the following years*
> *I shot up,*
> *eventually becoming taller than him.*
> *But I never got his charisma.*
> *He was larger than life*
> *and I was smaller than it.*

I go down to Ballina every now and then. My books sell in Eason's. Some of my classmates are aware of the fact that I've been busy writing since I left the town.

Now and again I might have something in a local magazine or paper. I'd like to have been more involved with them over the years but after I left I lost contact with so many people. It's hard to pick up the pieces on visits that only happen once in a blue moon.

The last time I was down there was at the launch of a book by Henry Wills, the photographer for the *Western People*. He'd been in my class in Muredach's. I hadn't seen him for half a century but we'd talked on the phone a number of times. It was great to see him at the launch but he didn't look well. Shortly after it he died of cancer.

It was a wake-up call to me. I was probably the only person at it who didn't know how ill he was. It reminded me of the death of John McGahern. So many people have gone from my life in recent years – Keith, my nephew Derek, my two brothers-in law John and Pat and many others.

When people of your own age die it gives you an extra scare. You feel time's winged chariot gaining. I don't know if that makes me want to write more or less.

A part of me wants to capture things I missed and a part wants to let it all go. What's happened to all my classmates since I knew them? What jobs did they go into? How many of them left the town? How many stayed there?

We were supposed to meet up in 2020 at a proposed Past Pupils Reunion. That year would have been the fiftieth anniversary of our class. It was cancelled due to Covid. I wrote a poem in my father's doggerel style about what it might have entailed:

> *Advertised for ages*
> *the reunion was on.*
> *I couldn't believe it,*
> *fifty years gone.*
>
> *Almost a lifetime*
> *since I'd seen the old chums,*
> *entertainment was promised*
> *and frolicsome fun.*
>
> *So many people*
> *from back in the day.*

when I met them again
what would I say'?

Who'd have succumbed
to the Reaper's call?
Who'd have a beer belly?
Who'd be bald?

Would the boy from 3E
remember my name?
Would he tell stories
about country lanes?

Would the classroom swot
whose name I forgot
still bore me senseless
with the grades he got?

I wrote another poem on the theme of how I'd felt about Ballina since I left it, how I'd tried to replace it with Dublin and other places over the years. Such attempts usually failed. I kept returning to it like a murderer to the scene of a crime. And yet I knew I could never be a part of it again. I was doomed to be always a tourist, always stuck between a rock and a hard place. I called the poem "Closed Doors":

How many years
did you spend thinking
of the way it used to be,
the simplicity of life
lived on the edge of nowhere,
your family gone
to fresh pastures
as you walked
empty streets.

You were a child

thrown onto a man's stage.
Old before your time,
you tried to contrive a future.
The people you knew
embraced emigration.
the holy grail of jobs overseas,
marriage to another culture.

England came to the rescue.
America came to the rescue.

On a clear day,
we joked,
you could see
the Statue of Liberty
from Blacksod Bay.
Ballina was static.
It was doing the same thing
day in day out
until they put you down.

You left it,
sampled the exoticism
of France, Thessalonica,
the Greek islands.
Then you came home.
You sat in a hotel
in Bunree
watching the Grand National.

You called to your aunt
on the Killala Road
but she didn't answer
You phoned her
from a box
outside Jimmy Geraghty's
but she couldn't hear you.

Walking up Lord Edward Street
to another family afterwards
you wondered
who might still be there.

The answer was nobody.
Their doors were closed too.
They'd embraced emigration
as well.
You'd left it too long to come back.
You recalled
snatches of conversations
you had with them
when the world was young,
when nobody knew
the importance
of what they said
or did.

Magic was yesterday.
Later you sat
with the cool people
who knew what was what.

Norfolk blew before you
like a flower
in the wind.
You sat blinded
under a sun
that wiped everything out,
leaving only the vacuum
of a street
that went nowhere.

I wrote another poem dealing with how I felt about the new generation growing up in the town:

I went back to Muredach's
to see the new generation.
They were dressed in denims
cut off at the knees.
They had skintight haircuts.
One of them wore an ear-ring.
Another held a bottle of spring water.
He was listening to iTunes
through an earplug with no wires.

'You're privileged,'
I said to them,
'Your teachers ask you
for your views on things.
They pander to your needs.'
They didn't know
what I was talking about.
They took it for granted.
They talked about the planet,
about electric cars.
the ozone layer,
climate change.
When I brought up films
they used words like 'revisionist.'
They knew about Quentin Tarantino
but not Frank Borzage.
They knew about Greta Gerwig
but not Preston Sturges.

They didn't sit at desks.
They sat at computers.
They used words like
'hashtag,' 'encrypted,''emoji.'

Like Keith I'm back in the Hollywood trivia factory. Like my father I'm anti-computer. I think of him sometimes as I'm clattering away on my typewriter, even if my nerve damage means I can't use the same two fingers he did.

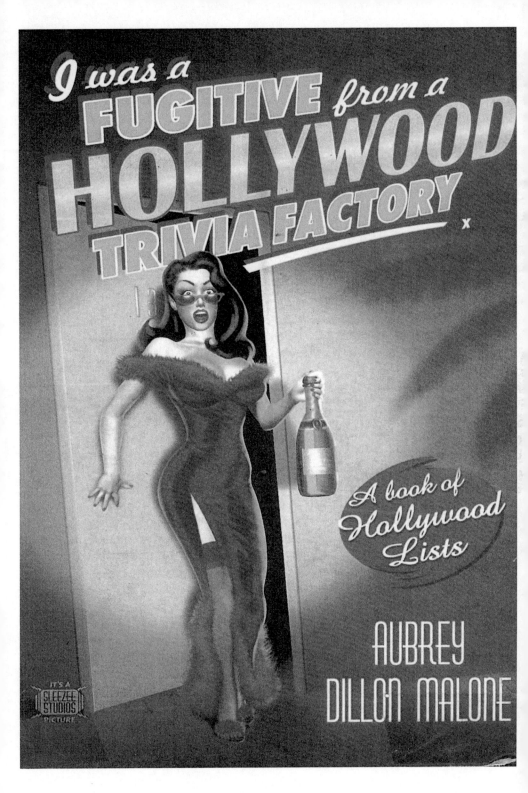

I continue to resist technology, only learning what I have to in order to keep in touch with the insane industry I have somehow managed to stay apart of. A publisher asked me to send him some images once so I asked Basil to teach me how to cut and paste. When he said, "Is there anything else you'd like to know?" I said, "Not at the moment." I felt if I cluttered my mind up with too many facts there'd be no room left for my imagination.

I stopped writing for *Books Ireland* when it went digital. What I liked most about the magazine was the thump on the floor when it came in the letterbox every month. I used to like flipping through the pages. Now I would only be able to do that on a screen. One of the publishers I wrote for sent me an online catalogue of their books every year. It had a little emoji of a thumb on the bottom left hand corner of the screen so you 'could get the sense of turning the pages for real. What next, I thought – the sound of a swish as you did so? With AI anything was possible.

The world of technology is one of contradictions. Netflix keeps sending me emails begging me to sign up with them but when I lost my Visa card they cancelled my membership, refusing to accept the new one. People tell you their inside leg measurement on Facebook but data protection means that when you ring the bank to ask for your balance you have to give your mother's maiden name, your favourite film at age 12 before they process your enquiry.

We live in an age where we know everything and nothing at the same time. I'm sure George Orwell would be amused. (Surprisingly, the clocks haven't struck thirteen yet.)

An ad for a Black and Decker drill hijacked the home page of my computer. Another person might have been able to get rid of it. I took the old-fashioned solution, sellotaping a sheet of paper over it. Sometimes I reminded myself of the Kerryman who got rid of typos on his computer screen by the use of Tipp-Ex.

The fact that I have no social media fingerprints means I'm invisible as far as "go ahead" publishers are concerned. They ask me to set up a webpage but I'm not really interested. As for places like LinkedIn and Instagram, do I really want to know what my 237 "best friends" did yesterday? These sites are supermarkets but you don't usually meet interesting people at supermarkets. You meet them in the shop on the corner.

Canon typewriters are now referred to as "vintage models." I find that expression strange. It seems like only yesterday when I went into Harry Moore's shop in Grafton Street to buy my first one. It was black and flat like a laptop.

Hugo said to me once about the film *The Graduate*, "I still think of it as a modern film." So do I. That's why I get surprised whenever it turns up on late night TV as a "classic," as in *Turner's Classic Movies*. "Classic" is a euphemism for "Old." Can it really be almost sixty years ago when Dustin Hoffman said to Anne Bancroft, "Are you trying to seduce me, Mrs Robinson?"

I was a teenager when I saw it first. It was such a contrast to the black and white Bogart films I watched in my childhood, films that Keith would have grown up on. Keith was sixteen years older than me, almost old enough to be my father. I substituted his Bogart for Brando.

But Brando was born in 1924, a whole century ago. I realise I'm deluding myself about what's modern and what isn't. "Old age," someone said, "is always ten years older than what you are." Or twenty. Or thirty. It's frightening for me to think of people like Tom Hanks and Sean Penn as old fogies today, never mind myself. And frightening to think that I'll never be able to get spare parts for all my malfunctioning Canon typewriters in the attic, or anyone to insert them even if I did, because all the people who used to do this kind of work are all out on grass. Or under it.

A genius called Melissa digitises my books after I send them to her in hard copy. She uses a process called "optical character recognition" (which I never understood) that enables her to make Word documents of them without her having to re-type the pages. It's yet another manifestation of modern technology that fazes me.

People don't seem to want to read books today unless they're on tablets or kindle. Go on to the Dart and you'll see them with their heads buried in Smartphones. Go *anywhere* and you'll see them with their heads buried in Smartphones. That's okay. Whatever works. But I don't ever want to read a book on a flat screen. In fact if I'm reading a book that has anything technological in it, even two people exchanging texts, I leave it down.

The internet has decimated the sales of books just like Smartphones have. I've even become a victim of this myself. I don't browse in bookshops anymore, preferring to surf the internet. It saves you so much time finding what you're looking for. The pity is that you rarely find what you weren't looking for, which was the main pleasure of browsing.

I don't want to turn into a grouch. (And don't say, "Too late.") I'm well aware of the fact that if I was these people's age I'd probably be doing that kind of thing too. I'd probably also 'mis-spell' words in texts, as seems to be the "done thing" today.

It's difficult trying to preserve one's individuality in a world that seems bent on stamping it out. This hits me in all sorts of ways, even with regard to grammar.

Every time I get one of my books from an American publisher for proofing, there are about forty commas on the page. I write a sentence like, "He made his next film in 1945 with two major stars but it wasn't a success and he was disappointed and contemplated leaving films." It comes back as, "He made his next film, in 1945, with two major stars, but it wasn't a success, and he was disappointed, and contemplated leaving films."

I say, "Please get rid of all the commas. They disrupt the flow of the sentence – and they're not grammatical." They reply, "We're using the *Chicago Manual* style. We have to leave them in." And I say, "What the hell is the *Chicago Manual*?"

If I ever become Taoiseach of Ireland I'll make this book, whatever it is, illegal. (I hope you like the two commas I've just used. That's to please my American publishers). I will also campaign for the virtual culling of the comma from books. Okay, so my ambition isn't up there with World Peace or stopping the planet burning up, but someone has to get around to this issue, and soon.

What's next?

There are more translations of *The Cynic's Dictionary* pending. I have a book on the perils of being a child star coming out from the Histria Press. I've said already that my main problem in writing books is doing the first chapter. That was made easy here, as it was in *Writing Under the Influence*, because some of the themes overlapped with other books. I was able to use some of my Brandon de Wilde material from my study of *Shane*, for instance, and some of the Judy Garland and Hayley Mills material from *She Married the Boss* as both of these stars married directors.

The important thing was not to repeat myself. In each book I wrote, even if I was dealing with people I wrote about before, I tried to find new sides to them.

Writing doesn't get easier. I continue to approach publishers and often get rebuffed. Even when a book comes out there can be problems with it.

A couple of years ago I got a letter from a man who told me that a company which had published my quotes compilation books was cheating me.

The reason he knew this was because they were cheating him as well. I checked out what he said and realised he was right. They were selling our books but not paying us royalties. When the royalty cheques from this company stopped some years before I imagined it was because the books had been discontinued. That wasn't so. I emailed them to ask them what was happening and of course got no reply. When I phoned, the line just rang out.

So it was down to my local friendly solicitor again. I asked him to write to them and tell them their eyes and ears would be pulled out if they didn't clean up their act, or words to that effect. They didn't reply to his letters so he asked me if I wanted to take things further.

Since the amount of money we were talking about wasn't likely to get me a holiday on the Cote d'Azur I told him not to. I'd been in court twice with publishers already and it drained me, whatever money I got from them not quite making up for the years they added to my age.

My father had it right: the law was an ass. But it's sad to see such corruption going on and not a lot being able to be done about it. Some day I might travel over to this firm and spray-paint "Bastards" on the wall. I'm sure it would do me good, but the way these things go, I'd probably be spotted and end up in the clink for vandalism.

Despite all these setbacks I'll try to go on for a while yet. The appetite I've always had is still there but I have an older head on my shoulders now when I submit things to places. In other words I've learned to read the signals from editor who aren't interested in what I send them.

"We liked your piece but unfortunately it is not suitable for us at this time" means... your piece was crap. "Showed lots of potential but unfortunately lost its way in the middle," means they didn't bother finishing it. "Your manuscript caused a lot of controversy" usually means your manuscript caused a lot of swearing and hurling of furniture across the editor's room.

If you're informed your writing is "enigmatic" this means the people who read it didn't have a rats what it was about. (Maybe you didn't either, but that's beside the point). "Evocative" means dense. "Poetic" means saccharine. "Great gems of wit, but..." means you should probably try *Reader's Digest*.

"This makes for fascinating reading, but unfortunately we carried a similar idea recently" means they didn't.

You know they're digging deeper when they go to the bother of saying something like, "Personally I loved this, but my higher-ups – for reasons best known to themselves – went against it". (English translation: I think you suck but I haven't the guts to tell you so I'm passing the buck).

Cypriots bearing gifts are much more worrisome than those who tell it like it is from day one. As we all know, the only really worthwhile journalists are the hardnosed ones, and rejection might as well happen sooner rather than later.

This is why I take my hat off to the editor who received a submission from a rather genial, unassuming young man along with a note saying, "If' you're not interested in this, don't worry – I have other irons in the fire". The gent in question read the piece quickly and sent back this reply: "Put it with the other irons."

There are no more good or bad people in the writing game than any other one - music or politics or sports or anything else. If I decided to go into any of these fields I know I'd have had the same problems I had in writing. If I was an actor I'd have crumbled at auditions.

If I was a singer, even a good one, I'd probably have had problems getting gigs because of not pushing myself. Sinead

O'Connor once said that the music business had "all the sincerity of a whore's kiss." Maybe the book business is the same but so what? If you're in it, deal with it. The journalist Vincent Browne, has a saying: "Survival is the best revenge." I live by that.

Whenever I got a rejection letter from a publisher I read it from the bottom up, being mindful of the American expression "the bottom line." It was usually the only one that mattered. It tended to go, "We wish you well with your book." In other words they weren't taking it. It was the kiss-off line, the one that told you to get lost.

Looking upwards, you saw something like, "Our team really liked your book and feel it has great potential. However..." Once you saw the "However" you didn't need to read further. I never cared what their reasons for turning me down were.

They generally gave false ones. "We don't like your book" came out as "We feel the time isn't right for this genre now." "We don't like you" came out as "We're aware of your great facility with this kind of writing."

If people are taking your book, all you need is a "yes." If they aren't, "No" will do.

When Bear Manor took my Brando book, they did so with one word, "Deal!" It's the refusers who are generally loquacious.

If you're the editor of a publishing company and you don't like the book someone has sent you, bear in mind they'd prefer you to say, "Your book is shit" rather than, "We feel this could be a masterpiece with some editing but our reading period has just ended so kindly keep an eye on our website for submission details when the portal opens again." Because we know you're lying through your (probably false) teeth.

Diccionario

de los

Cínicos

PERIODISMO:
CHISME ORGANIZADO.
—*Edward Eggleston*

CASTIDAD:
LA MÁS ANTINATURAL
DE LAS PERVERSIONES
SEXUALES.
—*Aldous Huxley*

VAGO:
ALGUIEN QUE
SIEMPRE TIENE TIEMPO.
—*Kin Hubbard*

Aubrey Dillon-Malone

Where To From Here?

I wake with some surprise
each noon
to find I'm still around.
I still frequent the trendy pubs
swap pleasantries with hardy Dubs
make fashion statements
with the old and sick.
Am I hip
or do I need a hip replacement?
Take your pick.

I'm told I ought to get a grip,
accept the greying locks,
the fact that youth
will mock the elderly,
their loss of memory,
the failure to zip up
after we pee
forgetting the names of friends
or enemies
our last end
or our last disease.

The tragedy of ageing
isn't ageing at all
but staying young.
Our minds still want to go
but our bodies say no –
this is our downfall.

I need to smell the flowers,
I'm informed
and pick a few
to bring back home.
I have to grow into my time
the common wisdom says

accept the way our flesh decays
without reason or rhyme.

I once collected a set of quotations on travel, *It's Great To Be Back on Terra Cotta.* It sums me up. I hope you get the pun. I mean *terra firma.* As someone said to me once, "The firma the grounda, the lessa the terra" (i.e. terror.) I won't be going to the moon soon with Richard Branson.

I've done my share of globetrotting. Today I'm a homebody. I don't tend to answer the door anymore unless it's the postman. I don't answer the phone much either. If someone I know leaves a message I ring them back. I don't ring unknown numbers. Anonymous callers rarely leave messages but they tend to keep ringing, making you wonder why they're so persistent. Maybe, you think, they're different people to the last ones who called. That would explain it. Or maybe they just don't want to be identified until they get you on the line. Either way it means you have people who don't want you to know who they are ringing you off the hook and you not answering. How do we ever communicate with one another?

It's particularly difficult to have conversations with writers today. They just keep referring you to their websites. Such sites seem to be more important than their books to them. If you google them you're asked to check them out on Instagram, which you're not on, or Facebook, which you're not on either. For a while you feel you're missing out on something but then you realise it's probably for the best. Because you'd prefer to eat your own vomit than read most of these people.

I'm glad I'm not still teaching. You'd be getting reviewed on social media every time you blew your nose. It's not just books that get reviewed today, it's people. They're even "reviewing" couriers today. Everytime an Amazon guy brings me a book I've ordered I get an email asking: "How was your delivery?" There are icons of "thumbs up" and "thumbs down" that you can click on before you give your review. I wonder what they expect me to say. "Well yes, the courier looked very well – nice hair, lovely tan jacket, he flashed a big smile at me and thrust the book into my hand with a wonderful flourish."

It's Great to be Back on Terra Cotta!

Quirky Quotes about Travel and Transport

AUBREY
MALONE

ILLUSTRATIONS BY
BRIAN
FITZGERALD

People sometimes ask me how I write my books. I say, "I sit down on a chair and turn the typewriter on. I write 'Page 1' on a page, which I fill with words. When that's finished I write 'Page 2' on the next one. And so on until it's finished. I write 'The End' when it is, and then I send it to the publisher. He sends it to a printer and shortly afterwards it appears on bookshelves with nice covers."

A more truthful answer would be, "I get an idea, which I try to turn into a book, which usually fails. Then I get another one, which fails also. After about ten tries, I get one which seems to be the basis of one, so after a few months turning it around in my head I sit down and try to write it.

After the first day nothing comes so the page stays blank. The second day might produce a few words but more often than not they end up in the bin. After a week or a month I get something usable down on paper. I run the idea by twenty publishers or so. About fifteen fail to reply.

The other five say something like 'This might be something.' One or two ask for synopses and sample chapters, which I supply. After six months of them not getting back to me I write to them and ask them did they get what I sent. Two say no. A third says, 'Yes but we're not interested.'

The fourth and fifth say, 'We're not publishing at the moment. Try us again next year or the year after.' So I park the idea and go down to Dollymount for a walk. The sea looks nice and the wind blows in my face and I think: 'This is better than writing.' But then I go back home and realise I need to be active so I have another go at something. Then the process begins again. I get an idea, etc. See above.'"

Good writing means something different to me every day. Sometimes it's Wallace Stevens, sometimes it's Woody Allen, sometimes it's Andre Gide. Today it's Iris DeMent because I've been listening to her song 'Easy's Gettin' Harder Every Day.' It reminds me of Bob Dylan's 'Not Dark Yet' and I can think of no higher praise than that. Last week it was Elvis Costello's 'A Good Year for the Roses,' another song that tells a story. I like songs that tell stories. Sometimes there's good writing in bad books, or bad songs, and bad writing in good ones. Sometimes prose sounds like poetry and poetry sounds like prose. We need to get rid of tight definitions of things.

How did I get to be seventy without knowing anything about Iris? Maybe because of one of the things I like most about her: she doesn't push herself. She's Dolores Claiborne from America's outback, a soul sweeter than any you could ever imagine, singing from the bottom of her heart with that catch in her throat that reminds you of Emmylou Harris. Iris is like Emmylou's little sister. Emmylou has to look out for her because there are lots of wolves out there that prey on gentle souls.

Her stories of simple folk in small towns and the wide open country beyond them brings a tear to my eyes every time. One of the great things about discovering Iris at seventy is that you have so much more to hear and discover. After "Our Town," "Mama's Opry," "Infamous Angel" and all those other torch songs invested with her purity, you wonder just how many other treasures there are out there. I dare anyone to listen to "Sweet Is the Melody" without tears coming to their eyes.

Someone once defined graffiti as the literature of the disenfranchised. Music lyrics can perform that function too, even lyrics of rap songs. A line can come back to you years later from the most banal song you ever heard and it can be so powerful as to draw tears to your eyes, something like Neil Diamond's 'You Don't Send Me Flowers.' Then a minute later you might say to yourself, 'Why did that move me? You feel stupid because the moment has passed and so has your reaction.

It may have been caused by something that just happened to you. Emotions come from strange places. What we have to guard against is thinking something is good because someone else, or everyone else, tells us it's good. There's a lot of pressure in that area from social media.

We should never deny ourselves the right to be moved by something that's commonly regarded as base or saccharine. We may not like best-selling books from writers we see as poor but we should accept the fact that they have something the pretentious poets who produce one oblique collection a decade lack, which is the ability to tap into a mood that runs through different genres into an area we can't define. Areas we can't define are good ones.

They open the process up to produce good work from bad sources.

I'd like to unwrite, or unpublish, some of my books. Others I thought got unfairly ignored or reviewed. Some came too easy. Others disappeared through the cracks because of the cavalier disregard of the people handling them or unfortunate events. My Sidney Lumet biography came out the very same week as a major biography of him from a New York publisher who had thousands of dollars to put into publicity. It was David versus Goliath. My book died through no fault of my own.

After I published my Harry Potter guide, the editor of the *Irish Independent* interviewed me over the phone. It was around the time J.K. Rowling was suing somebody for publishing a guide to her books. My one became quite controversial in these circumstances. He said he could give me a whole page.

At the end of the interview he said he was sending a photographer out to the house for a shot of me. I froze. It was during my 'camera shy' phase when I was going around Dublin in my Peter Murphy guise. "I wouldn't be agreeable to that," I said. He couldn't understand it. As a result, the interview was shrunk to a few paragraphs. I rang him and asked him why. "My boss wasn't impressed by your coyness," he told me.

Basil .is the opposite of me. When he writes a book he networks. He has a web page and lots of ideas about how to sell his books to people from all countries. He's also on social media.

He tells me I should be too. I tell him it's because I'm not sociable. I tell him I enjoy my anonymity. He always liked being in a crowd so he finds that hard to get his head around, especially when benefits would accrue from me having a profile.

"Why turn yourself into J.D. Salinger?" he says. I say I didn't turn myself into him. I always was him. The difference between us is that he could afford to hide himself away because he'd written *The Catcher in the Rye*. What had I written? No immediate title would spring to mind if you brought my name up to people.

The bottom line is that we have to be who we are. There are also things I'd like Basil to do that he doesn't, like write more books. I know he could. He's shown me the drafts of some of them he has in progress and they're very good. "Maybe when I retire," he says. I'd like to see them on a shelf. I never attended a creative writing course. The phrase to me was a contradiction in terms I didn't think you could teach people to write any more than you could teach them to eat their dinner. (Okay, so some people have to be taught how to eat their dinner).

Most creative writing courses, I believed, destroyed creativity. They sought to put a rope round the process, which atrophied it. When someone produced something at one of those courses it was usually analysed to the death by the other people at it, including the teacher. The analysts were probably critics-in-waiting, sharpening their knives for a career on the sidelines Meanwhile the person who'd sweated to fill a page was being told everything that was wrong with it.

I also saw the opposite reaction. Sometimes people excessively praised the things that were done at these courses. It was the same

way the editor of a vanity press would praise something one of their clients wrote. They knew it was rubbish but it was their mealticket. If they praised it they'd get the person's money, be it for the course or for copies of the book. Meanwhile it would gather dust in someone's garage while the vanity people laughed their way to the bank.

I don't believe in either praise or blame. If I was asked to direct a creative writing class I'd come into the room, hand everyone a pen and say, "I'm off to sleep now. Write something if you feel like it. If you don't, make a doodle. I don't have any suggestions as to what you might do. If you want your money back, wake me up."

I now have an agent who lives in South America. The girl who proofed my last book is from India. The publisher lives in Japan but has his office in Florida. It all sounds very fancy but these places are just dots on a map. They mean nothing to me any more than it means nothing when people tell me they're jetting off on holidays to far-flung places. When I was young, people went to Ballycastle on holidays. Now they go to Bali. So what? As my

357

Sidney Lumet
The Actor's Director

Aubrey Malone

father said, many of them have travelled bodies but untravelled minds. Whether my editor lives in India or Crossmolina, it doesn't make the book any better or worse. At the end of the day I'll be happy if it sells a few hundred copies. As well as not being on social media, and avoiding cameras like the plague, I've never organised book launches. The only one I ever had was for the Behan book and I hated that. I spent most of the night wandering about looking like I crashed someone else's party. Margot came to it and couldn't understand me. I didn't even give a speech. She wrote a piece about me in *Modern Woman* afterwards called 'The Quiet Man.'

'If there's a heaven,' John McGahern said, 'Let's pray there'll be no writers in it.' I agree. It's even worse when you see them poncing about in groups in their woolly jumpers.

Richard Ford said to John Banville recently, "In the old days we would have been seen as the lions of literature. Now we're just old farts." It's true. There are no icons anymore. Jack's as good as his master. We're growing writers like potatoes. They may win prestigious prizes or self-publish for ten people to read but they're all in the same melting pot. The pyramidic structure is gone.

A lot of this is due to Facebook. Here people who can't string two words together without help elevate themselves to the status of Pulitzer Prize winners in their heads. They tell us what they had for breakfast and see this as "literature." The actor Dennis Hopper said, "When I was growing up, a biography was a book about Abraham Lincoln. Now it's one about the guy next door."

Sometimes I think it isn't just me who's writing too much, it's everyone.

The singer Jordan has written a number of novels. The Irish politician Alan Shatter wrote a "naughty" one as a potboiler. Why not? Everyone else seemed to be at it. Joan Collins wrote one for a £1 million advance which was taken back when the publishers realised it wasn't any good. She sued to get her lolly back – and won. It sent out a bad message to the world of literature: Bad writing succeeds if you're a celebrity. Had Jackie put a word in her ear and said, "Joanie, it's easy, have a go"?

In recent years, Ronnie O'Sullivan has even taken to writing novels, gritty noir ones that read like Mickey Spillane on steroids. How can someone be the greatest snooker player in history and then just turn on this other side of him like a tap? It's not fair.

I wrote to Marcia Clark, the lawyer who prosecuted O.J. Simpson unsuccessfully in 1994, to try to console her over his acquittal. The next thing I heard, she too was lending her name to the list of novelists out there. Had she become disillusioned with the law after OJ got off? Is this a good enough reason to 'become' a novelist?

I wrote my book on gay cinema simply because it was the only offer on the table that year That's what you have to do in writing: Be available. When it isn't going well, sometimes I feel like going down to the local newsagent and putting a sign on the window saying: "Writer available, Reasonable Rates, No Job Too Small". Right of the middle of the ones for plumbers and carpenters and butchers and bakers and Chinese food salesmen. Except that no one would probably answer it. Because there are too many of us around.

Some years ago a Galway magazine featured a farmer on the cover of a literary magazine with a pitchfork in his hand. His claim to fame was, he said, the fact that he was the one man in the country who wasn't writing a book.

Maybe they should run courses on how to write a novel like they do on how to put up shelves without injuring yourself, or the best way to make quiche.

You're a golfer going through a rough patch? Never fear. You too can be Jeffrey Archer. Tired of the slog of being an actuary? No problem. Run off a few chapters about your grandad's granary in Oldham and stick in a bit about him wanting to bump off grandma because she's starting to sprout a bit of snow on the roof and he fancies the squeeze down the road who's doing Pilates. Instant best-seller.

At the moment I'm thinking of going down to the local deli and putting a sign in the window saying, "Writer For Hire. Reasonable Rates. No Job Too Small." I could put it in between the one that says "Man with Van" and "Woman Will Take in Washing." Some time ago when I was in Galway I saw a magazine with a picture of a farmer on the cover with a pitchfork in his hand. His claim to fame? He said he was the only man in the county not writing a novel. I thought: Fair play to you.

My car packed up last year. I didn't feel it owed me anything. I drove it into the ground. The new one, like everything else in this world, has many controls I don't understand or ever want to. It also has a petrol tank that won't open I went at it with a kitchen knife before the dealer told me the switch to open it was beside the driver's seat.

As you drive, various bells go off to tell you if your seatbelt isn't on or if you're getting near a wall or another car. The point is, I generally tend to know if I'm near a wall or a car. I have eyes. And the incessant pinging makes me more likely to crash into them. Another bell goes off when you go into reverse. Hello, I know I'm in reverse. I was the guy who got me there.

You can't roll windows up or down in cars anymore. You can't even lock doors one by one. It's like what's happening with books, where they've stopped us turning pages because of the computer revolution.

I keep *On the Road* in the glove compartment. Can I still be Dean Moriarty or does my age mean I'm more likely to be compared to Eliot's Prufrock. I know you're not supposed to read this book if you're over 25 or if you're not traversing the globe with your girlfriend in a pair of Levis but I never went for what one was supposed to do. I like it because it's a book you can pick up at any page. And because it makes me want to be on the move myself.

Life gets boring sitting in the one place. I write some of my books when I'm on my holidays somewhere. A building can start something off, or a sunset, or a view from a hill. Sometimes I drive somewhere and write in the car in the kinds of copies we used to have in school as children. The only way I could write at home was when something else was happening around me. Most writers needed to be able to concentrate. I needed to de-concentrate. It was the ADHD thing again. If I had to go somewhere soon, or if the phone rang, or the doorbell, it galvanised me. I put the radio or the television on to activate me as well. I heard somewhere that Bob Dylan could write songs in a

Aubrey Malone

QUEER CINEMA
IN AMERICA

An Encyclopedia of
LGBTQ Films, Characters,
and Stories

room full of twenty people. I used to see his foot tapping in any live footage I saw of him typing. It was another sign of his nervous energy.

I've got more picky about where I go on holidays. If it's a self-catering apartment I have to have an en-suite and a balcony with a view of the sea. This contrasts somewhat with my cavorting across Europe in the seventies where I was happy to stay anywhere that wasn't run by Norman Bates.

Sometimes when I'm in an exotic place I get an idea for a story that I know I'd never have got anywhere else. These are the best moments of writing, when you don't even have to try.

Leonard Cohen had a saying, "I didn't write the song. The song wrote me." I knew what he meant. Edna O'Brien said her first book was given' to her. I understood that too. Some of my stories came to me without me knowing their origin. I took up a pen in a certain mood and the words appeared as a result of that mood. Maybe it's a bit like dreaming.

When I was in London in 1970 I started a dream diary as I was having a lot of interesting dreams that summer. Sometimes I felt I was in charge of the dreams, that a part of me was directing where they went. By the end of the summer I concluded that the subject of the dreams didn't really matter. What mattered was their tones or themes. If I was stressed I tended to have a stressed dream and if I was relaxed I had a relaxed one.

It's the same with writing. Your mood creates the texture of what you're writing and the subject follows. I've often seen dreams as therapy, like your mind going to the toilet. I think of writing in the same way. People sometimes use the word 'catharsis' to describe writing. Maybe it's more like a colonoscopy.

I wish I could have Jack Kerouac's peripatetic nature. My geographical radius has been low in the past few decades. My nephews and nieces go to Bali, I go to Ballyhaunis. They go to Iceland, I spend my time in Kentucky Fried Chicken.

Mary and myself confine ourselves to ferry trips "across the pond" most summers. That generally means Wales. I've collected lots of anthologies of Welsh quotations, the most recent being *Welsh Rarebits*.

The Welsh I always found to be friendlier than the English. "We're all Celts," they say to me occasionally. The English colonised many parts of Wales just as they did Ireland. We had a common enemy in them. They seemed to suss my discomfiture whenever I met them in Wales, not showing any warmth in conversations. Or maybe they wouldn't have anyway.

If they were running cafes they let you know very quickly what you could or couldn't order, or how soon they would be closing. Welsh owners just shrugged their shoulders as if to say, "Whatever."

Maybe they wouldn't have the food you wanted either but for some reason you didn't seem to mind. It was like Ireland, a country where everything was either out of stock or not available until "next Wednesday." I preferred that than being told, "We're closing now. You'll have to leave." England, I think, the land of the Industrial Revolution. The Irish and the Welsh would be too busy having the craic to have invented the spinning jenny.

Being away sometimes filled us with adventurous thoughts. We kidded ourselves by thinking we could up sticks in Dublin and move back to Galway or Ballina, or commute between the two places like Scott and Zelda. The prospect of such a lifestyle was exciting to us on balmy evenings where we sat on verandahs sipping cocktails as the sun went down on golden shores. It became less palatable on the mornings after all those nights before as, to our chagrin, we remembered having mini nervous breakdowns the last time we planned an overnight stay at a B&B in Skerries.

People's priorities change as they age. There was a time I would have said to Mary prior to a trip, "Have you packed your climbing boots?" Now it's more like, "Don't forget the Panadol."

Here's the way our lives change with age:

20: Bungi-jumping over the Himalayas
30: Snorkling in the Great Barrier Reef
40: Kayaking on the Hudson
70: Managing to stay awake after lunch.

Our Wonderful World

The world went a bit crazy in recent years. Donald Trump beat Hillary Clinton in a presidential election in America. We had Covid. A bunch of hooligans invaded the White House.

A pope stepped down. The world started burning up. People in hospitals died on trolleys. Nobody could afford a house. Putin invaded the Ukraine. We watched pictures of devastation every night on the television. Then Hamas invaded Israel. Benjamin Netanyahu turned into another Putin as he retaliated. He said he wanted to exterminate Hamas but as time went on it looked like he was more interested in exterminating Palestine and the Lebanon.

Everyone fiddled while the planet burned. We got bothered about the rising cost of petrol as Putin strangled supplies getting out to the free world but maybe he was doing us a favour. Should we all not sign up for electric cars and stop those noxious fumes burning even more of the ozone layer? "I can't drive an electric car," I told people, "My flex doesn't even stretch as far as the Harmonstown Road."

Trump rose from the dead. He was arraigned on a barrel-load of charges but said he was still going to run for President. Himself and Biden were both in their dotage by now. Could America not come up with anything better with all their millions of people?

Four years ago I was pinning all my hopes on Biden beating Trump. Now I didn't care. "Sleepy Joe" had rowed in behind Netanyahu and his bloodthirstiness to secure the Jewish vote at the polls. "I'm ashamed to be from Ballina," Basil said to me apropos Biden's connection to the town. So was I.

Biden did a debate with Trump where he basically ended his presidential hopes. We all thought Trump was going to go for him but he didn't, instead just watching open-mouthed like the rest of us as Biden committed career suicide. We made jokes about which of them would be elected. If it was Trump, the country would have to be run from a prison. If it was Biden it would be run from a nursing home.

At a NATO press conference, Biden introduced President Zelensky as "President Putin." At the same conference he spoke of "Vice President Trump" when he meant vice-president Kamala Harris. I feared Trump would press the button if he didn't like the colour of someone's hair when he was in the White House.

Now my fear was that Biden would press it when he thought he was pressing the bell to ring for lunch. Not since Reagan had we to worry about a president with dementia. Now it appeared like a very real possibility. Who was going to stop him? His wife? His children? The House of Representatives? Everyone seemed powerless – or unwilling. Trump said he wanted him to continue to run. Why wouldn't he? How could he fail to beat a man who walked – and now spoke – like a ghost?

Not long afterwards there was an assassination attempt on Trump. That helped him too. He got away with just a nick on the ear. It was hard to kill a bad thing. We knew that when Covid didn't even seem to bother him.

Of course Trump isn't the problem. He's just being Trump. There's an idiot in every town in the world. The problem is the people supporting him. From that point of view he's a symptom of something rotten in the body politic. As the old saying goes, we get the politicians we deserve. Or vote for Trump only becomes a problem if he's elected. Then the joke becomes something much worse.

The moment Thomas Matthew Crooks' bullet clipped him on the ear he had a foot in the White House door. He owes him a pint when he meets him in heaven. (Or, as is probably more likely the other place).

He became more "presidential" after his brush with death, toning down his hate rhetoric in favour of a new and improved Donald who would unite the "disunited States." Hello, wasn't this Joe's territory? Sorry, I forgot. Joe is history so we need someone to morph into him and hoover up some of his votes.

I spent a lot of time thinking how I'd liked Joe so much four years ago whereas now he was just an irritant to me. It wasn't only his stance on Gaza and his aging. It was the unforgiveable stubbornness in the face of mounting pressure from his fellow Democrats to step down. Could Jill not have had a word with him in quiet? ("Retire, Joe, or I'll hide your walking frame.")

I thought of a jingle:

Joe and Jill went up the hill
to fetch a pail of water
Joe fell down
And broke his crown
For walking faster
Than he oughter.

I was now seeing him like Calvin Coolidge. When Calvin died, you might remember, someone said, "How could they tell?"

Joe finally pulled out of the race for the White House at the end of July. There was only one person upset at the decision. His name was Donald Trump. Now he'd actually have to win the election instead of having it gifted to him by Joe.

Kamala Harris was anointed as his replacement. Trump would face another woman after seeing off Hillary Clinton (unfairly) in 2016. Once again it was Right versus Left, a fundamentalist versus a libertine. The Far Right was getting strong in Europe and Britain. It was destroying Ireland. What would happen in America? Trump was trying to become more centrist to win the swing states. Would Kamala?

Trump was so sure he'd beat Biden he picked a funny fish as his running mate. When Kamala came on board she was a bit more careful. Walz versus Vance? No contest.

Meanwhile I put words together on pages. There's no alternative. If you think too much about the way the world is going you'll go crazy. Even if you don't you might

Writers don't write because they want to. They do it because they have to. We're back to Henry James' "painful duty." For me it's like doing the hoovering or pottering round in the garden. The more you leave it, the more it piles up.

The most times that happens is when I get my bugs. When I run myself down the backlog gets worse. I take to the bed to recharge my batteries, making notes in copybooks in my illegible scrawl.

The longer I'm out of commission, the more the copies get filled up. Sometimes they're so full I think I'll get a relapse if I even look at them. I say to myself: How did I let this happen? If I went slower I'd get more done.

It's like when you come to a yellow light in traffic. Do you slow down or accelerate? I accelerate. I was once behind someone when the light went yellow. I expected them to go through it but they didn't. They pulled up suddenly even though they'd have had lots of time to put the foot down.

I ended up accelerating to go past them. The light was red by that time. For me it beat five minutes chewing my nails as I waited for it to go green again. The driver started honking me as I sped away from him. I don't know what his problem was. I did what I wanted and he did what he wanted.

But going through a red light can be dangerous. Or you could get a ticket. A police car followed me through a red light once when I was rushing to meet an appointment. I hadn't seen it. He pulled me over. "I thought I got the end of the yellow," I said to him. "No," he said, "You got the beginning of the red."

More haste less speed. I missed my appointment as a result of the time it took him to book me. People tell me to slow down but you can't if you're made a certain way.

We all slowed down during Covid. I bought about 500 masks during the pandemic. It was like, "I'm going to die if I don't have one." Now I look at the boxes of them and think: "These stupid things are in the way. Should I throw them out?"

Maybe put one on me and rob the local post office if my writing continues to draw a blank. Or flog them on eBay to some hypochondriac with an "underlying condition."

My life these days alternates between bouts of hard work and long lay-offs. It's like the way someone defined air travel once, "Five hours of waiting followed by one of terror." I like going fast. It's why I gravitated towards players like Alex Higgins and Ronnie O'Sullivan in snooker. I saw myself in them. That didn't mean I wanted to be like them. Sometimes I envy the people who stop at yellow lights.

The way I breeze through them is the way I write books. More Mailer than Hemingway, more punch, less poetry. People say to me, "You're so prolific!" I say, "Please don't use that word." Mothers are prolific. They make children. Binmen are prolific. They collect the rubbish. People who wash plates in restaurants are prolific.

Why is the word exclusive to writers? Don't we all do something every day? It takes no special skill to be a writer. Maybe the skill is to stop being one.

Nothing is better than anything else in life. That's what we need to emphasise. I always hated it when people said to me, "You write good English."

I see "good" English as bad English. That was another thing Hemingway taught me when he threw out all the adjectives the Victorians loved. "All blackbirds are black," he said.

It makes sense when you think about it. Hemingway prided himself on the fact that nobody who read his work needed to go to a dictionary. They did for Faulkner. And they did for me when I wrote for Hibernia and Books Ireland. Hopefully they wouldn't now.

I realise I'm in the minority when I speak this way. You don't hear people going on like this in the *Times Literary Supplement* or the *Sewanee Review*. They don't want me doing the Guy Fawkes, upsetting their cosy niches. It's easier to be fluffy and tweedy and keep the fires stoked with the old verities.

Publishers are that way too. They like you to play the game. That way nobody gets hurt, or at least nobody at the top of the tree. Publishers are happiest when they're sitting back counting the money you make for them.

Whenever I submit an idea to them these days I get a form back asking me if I'll do signings, if there's some event coming up that I can tie my book in with, what interviews I can do to share my wisdom with the Great Unwashed, what review outlets I can suggest, what illustrations I can provide, what "bullet points" I can provide that define my book, what competitive titles I can list that may threaten it, but not really, because it's much better than them, isn't it?. Oh, and yes, will I be over in London any time soon so I can have dinner with Rodney?

Sorry, Rodney, but you'll have to dine alone. I have other plans. Sitting in with a six pack and a box set of David Lynch.

Where does that leave me in the 'industry'? Probably somewhere near outer Siberia. But that's where it's most fun.

Do I feel sad that my books don't make the "Top Ten" in any

given year? Or even the "Top Hundred"? No. Would I like to be on John Banville's party list? No, no, a thousand times no.

Many of the writers going around today couldn't as the saying goes, "write 'fuck' on a dusty Venetian blind" and yet they're the names on everyone's lips. And the people cleaning up at the literary awards ceremonies.

What writers do I like today? Preferably someone I haven't heard of before. I occasionally make stabs at reading the old classics but I don't get very far. I bought *Great Expectations* last year in Wales but didn't even get through a page of it. Likewise with *1984*.

My ADHD is still alive and well. It means I'm more inclined to read poetry than prose these days. You can get through it faster – unless it's someone like Walt Whitman.

Song lyrics also work We're living at a time when Bob Dylan won the Nobel Prize for literature, not music. Why did it take them so long? Even more surprising was the fact that he accepted it.

We're also living at a time where the worth of women has been discovered. Have we over-emphasised this?

The chicklit revolution has seen a lot of good books hitting the shelves but a lot of bad ones too. That's a pity. Overpaying the debt of history never works. We do it all the time with repressed people – immigrants, women, blacks. And it always does more harm than good.

The acquittal of O.J. Simpson didn't make up for Rodney King. It just deflected attention away from all the other Rodney Kings out there.

The book was thrown at the guy who killed George Floyd but then there were other George Floyds who didn't make the headlines. We comfort ourselves with tokenistic gestures but the abuses go on. I'm sure they're still going on with women in many quarters. Publishing bad novels by women won't stop them. It will only make them worse. There are too many good women writers out there for us to need to do this. It's an insult to them to patronise them by giving exposure to the substandard ones.

I'd hate to have to go back to the era where women had to pretend they were men to get their books published but sometimes

I think we've gone to the opposite extreme. There are women's writing competitions today, for instance, that men aren't allowed enter – I know this because I've submitted things to some of them and being told so – but not men's ones that women can't enter. That would be regarded as an abomination.

Having said that, I generally prefer women writers to men ones. The problem is that it's the wrong ones are usually praised. I think I can safely live my life without reading another Sally Rooney book, for instance – even if she does come from Mayo.

Bottom line? The people who write shouldn't and the ones who don't should. I met the actress Angie Dickinson at a showing of her movie *Rio Bravo* some years ago. Afterwards I told her I'd love to read her memoirs. She said she was hoping to write them.

Would she be employing a co-writer, I enquired. "Not on your life!" she said, "They'd be too saucy. I'd be embarrassed." My appetite was whetted but she never got around to it.

What a pity. I always liked her laidback attitude to everything, and her unPC comments. Asked once if she dressed for women or men she replied, "I dress for women and undress for men."

In recent years she said she thought the #Metoo movement had gone too far.

Me too.

Acknowledgments

I'd like to thank all the people responsible for bringing this book together in their various ways. First and foremost is Ken, the indefatigable multi-tasker who took it from the chaotic mess it was when he first saw it and, as ever, pulled it together with my infuriating 101 amendments.

Thanks are also due to Melissa for performing an earlier kind of major surgery on it, and to Gerry for his as always professional presentation of the finished product.

More generally I'd like to convey my gratitude to early influences on this theme. I'm grateful to my father for surrounding me with the litmus paper that bled into my subconscious in my pre-writing years, and to my mother for being the silent presence that allowed all things to flow from it.

Thank you Keith for opening up so many worlds of wonder to me, both inside cinemas and outside them. Thanks to Clive for all his words of encouragement to me about areas so far from his own ones. To June for going through everything with a fine toothcomb and pinning me to the wall with endless questions, most of which I couldn't answer. To Ruth for always being there for me, even from 3000 miles away.

To Hugo for opening my eyes to the idols he had that subsequently became mine. To Basil for sharing your journey with me that's so similar to mine in many ways, and equally fascinating.

I'd also like to thank people from the literary world - 'Big time' writers like John McGahern, Benedict Kiely and Dermot Healy praised me even when I didn't deserve it.

Uinsin O Donabháin took me on when I was raw and untested – thank you Uinsin, even if you lived to regret it. Thank you to David Marcus, who alerted me to hard truths when I didn't want to hear them, and to David Llewellyn for opening up a rich vein for me.   Thank you to Charlie Perdue for pursuing that vein over five books.

Thank you to Dennis Greig for allowing me to enter a world no other publisher would, and for good reason. Thanks to Brian Behan for allowing me to pick your brain day in day out for over a year. To Margot Davis for allowing me the kind of freedom I never had before, causing me to wear out various typewriters to the endless suffering of your readers.

Thanks to Chelsey and Richard for those early important contacts and contracts. To Andrew Goodfellow for living up to his name, and for pointing me in directions I didn't want to go even when I knew they were good for me in the back of my mind. To Harry for showing me how it was done even when I couldn't do it like you could.

Thanks to Des for all those nights where we tossed ideas around even if they came to nothing in the cold light of dawn. To John for flattering my words with your photographs. To Seamus for your enthusiasm for all my wacky ideas and somehow making them relevant to your needs.

Thank you to Charles Bukowski for teaching me that prose could be poetry. To Ernest Hemingway for teaching me that it could be music. To Leonard Cohen for his gentle profundity. And to Bob Dylan for…everything.

I'd like to thank all the publishers who had faith in me, even the ones who drove me up the walls with their demands, and for enduring my impatience (sometimes anyway). Thanks to JR for finding the unfindable with that child-like enthusiasm you have even into your eighties. Thank you to Vernon for walking the extra mile for me, even when it was into brick walls. Thanks to Ben Ohmart for giving a voice to the 'little' people - who are so often bigger than the giants.

Most of all I'd like to thank Mary for being with me since the beginning. You typed out *Silas Marner* for me on your father's little Facit in the seventies and almost broke your fingers doing so. It was my first book and I thought it would be my last. Half a century on they're still coming out. Too late to stop now.